The Object-Oriented Thought Process

Fourth Edition

Developer's Library

ESSENTIAL REFERENCES FOR PROGRAMMING PROFESSIONALS

Developer's Library books are designed to provide practicing programmers with unique, high-quality references and tutorials on the programming languages and technologies they use in their daily work.

All books in the *Developer's Library* are written by expert technology practitioners who are especially skilled at organizing and presenting information in a way that's useful for other programmers.

Key titles include some of the best, most widely acclaimed books within their topic areas:

PHP & MySQL Web Development
Luke Welling & Laura Thomson
ISBN 978-0-672-32916-6

MySQL
Paul DuBois
ISBN-13: 978-0-672-32938-8

Linux Kernel Development
Robert Love
ISBN-13: 978-0-672-32946-3

Python Essential Reference
David Beazley
ISBN-13: 978-0-672-32978-4

Programming in Objective-C
Stephen Kochan
ISBN-13: 978-0-672-32756-8

C++ Primer Plus
Stephen Prata
ISBN-13: 978-0321-77640-2

Developer's Library books are available at most retail and online bookstores, as well as by subscription from Safari Books Online at **safari.informit.com**

**Developer's
Library**
informit.com/devlibrary

The Object-Oriented Thought Process

Fourth Edition

Matt Weisfeld

✦✦ Addison-Wesley

Upper Saddle River, NJ • Boston • Indianapolis • San Francisco
New York • Toronto • Montreal • London • Munich • Paris • Madrid
Cape Town • Sydney • Tokyo • Singapore • Mexico City

ISBN-13: 978-0-321-86127-6
ISBN-10: 0-321-86127-2

Library of Congress Cataloging-in-Publication data is on file.

First Printing March 2013

Trademarks

All terms mentioned in this book that are known to be trademarks or service marks have been appropriately capitalized. Pearson cannot attest to the accuracy of this information. Use of a term in this book should not be regarded as affecting the validity of any trademark or service mark.

Warning and Disclaimer

Every effort has been made to make this book as complete and as accurate as possible, but no warranty or fitness is implied. The information provided is on an "as is" basis. The author and the publisher shall have neither liability nor responsibility to any person or entity with respect to any loss or damages arising from the information contained in this book.

Bulk Sales

Pearson offers excellent discounts on this book when ordered in quantity for bulk purchases or special sales. For more information, please contact

U.S. Corporate and Government Sales

1-800-382-3419

corpsales@pearsontechgroup.com

For sales outside of the U.S., please contact

International Sales

international@pearsoned.com

Acquisitions Editor
Mark Taber

Development Editor
Songlin Qiu

Managing Editor
Sandra Schroeder

Project Editor
Seth Kerney

Copy Editor
Barbara Hacha

Indexer
Brad Herriman

Proofreader
Sarah Kearns

Technical Reviewer
Jon Upchurch

Editorial Assistant
Vanessa Evans

Interior Designer
Gary Adair

Cover Designer
Chuti Prasertsith

Compositor
Bronkella Publishing LLC

Contents at a Glance

Table of Contents

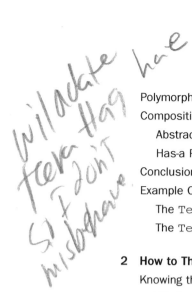

About the Author

Matt Weisfeld is a college professor, software developer, and author based in Cleveland, Ohio. Prior to teaching college full time, he spent 20 years in the information technology industry as a software developer, entrepreneur, and adjunct professor. Weisfeld holds an MS in computer science and an MBA. Besides the first three editions of *The Object-Oriented Thought Process*, he has authored two other software development books and published many articles in magazines and journals, such as *developer.com*, *Dr. Dobb's Journal*, *The C/C++ Users Journal*, *Software Development Magazine*, *Java Report*, and the international journal *Project Management*.

Dedication

❖

To Sharon, Stacy, Stephanie, and Duffy

❖

Acknowledgments

As with the first three editions, this book required the combined efforts of many people. I would like to take the time to acknowledge as many of these people as possible, for without them, this book would never have happened.

First and foremost, I would like to thank my wife Sharon for all her help. Not only did she provide support and encouragement throughout this lengthy process, she is also the first line editor for all my writing.

I would also like to thank my mom and the rest of my family for their continued support.

It is hard to believe that the work on the first edition of this book began in 1998. For all these years, I have thoroughly enjoyed working with everyone at Pearson—on all four editions. Working with editors Mark Taber, Songlin Qiu, Barbara Hacha, and Seth Kerney has been a pleasure.

A special thanks goes to Jon Upchurch for his expertise with much of the code as well as the technical editing of the manuscript. Jon's insights into an amazing range of technical topics have been of great help to me.

I would also like to thank Donnie Santos for his insights into mobile and hybrid development, as well as Objective-C.

Finally, thanks to my daughters, Stacy and Stephanie, and my cat, Duffy, for always keeping me on my toes.

We Want to Hear from You!

As the reader of this book, *you* are our most important critic and commentator. We value your opinion and want to know what we're doing right, what we could do better, what areas you'd like to see us publish in, and any other words of wisdom you're willing to pass our way.

We welcome your comments. You can email or write to let us know what you did or didn't like about this book—as well as what we can do to make our books better.

Please note that we cannot help you with technical problems related to the topic of this book.

When you write, please be sure to include this book's title and author as well as your name and email address. We will carefully review your comments and share them with the author and editors who worked on the book.

Email: feedback@developers-library.info

Mail: Reader Feedback
         Addison-Wesley Developer's Library
         Pearson Education
         800 East 96th Street
         Indianapolis, IN 46240

Reader Services

Visit our website and register this book at informit.com/register for convenient access to any updates, downloads, or errata that might be available for this book.

Introduction

This Book's Scope

As the title suggests, this book is about the object-oriented (OO) thought process. Although choosing the theme and title of a book are important decisions, these decisions are not at all straightforward when dealing with a highly conceptual topic. Many books deal with one level or another of programming and object orientation. Several popular books cover topics including OO analysis, OO design, OO programming, design patterns, OO data (XML), the Unified Modeling Language (UML), OO Web development, OO Mobile development, various OO programming languages, and many other topics related to OO programming.

However, while poring over all these books, many people forget that all these topics are built on a single foundation: how you think in OO ways. Often, many software professionals, as well as students, dive into these books without taking the appropriate time and effort to *really* understand the design concepts behind the code.

I contend that learning OO concepts is not accomplished by learning a specific development method, a programming language, or a set of design tools. Doing things in an OO manner is, simply put, a way of thinking. This book is all about the OO thought process.

Separating the languages, development practices, and tools from the OO thought process is not an easy task. Often, people are introduced to OO concepts by diving headfirst into a programming language. For example, many years ago, a large number of C programmers were first introduced to object orientation by migrating directly to C++ before they were even remotely exposed to OO concepts. Other software professionals' first exposure to object orientation was in the context of presentations that included object models using UML—again, before they were even exposed directly to OO concepts. Even now, a couple of decades after the emergence of the Internet as a business platform, it is not unusual to see programming books and professional training materials defer OO concepts until later in the discussion.

It is important to understand the significant difference between learning OO concepts and programming in an OO language. This came into sharp focus for me well before I worked on the first edition of this book, when I read articles like Craig Larman's "What the UML Is—and Isn't." In this article, he states,

Unfortunately, in the context of software engineering and the UML diagramming language, acquiring the skills to read and write UML notation seems to sometimes be equated with skill in object-oriented analysis and design. Of course, this is not so, and the latter is much more important than the former. Therefore, I recommend seeking education and educational materials in which intellectual skill in object-oriented analysis and design is paramount rather than UML notation or the use of a case tool.

Thus, although learning a modeling language is an important step, it is much more important to learn OO skills first. Learning UML before fully understanding OO concepts is similar to learning how to read an electrical diagram without first knowing anything about electricity.

The same problem occurs with programming languages. As stated earlier, many C programmers moved into the realm of object orientation by migrating to C++ before being directly exposed to OO concepts. This would always come out in an interview. Many times, developers who claim to be C++ programmers are simply C programmers using C++ compilers. Even now, with languages such as C# .NET, VB .NET, Objective-C, and Java well established, a few key questions in a job interview can quickly uncover a lack of OO understanding.

Early versions of Visual Basic are not OO. C is not OO, and C++ was *developed* to be backward compatible with C. Because of this, it is quite possible to use a C++ compiler writing only C syntax while forsaking all of C++'s OO features. Objective-C was designed as an extension to the standard ANSI C language. Even worse, a programmer can use just enough OO features to make a program incomprehensible to OO and non-OO programmers alike.

Thus, it is of vital importance that while you're learning to use OO development environments, you first learn the fundamental OO concepts. Resist the temptation to jump directly into a programming language (such as Objective-C, VB .NET, C++, C# .NET, or Java) or a modeling language (such as UML), and instead take the time to learn the object-oriented thought process.

After programming in C for many years, I took my first Smalltalk class in the late 1980s. The company I was with at the time had determined that its software developers needed to learn this up-and-coming technology. The instructor opened the class by stating that the OO paradigm was a totally new way of thinking (*despite the fact that it has been around since the 60s*). He went on to say that although all of us were most likely very good programmers, about 10%–20% of us would never really grasp the OO way of doing things. If this statement is indeed true, it is most likely because some good programmers never take the time to make the paradigm shift and learn the underlying OO concepts.

What's New in the Fourth Edition

As stated often in this introduction, my vision for the first edition was to stick to the concepts rather than focus on a specific emerging technology. Although I still adhere to this goal for the second, third, and fourth editions, I have included chapters on several application topics that fit well with object-oriented concepts. Chapters 1–10 cover the fundamental object-oriented concepts, and Chapters 11–15 are focused on applying these concepts to some general object-oriented technologies. For example, Chapters 1–10 provide the foundation for a course on object-oriented fundamentals (such as encapsulation, polymorphism, inheritance, and the like), with Chapters 11–15 adding some practical applications.

For the fourth edition, I expanded on many of the topics of the previous editions. These revised and updated topics include coverage of the following:

- Mobile device development, which includes phone apps, mobile apps and mobile/web, hybrids, and so on

- Objective-C code examples to include the iOS environment

- Human-readable data interchange using XML and JSON
- Rendering and transformation of data using CSS, XSLT, and so on
- Web services, including Simple Object Access Protocol (SOAP), RESTful Web Services, and the like
- Client/server technologies and marshaling objects
- Persistent data and serializing objects
- Expanded code examples, for certain chapters, in Java, C# .NET, VB .NET, and Objective-C available online on the publisher's website

The Intended Audience

This book is a general introduction to fundamental OO concepts, with code examples to reinforce the concepts. One of the most difficult juggling acts was to keep the code conceptual while still providing a solid code base. The goal of this book is to enable a reader to understand the concepts and technology without having a compiler at hand. However, if you do have a compiler available, there is code to be executed and explored.

The intended audience includes business managers, designers, developers, programmers, project managers, and anyone who wants to gain a general understanding of what object orientation is all about. Reading this book should provide a strong foundation for moving to other books covering more advanced OO topics.

Of these more advanced books, one of my favorites is *Object-Oriented Design in Java*, by Stephen Gilbert and Bill McCarty. I really like the approach of the book and have used it as a textbook in classes I have taught on OO concepts. I cite *Object-Oriented Design in Java* often throughout this book, and I recommend that you graduate to it after you complete this one.

Other books that I have found very helpful include *Effective C++*, by Scott Meyers; *Classical and Object-Oriented Software Engineering*, by Stephen R. Schach; *Thinking in C++*, by Bruce Eckel; *UML Distilled*, by Martin Fowler; and *Java Design*, by Peter Coad and Mark Mayfield.

While teaching intro-level programming and web development classes to programmers at corporations and universities, it quickly became obvious to me that most of these programmers easily picked up the language syntax; however, these same programmers struggled with the OO nature of the language.

The Book's Approach

It should be obvious by now that I am a firm believer in becoming comfortable with the object-oriented thought process before jumping into a programming language or modeling language. This book is filled with examples of code and UML diagrams; however, you do not need to know a specific programming language or UML to read it. After all I have said about learning the concepts first, why is there so much Java, C# .NET, VB .NET, and Objective-C code, as well as so many UML diagrams? First, they are great for illustrating OO concepts. Second, they are vital to the OO process and should be addressed at an introductory level. The key is not to focus on Java, C# .NET, VB .NET, and Objective-C or UML, but to use them as aids in the understanding of the underlying concepts.

Note that I really like using UML class diagrams as a visual aid in understanding classes, and their attributes and methods. In fact, the class diagrams are the only component of UML that is used in this book. I believe that the UML class diagrams offer a great way to model the conceptual nature of object models. I continue to use object models as an educational tool to illustrate class design and how classes relate to one another.

The code examples in the book illustrate concepts such as loops and functions. However, understanding the code itself is not a prerequisite for understanding the concepts; it might be helpful to have a book at hand that covers specific languages' syntax if you want to get more detailed.

I cannot state too strongly that this book does *not* teach Java, C# .NET, VB .NET, Objective-C, or UML, all of which can command volumes unto themselves. It is my hope that this book will whet your appetite for other OO topics, such as OO analysis, object-oriented design, and OO programming.

This Book's Conventions   *espaciales*

The following conventions are used in this book:

- Code lines, commands, statements, and any other code-related terms appear in a monospace typeface.   *(sp)*
- Throughout the book, there are special sidebar elements, such as the following: *projects*

▌ **Tip**
▌ A Tip offers advice or shows you an easy way of doing something.

▌ **Note**
▌ A Note presents interesting information related to the discussion—a little more insight or a pointer to some new technique.

▌ **Caution**
▌ A Caution alerts you to a possible problem and gives you advice on how to avoid it.

Source Code Used in This Book

The sample code described throughout this book is available on the publisher's website. Go to informit.com/register and register your book for access to downloads.

1

Introduction to Object-Oriented Concepts

Although many programmers don't realize it, object-oriented (OO) software development has been around since the early 1960s. It wasn't until the mid to late 1990s that the object-oriented paradigm started to gain momentum, despite the fact that popular object-oriented programming languages such as Smalltalk and C++ were already widely used.

The rise of OO methodologies coincides with the emergence of the Internet as a business and entertainment platform. In short, objects work well over a network. And after it became obvious that the Internet was here to stay, object-oriented technologies were already well positioned to develop the new web-based technologies.

It is important to note that the title of this first chapter is "Introduction to Object-Oriented Concepts." The operative word here is "concepts" and not "technologies." Technologies change very quickly in the software industry, whereas concepts evolve. I use the term "evolve" because, although they remain relatively stable, they do change. And this is what is really cool about focusing on the concepts. Despite their consistency, they are always undergoing reinterpretations, and this allows for some very interesting discussions.

This evolution can be easily traced over the past 20 years or so as we follow the progression of the various industry technologies from the first primitive browsers of the mid to late 1990s to the mobile/phone/web applications that dominate today. As always, new developments are just around the corner as we explore hybrid apps and more. Throughout this journey, OO concepts have been there every step of the way. That is why the topics of this chapter are so important. These concepts are just as relevant today as they were 20 years ago.

The Fundamental Concepts

The primary point of this book is to get you thinking about how the concepts are used in designing object-oriented systems. Historically, object-oriented languages are defined by the following: *encapsulation*, *inheritance*, and *polymorphism*. Thus, if a language does not implement all of these, it is generally not considered completely object-oriented. Along with these three terms, I always include composition in the mix; thus, my list of object-oriented concepts looks like this:

- Encapsulation
- Inheritance
- Polymorphism
- Composition

We will discuss all these in detail as we proceed through the rest of the book.

One of the issues that I have struggled with right from the first edition of this book is how these concepts relate directly to current design practices, which are always changing. For example, there has always been debate about using inheritance in an OO design. Does inheritance actually break encapsulation? (This topic will be covered in later chapters.) Even now, many developers try to avoid inheritance as much as possible.

My approach is, as always, to stick to concepts. Whether or not you use inheritance, you at least need to understand what inheritance is, thus enabling you to make an educated design choice. As mentioned in the introduction, the intended audience is those who want *a general introduction to fundamental OO concepts*. With this statement in mind, in this chapter I present the fundamental object-oriented concepts with the hope that the reader will then gain a solid foundation for making important design decisions. The concepts covered here touch on most, if not all, of the topics covered in subsequent chapters, which explore these issues in much greater detail.

Objects and Legacy Systems

As OO moved into the mainstream, one of the issues facing developers was the integration of new OO technologies with existing systems. At the time, lines were being drawn between OO and structured (or procedural) programming, which was the dominant development paradigm at the time. I always found this odd because, in my mind, object-oriented and structured programming do not compete with each other. They are complementary because objects integrate well with structured code. Even now, I often hear this question: Are you a structured programmer or an object-oriented programmer? Without hesitation, I would answer: both.

In the same vein, object-oriented code is not meant to replace structured code. Many non-OO *legacy systems* (that is, older systems that are already in place) are doing the job quite well, so why risk potential disaster by changing or replacing them? In most cases, you should not change them, at least not for the sake of change. There is nothing inherently wrong with systems written in non–OO code. However, brand-new development definitely warrants the consideration of using OO technologies (in some cases, there is no choice but to do so).

Although there has been a steady and significant growth in OO development in the past 20 years, the global community's dependence on networks such as the Internet and mobile infrastructures has helped catapult it even further into the mainstream. The literal explosion of transactions performed on browsers and mobile apps has opened up brand-new markets, where much of the software development is new and mostly unencumbered by legacy concerns. Even when there are legacy concerns, there is a trend to wrap the legacy systems in object wrappers.

Object Wrappers

Object wrappers are object-oriented code that includes other code inside. For example, you can take structured code (such as loops and conditions) and *wrap* it inside an object to make it look like an object. You can also use object wrappers to *wrap* functionality such as security features, nonportable hardware features, and so on. Wrapping structured code is covered in detail in Chapter 6, "Designing with Objects."

Today, one of the most interesting areas of software development is the integration of legacy code with mobile- and web-based systems. In many cases, a mobile web front-end ultimately connects to data that resides on a mainframe. Developers who can combine the skills of mainframe and mobile web development are in demand.

You probably experience objects in your daily life without even realizing it. These experiences can take place in your car, when you're talking on your cell phone, using your home entertainment system, playing computer games, and many other situations. The electronic highway has, in essence, become an object-based highway. As businesses gravitate toward the mobile web, they are gravitating toward objects because the technologies used for electronic commerce are mostly OO in nature.

Mobile Web

No doubt, the emergence of the Internet provided a major impetus for the shift to object-oriented technologies. This is because objects are well suited for use on networks. Although the Internet was at the forefront of this paradigm shift, mobile networks have now joined the mix in a major way. In this book, the term *mobile web* will be used in the context of concepts that pertain to both mobile app development and web development. The term *hybrid* app is sometimes used to refer to applications that render in browser on both web and mobile devices.

Procedural Versus OO Programming

Before we delve deeper into the advantages of OO development, let's consider a more fundamental question: What exactly is an object? This is both a complex and a simple question. It is complex because learning any method of software development is not trivial. It is simple because people already think in terms of objects.

For example, when you look at a person, you see the person as an object. And an object is defined by two components: attributes and behaviors. A person has attributes, such as eye color, age, height, and so on. A person also has behaviors, such as walking, talking, breathing, and so on. In its basic definition, an *object* is an entity that contains *both* data and behavior.

The word *both* is the key difference between OO programming and other programming methodologies. In procedural programming, for example, code is placed into totally distinct functions or procedures. Ideally, as shown in Figure 1.1, these procedures then become "black boxes," where inputs go in and outputs come out. Data is placed into separate structures and is manipulated by these functions or procedures.

Difference Between OO and Procedural

In OO design, the attributes and behaviors are contained within a single object, whereas in procedural, or structured, design, the attributes and behaviors are normally separated.

Inputs → [black box] → Outputs

Figure 1.1   Black boxes.

As OO design grew in popularity, one of the realities that initially slowed its acceptance was that there were a lot of non-OO systems in place that worked perfectly fine. Thus, it did not make any business sense to change the systems for the sake of change. Anyone who is familiar with any computer system knows that any change can spell disaster—even if the change is perceived to be slight.

This situation came into play with the lack of acceptance of OO databases. At one point in the emergence of OO development, it seemed somewhat likely that OO databases would replace relational databases. However, this never happened. Businesses have a lot of money invested in relational databases, and one overriding factor discouraged conversion—they worked. When all the costs and risks of converting systems from relational to OO databases became apparent, there was no compelling reason to switch.

In fact, the business forces have now found a happy middle ground. Much of the software development practices today have flavors of several development methodologies, such as OO and structured.

As illustrated in Figure 1.2, in structured programming the data is often separated from the procedures, and often the data is global, so it is easy to modify data that is outside the scope of your code. This means that access to data is uncontrolled and unpredictable (that is, multiple functions may have access to the global data). Second, because you have no control over who has access to the data, testing and debugging are much more difficult. Objects address these problems by combining data and behavior into a nice, complete package.

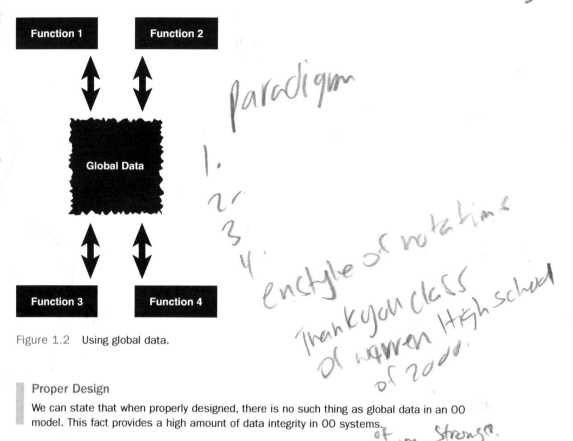

Figure 1.2   Using global data.

Proper Design

We can state that when properly designed, there is no such thing as global data in an OO model. This fact provides a high amount of data integrity in OO systems.

Rather than replacing other software development paradigms, objects are an evolutionary response. Structured programs have complex data structures, such as arrays, and so on. C++ has structures, which have many of the characteristics of objects (classes).

However, objects are much more than data structures and primitive data types, such as integers and strings. Although objects do contain entities such as integers and strings, which are used to represent attributes, they also contain methods, which represent behaviors. In an object, methods are used to perform operations on the data as well as other actions. Perhaps more important, you can control access to members of an object (both attributes and methods). This means that some members, both attributes and methods, can be hidden from other objects. For instance, an object called Math might contain two integers, called myInt1 and myInt2. Most likely, the Math object also contains the necessary methods to set and retrieve the values of myInt1 and myInt2. It might also contain a method called sum() to add the two integers together.

Data Hiding

In OO terminology, data are referred to as *attributes*, and behaviors are referred to as *methods*. Restricting access to certain attributes and/or methods is called *data hiding*.

By combining the attributes and methods in the same entity, which in OO parlance is called *encapsulation*, we can control access to the data in the Math object. By defining these integers as off-limits, another logically unconnected function cannot manipulate the integers myInt1 and myInt2—only the Math object can do that.

Sound Class Design Guidelines

Keep in mind that it is possible to create poorly designed OO classes that do not restrict access to class attributes. The bottom line is that you can design bad code just as efficiently with OO design as with any other programming methodology. Simply take care to adhere to sound class design guidelines (see Chapter 5, "Class Design Guidelines").

What happens when another object—for example, myObject wants to gain access to the sum of myInt1 and myInt2? It asks the Math object: myObject sends a message to the Math object. Figure 1.3 shows how the two objects communicate with each other via their methods. The message is really a call to the Math object's sum method. The sum method then returns the value to myObject. The beauty of this is that myObject does not need to know how the sum is calculated (although I'm sure it can guess). With this design methodology in place, you can change how the Math object calculates the sum without making a change to myObject (as long as the means to retrieve the sum do not change). All you want is the sum—you *don't care* how it is calculated.

Using a simple calculator example illustrates this concept. When determining a sum with a calculator, all you use is the calculator's interface—the keypad and LED display. The calculator has a sum method that is invoked when you press the correct key sequence. You may get the correct answer back; however, you have no idea how the result was obtained—either electronically or algorithmically.

Calculating the sum is not the responsibility of myObject—it's the Math object's responsibility. As long as myObject has access to the Math object, it can send the appropriate messages and obtain the proper result. In general, objects should not manipulate the internal data of other objects (that is, myObject should not directly change the value of myInt1 and myInt2). And, for reasons we will explore later, it is normally better to build small objects with specific tasks rather than build large objects that perform many.

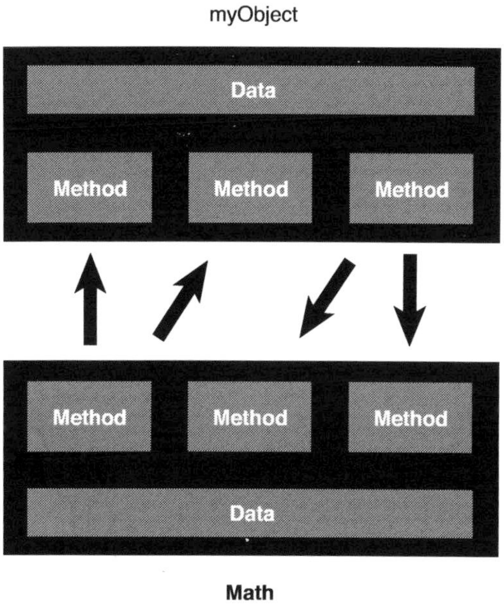

myObject

Data

| Method | Method | Method |

| Method | Method | Method |

| Data |

Math

Figure 1.3   Object-to-object communication.

Moving from Procedural to Object-Oriented Development

Now that we have a general understanding about some of the differences about procedural and object-oriented technologies, let's delve a bit deeper into both.

Procedural Programming

Procedural programming normally separates the data of a system from the operations that manipulate the data. For example, if you want to send information across a network, only the relevant data is sent (see Figure 1.4), with the expectation that the program at the other end of the network pipe knows what to do with it. In other words, some sort of handshaking agreement must be in place between the client and server to transmit the data. In this model, it is quite possible that no code is actually sent over the wire.

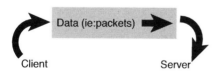

Data (ie:packets)

Client   Server

Figure 1.4   Data transmitted over a wire.

OO Programming

The fundamental advantage of OO programming is that the data and the operations that manipulate the data (the code) are both encapsulated in the object. For example, when an object is transported across a network, the entire object, including the data and behavior, goes with it.

> **A Single Entity**
>
> Although thinking in terms of a single entity is great in theory, in many cases, the behaviors themselves may not be sent because both sides have copies of the code. However, it is important to think in terms of the entire object being sent across the network as a single entity.

In Figure 1.5, the `Employee` object is sent over the network.

> **Proper Design**
>
> A good example of this concept is an object that is loaded by a browser. Often, the browser has no idea of what the object will do ahead of time because the code is not there previously. When the object is loaded, the browser executes the code within the object and uses the data contained within the object.

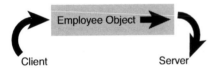

Client   Server

Figure 1.5   Objects transmitted over a wire.

What Exactly Is an Object?

Objects are the building blocks of an OO program. A program that uses OO technology is basically a collection of objects. To illustrate, let's consider that a corporate system contains objects that represent employees of that company. Each of these objects is made up of the data and behavior described in the following sections.

Object Data

The data stored within an object represents the state of the object. In OO programming terminology, this data is called *attributes*. In our example, as shown in Figure 1.6, employee attributes could be Social Security numbers, date of birth, gender, phone number, and so on. The attributes contain the information that differentiates between the various objects, in this case the employees. Attributes are covered in more detail later in this chapter in the discussion on classes.

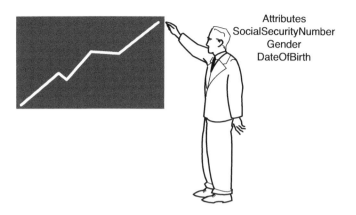

Attributes
SocialSecurityNumber
Gender
DateOfBirth

Figure 1.6   Employee attributes.

Object Behaviors

The *behavior* of an object represents what the object can do. In procedural languages, the behavior is defined by procedures, functions, and subroutines. In OO programming terminology, these behaviors are contained in *methods*, and you invoke a method by sending a message to it. In our employee example, consider that one of the behaviors required of an employee object is to set and return the values of the various attributes. Thus, each attribute would have corresponding methods, such as setGender() and getGender(). In this case, when another object needs this information, it can send a message to an employee object and ask it what its gender is.

Not surprisingly, the application of getters and setters, as with much of object-oriented technology, has evolved since the first edition of this book was published. This is especially true when in comes to data. As we will see in Chapter 11, "Objects and Portable Data: XML and JSON," and Chapter 12, "Persistent Objects: Serialization, Marshalling, and Relational Databases," data is now constructed in an object-oriented manner. Remember that one of the most interesting, not to mention powerful, advantages of using objects is that the data is part of the package—it is not separated from the code.

The emergence of XML has not only focused attention on presenting data in a portable manner; it also has facilitated alternative ways for the code to access the data. In .NET techniques, the getters and setters are considered properties of the data itself.

For example, consider an attribute called Name, using Java, that looks like the following:

```
public String Name;
```

The corresponding getter and setter would look like this:

```
public void setName (String n) {name = n;};
public String getName() {return name;};
```

Now, when creating an XML attribute called `Name`, the definition in C# .NET may look something like this:

```
Private string strName;
public String Name
{
    get
    {
        return this.strName;
    }
    set
    {
        if (value == null) return;
        this.strName = value;
    }
}
```

In this approach, the getters and setters are actually *properties* of the attributes—in this case, `Name`.

Regardless of the approach, the purpose is the same—controlled access to the attribute. For this chapter, I want to first concentrate on the conceptual nature of accessor methods; we will get more into properties when we cover object-oriented data in Chapter 11 and beyond.

Getters and Setters

The concept of getters and setters supports the concept of data hiding. Because other objects should not directly manipulate data within another object, the getters and setters provide controlled access to an object's data. Getters and setters are sometimes called accessor methods and mutator methods, respectively.

Note that we are showing only the interface of the methods, and not the implementation. The following information is all the user needs to know to effectively use the methods:

- The name of the method
- The parameters passed to the method
- The return type of the method

To illustrate behaviors, consider Figure 1.7.

In Figure 1.7, the `Payroll` object contains a method called `CalculatePay()` that calculates the pay for a specific employee. Among other information, the `Payroll` object must obtain the Social Security number of this employee. To get this information, the payroll object must send a message to the `Employee` object (in this case, the `getSocialSecurityNumber()` method). Basically, this means that the `Payroll` object calls the `getSocialSecurityNumber()` method of the `Employee` object. The employee object recognizes the message and returns the requested information.

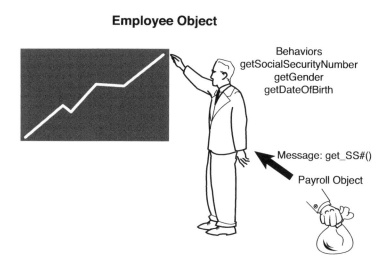

Employee Object

Behaviors
getSocialSecurityNumber
getGender
getDateOfBirth

Message: get_SS#()

Payroll Object

Figure 1.7   Employee behaviors.

To illustrate further, Figure 1.8 is a class diagram representing the Employee/Payroll system we have been talking about.

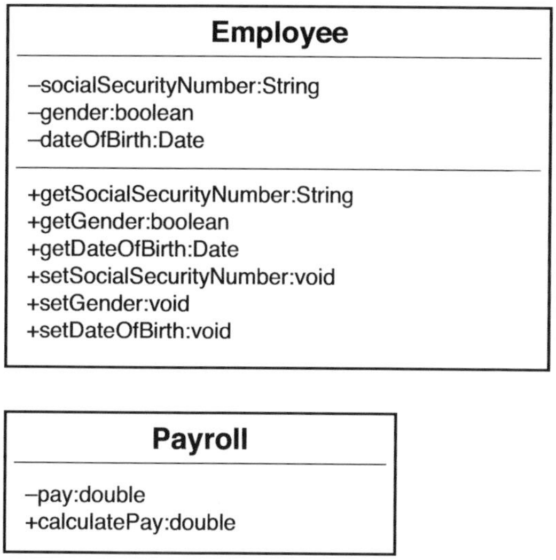

Employee

−socialSecurityNumber:String
−gender:boolean
−dateOfBirth:Date

+getSocialSecurityNumber:String
+getGender:boolean
+getDateOfBirth:Date
+setSocialSecurityNumber:void
+setGender:void
+setDateOfBirth:void

Payroll

−pay:double
+calculatePay:double

Figure 1.8   Employee and payroll class diagrams.

UML Class Diagrams

Because this is the first class diagram we have seen, it is very basic and lacks some of the constructs (such as constructors) that a proper class should contain. Fear not—we will discuss class diagrams and constructors in more detail in Chapter 3, "Advanced Object-Oriented Concepts."

Each class diagram is defined by three separate sections: the name itself, the data (attributes), and the behaviors (methods). In Figure 1.8, the Employee class diagram's attribute section contains SocialSecurityNumber, Gender, and DateofBirth, whereas the method section contains the methods that operate on these attributes. You can use UML modeling tools to create and maintain class diagrams that correspond to real code.

Modeling Tools

Visual modeling tools provide a mechanism to create and manipulate class diagrams using the Unified Modeling Language (UML). Class diagrams are discussed throughout this book, and you can find a description of this notation in Chapter 10, "Creating Object Models." UML class diagrams are used as a tool to help visualize classes and their relationships to other classes. The use of UML in this book is limited to class diagrams.

We will get into the relationships between classes and objects later in this chapter, but for now you can think of a class as a template from which objects are made. When an object is created, we say that the objects are instantiated. Thus, if we create three employees, we are actually creating three totally distinct instances of an Employee class. Each object contains its own copy of the attributes and methods. For example, consider Figure 1.9. An employee object called John (John is its identity) has its own copy of all the attributes and methods defined in the Employee class. An employee object called Mary has its own copy of attributes and methods. They both have a separate copy of the DateOfBirth attribute and the getDateOfBirth method.

An Implementation Issue

Be aware that there is not necessarily a physical copy of each method for each object. Rather, each object points to the same implementation. However, this is an issue left up to the compiler/operating platform. From a conceptual level, you can think of objects as being wholly independent and having their own attributes and methods.

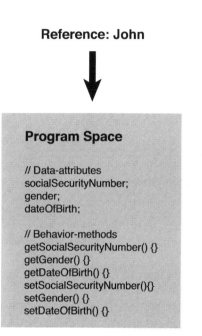

Figure 1.9   Program spaces.

What Exactly Is a Class?

In short, a class is a blueprint for an object. When you instantiate an object, you use a class as the basis for how the object is built. In fact, trying to explain classes and objects is really a chicken-and-egg dilemma. It is difficult to describe a class without using the term *object* and visa versa. For example, a specific individual bike is an object. However, someone had to have created the blueprints (that is, the class) to build the bike. In OO software, unlike the chicken-and-egg dilemma, we do know what comes first—the class. An object cannot be instantiated without a class. Thus, many of the concepts in this section are similar to those presented earlier in the chapter, especially when we talk about attributes and methods.

To explain classes and methods, it's helpful to use an example from the relational database world. In a database table, the definition of the table itself (fields, description, and data types used) would be a class (metadata), and the objects would be the rows of the table (data).

This book focuses on the concepts of OO software and not on a specific implementation (such as Java, C#, Visual Basic .NET, Objective C, or C++), but it is often helpful to use code examples to explain some concepts, so Java code fragments are used throughout the book to help explain some concepts when appropriate. However, when appropriate, the end of each chapter contains the chapter's example code in C#. Much of the code presented in the book is available electronically on the publisher's website. For many chapters, the code examples are provided electronically in Java, C# .Net, VB .NET, and Objective C.

The following sections describe some of the fundamental concepts of classes and how they interact.

Creating Objects

Classes can be thought of as the templates, or cookie cutters, for objects, as seen in Figure 1.10. A class is used to create an object.

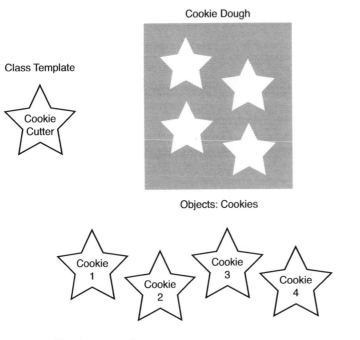

Figure 1.10   Class template.

A class can be thought of as a sort of higher-level data type. For example, just as you create an integer or a float:

```
int x;
float y;
```

you can also create an object by using a predefined class:

```
myClass myObject;
```

In this example, the names themselves make it obvious that myClass is the class and myObject is the object.

Remember that each object has its own attributes (data) and behaviors (functions or routines). A class defines the attributes and behaviors that all objects created with this class will possess. Classes are pieces of code. Objects instantiated from classes can be distributed individually or as part of a library. Because objects are created from classes, it follows that classes must define the basic building blocks of objects (attributes, behavior, and messages). In short, you must design a class before you can create an object.

For example, here is a definition of a Person class:

```
public class Person{

    //Attributes
    private String name;
    private String address;

    //Methods
    public String getName(){
        return name;
    }
    public void setName(String n){
        name = n;
    }

    public String getAddress(){
        return address;
    }
    public void setAddress(String adr){
        address = adr;
    }

}
```

Attributes

As you already saw, the data of a class is represented by attributes. Each class must define the attributes that will store the state of each object instantiated from that class. In the Person class example in the previous section, the Person class defines attributes for name and address.

Access Designations

When a data type or method is defined as public, other objects can directly access it. When a data type or method is defined as private, only that specific object can access it. Another access modifier, protected, allows access by related objects, which you'll learn about in Chapter 3.

Methods

As you learned earlier in the chapter, methods implement the required behavior of a class. Every object instantiated from this class has the methods as defined by the class. Methods may implement behaviors that are called from other objects (messages) or provide the fundamental, internal behavior of the class. Internal behaviors are private methods that are not accessible by other objects. In the `Person` class, the behaviors are `getName()`, `setName()`, `getAddress()`, and `setAddress()`. These methods allow other objects to inspect and change the values of the object's attributes. This is common technique in OO systems. In all cases, access to attributes within an object should be controlled by the object itself—no other object should directly change an attribute of another.

Messages

Messages are the communication mechanism between objects. For example, when Object A invokes a method of Object B, Object A is sending a message to Object B. Object B's response is defined by its return value. Only the public methods, not the private methods, of an object can be invoked by another object. The following code illustrates this concept:

```
public class Payroll{

    String name;

    Person p = new Person();

    String = p.setName("Joe");

    ... code

    String = p.getName();

}
```

In this example (assuming that a `Payroll` object is instantiated), the `Payroll` object is sending a message to a `Person` object, with the purpose of retrieving the name via the `getName()` method. Again, don't worry too much about the actual code, because we are really interested in the concepts. We address the code in detail as we progress through the book.

Using Class Diagrams as a Visual Tool

Over the years, many tools and modeling methodologies have been developed to assist in designing software systems. Right from the start, I have used UML class diagrams to assist in the educational process. Although it is beyond the scope of this book to describe UML in any detail, we will use UML class diagrams to illustrate the classes that we build. In fact, we have already used class diagrams in this chapter. Figure 1.11 shows the `Person` class diagram we discussed earlier in the chapter.

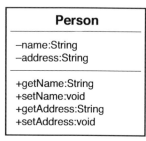

Person

−name:String
−address:String

+getName:String
+setName:void
+getAddress:String
+setAddress:void

Figure 1.11   The `Person` class diagram.

As we saw previously, notice that the attributes and methods are separated (the attributes on the top, and the methods on the bottom). As we delve more deeply into OO design, these class diagrams will get much more sophisticated and convey much more information on how the different classes interact with each other.

Encapsulation and Data Hiding

One of the primary advantages of using objects is that the object need not reveal all its attributes and behaviors. In good OO design (at least what is generally accepted as good), an object should reveal only the interfaces that other objects must have to interact with it. Details not pertinent to the use of the object should be hidden from all other objects.

Encapsulation is defined by the fact that objects contain both the attributes and behaviors. Data hiding is a major part of encapsulation.

For example, an object that calculates the square of a number must provide an interface to obtain the result. However, the internal attributes and algorithms used to calculate the square need not be made available to the requesting object. Robust classes are designed with encapsulation in mind. In the next sections, we cover the concepts of interface and implementation, which are the basis of encapsulation.

Interfaces

We have seen that the interface defines the fundamental means of communication between objects. Each class design specifies the interfaces for the proper instantiation and operation of objects. Any behavior that the object provides must be invoked by a message sent using one of the provided interfaces. The interface should completely describe how users of the class interact with the class. In most OO languages, the methods that are part of the interface are designated as `public`.

> ### Private Data
>
> For data hiding to work, all attributes should be declared as `private`. Thus, attributes are never part of the interface. Only the `public` methods are part of the class interface. Declaring an attribute as `public` breaks the concept of data hiding.

Let's look at the example just mentioned: calculating the square of a number. In this example, the interface would consist of two pieces:

- How to instantiate a `Square` object
- How to send a value to the object and get the square of that value in return

As discussed earlier in the chapter, if a user needs access to an attribute, a method is created to return the value of the attribute (a getter). If a user then wants to obtain the value of an attribute, a method is called to return its value. In this way, the object that contains the attribute controls access to it. This is of vital importance, especially in security, testing, and maintenance. If you control the access to the attribute, when a problem arises, you do not have to worry about tracking down every piece of code that might have changed the attribute—it can be changed in only one place (the setter).

From a security perspective, you don't want uncontrolled code to change or retrieve data such as passwords and personal information.

> ### Signatures—Interfaces Versus Interfaces
>
> It is important to note that there are interfaces to the classes as well as the methods; don't confuse the two. The interfaces to the classes are the public methods. You invoke these methods by using their signature, which primarily consists of the method name and its parameter list. This concept is covered in more detail later.

Implementations

Only the public attributes and methods are considered the interface. The user should not see any part of the internal implementation—interacting with an object solely through class interfaces. Thus, anything defined as private is inaccessible to the user and considered part of the class's internal implementation.

In the previous example, for instance the `Employee` class, only the attributes were hidden. In many cases, there will be methods that also should be hidden and thus not part of the interface. Continuing the example of the square root from the previous section, the user does not care how the square root is calculated—as long as it is the correct answer. Thus, the implementation can change, and it will not affect the user's code. For example, the company that produces the calculator can change the algorithm (perhaps because it is more efficient) without affecting the result.

A Real-World Example of the Interface/Implementation Paradigm

Figure 1.12 illustrates the interface/implementation paradigm using real-world objects rather than code. The toaster requires electricity. To get this electricity, the cord from the toaster must be plugged into the electrical outlet, which is the interface. All the toaster needs to do to obtain the required electricity is to implement a cord that complies with the electrical outlet specifications; this is the interface between the toaster and the power company (actually the power industry). That the actual implementation is a coal-powered electric plant is not the concern of the toaster. In fact, for all the toaster cares, the implementation could be a nuclear power plant or a local power generator. With this model, any appliance can get electricity, as long as it conforms to the interface specification, as shown in Figure 1.12.

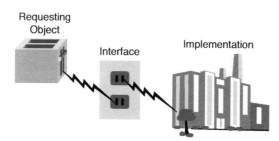

Figure 1.12   Power plant example.

A Model of the Interface/Implementation Paradigm

Let's explore the Square class further. Assume that you are writing a class that calculates the squares of integers. You must provide a separate interface and implementation. That is, you must specify a way for the user to invoke and obtain the square value. You must also provide the implementation that calculates the square; however, the user should not know anything about the specific implementation. Figure 1.13 shows one way to do this. Note that in the class diagram, the plus sign (+) designates public and the minus sign (-) designates private. Thus, you can identify the interface by the methods, prefaced with plus signs.

IntSquare
–squareValue:int
+getSquare:int –calculateSquare:int

Figure 1.13   The square class.

This class diagram corresponds to the following code:

```
public class IntSquare {

    // private attribute
    private int squareValue;

    // public interface
    public int getSquare (int value) {

        SquareValue =calculateSquare(value);

        return squareValue;

    }

    // private implementation
    private int calculateSquare (int value) {

        return value*value;

    }
}
```

Note that the only part of the class that the user has access to is the public method getSquare, which is the interface. The implementation of the square algorithm is in the method calculateSquare, which is private. Also notice that the attribute SquareValue is private because users do not need to know that this attribute exists. Therefore, we have hidden the part of the implementation: The object reveals only the interfaces the user needs to interact with it, and details that are not pertinent to the use of the object are hidden from other objects.

If the implementation were to change—suppose you wanted to use the language's built-in square function—you would not need to change the interface. Here the code uses the Java library method Math.pow, which performs the same function, but note that the interface is still calculateSquare:

```
// private implementation
private int calculateSquare (int value) {

    return = Math.pow(value,2);

}
```

The user would get the same functionality using the same interface, but the implementation would have changed. This is very important when you're writing code that deals with data; for example, you can move data from a file to a database without forcing the user to change any application code.

Inheritance

One of the most powerful features of OO programming is, perhaps, code reuse. Structured design provides code reuse to a certain extent—you can write a procedure and then use it as many times as you want. However, OO design goes an important step further, allowing you to define relationships between classes that facilitate not only code reuse, but also better overall design, by organizing classes and factoring in commonalties of various classes. *Inheritance* is a primary means of providing this functionality.

Inheritance allows a class to inherit the attributes and methods of another class. This allows creation of brand-new classes by abstracting out common attributes and behaviors.

One of the major design issues in OO programming is to factor out commonality of the various classes. For example, suppose you have a Dog class and a Cat class, and each will have an attribute for eye color. In a procedural model, the code for Dog and Cat would each contain this attribute. In an OO design, the color attribute could be moved up to a class called Mammal— along with any other common attributes and methods. In this case, both Dog and Cat inherit from the Mammal class, as shown in Figure 1.14.

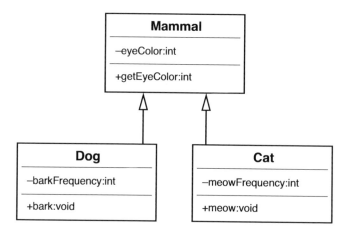

Figure 1.14   Mammal hierarchy.

The Dog and Cat classes both inherit from Mammal. This means that a Dog class has the following attributes:

```
eyeColor        // inherited from Mammal
barkFrequency   // defined only for Dogs
```

In the same vein, Dog object has the following methods:

```
getEyeColor     // inherited from Mammal
bark            // defined only for Dogs
```

When the Dog or the Cat object is instantiated, it contains everything in its own class, as well as everything from the parent class. Thus, Dog has all the properties of its class definition, as well as the properties inherited from the Mammal class.

Superclasses and Subclasses

The superclass, or parent class (sometimes called base class), contains all the attributes and behaviors that are common to classes that inherit from it. For example, in the case of the Mammal class, all mammals have similar attributes, such as eyeColor and hairColor, as well as behaviors, such as generateInternalHeat and growHair. All mammals have these attributes and behaviors, so it is not necessary to duplicate them down the inheritance tree for each type of mammal. Duplication requires a lot more work, and perhaps more worrisome, it can introduce errors and inconsistencies.

The subclass, or child class (sometimes called derived class), is an extension of the superclass. Thus, the Dog and Cat classes inherit all those common attributes and behaviors from the Mammal class. The Mammal class is considered the superclass of the Dog and the Cat subclasses, or child classes.

Inheritance provides a rich set of design advantages. When you're designing a Cat class, the Mammal class provides much of the functionality needed. By inheriting from the Mammal object, Cat already has all the attributes and behaviors that make it a true mammal. To make it more specifically a cat type of mammal, the Cat class must include any attributes or behaviors that pertain solely to a cat.

Abstraction

An inheritance tree can grow quite large. When the Mammal and Cat classes are complete, other mammals, such as dogs (or lions, tigers, and bears), can be added quite easily. The Cat class can also be a superclass to other classes. For example, it might be necessary to abstract the Cat class further, to provide classes for Persian cats, Siamese cats, and so on. Just as with Cat, the Dog class can be the parent for GermanShepherd and Poodle (see Figure 1.15). The power of inheritance lies in its abstraction and organization techniques.

In most recent OO languages (such as Java, .NET, and Objective C), a class can have only a single parent class; however, a class can have many child classes. Some languages, such as C++, can have multiple parents. The former case is called *single-inheritance*, and the latter is called *multiple-inheritance*.

Note that the classes GermanShepherd and Poodle both inherit from Dog—each contains only a single method. However, because they inherit from Dog, they also inherit from Mammal. Thus, the GermanShepherd and Poodle classes contain all the attributes and methods included in Dog and Mammal, as well as their own (see Figure 1.16).

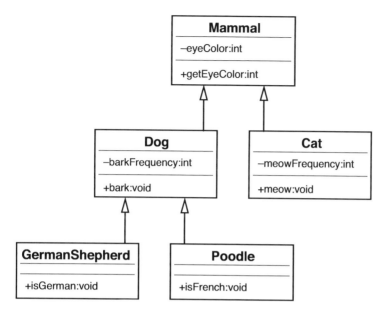

Figure 1.15   Mammal UML diagram.

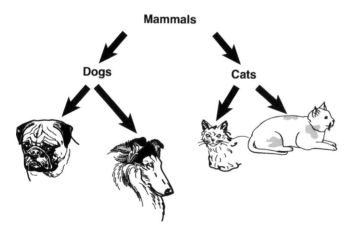

Figure 1.16   Mammal hierarchy.

Is-a Relationships

Consider a Shape example where Circle, Square, and Star all inherit directly from Shape. This relationship is often referred to as an *is-a relationship* because a circle is a shape, and a square is a shape. When a subclass inherits from a superclass, it can do anything that the super-class can do. Thus, `Circle`, `Square`, and `Star` are all extensions of `Shape`.

In Figure 1.17, the name on each of the objects represents the `Draw` method for the `Circle`, `Star`, and `Square` objects, respectively. When we design this `Shape` system, it would be very helpful to standardize how we use the various shapes. Thus, we could decide that if we want to draw a shape, no matter what shape, we will invoke a method called `draw`. If we adhere to this decision, whenever we want to draw a shape, only the `Draw` method needs to be called, regardless of what the shape is. Here lies the fundamental concept of polymorphism—it is the individual object's responsibility, be it a `Circle`, `Star`, or `Square`, to draw itself. This is a common concept in many current software applications, such as drawing and word processing applications.

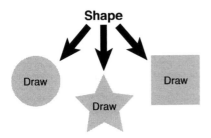

Figure 1.17   The shape hierarchy.

Polymorphism

Polymorphism is a Greek word that literally means many shapes. Although polymorphism is tightly coupled to inheritance, it is often cited separately as one of the most powerful advantages to object-oriented technologies. When a message is sent to an object, the object must have a method defined to respond to that message. In an inheritance hierarchy, all subclasses inherit the interfaces from their superclass. However, because each subclass is a separate entity, each might require a separate response to the same message.

For example, consider the `Shape` class and the behavior called `Draw`. When you tell somebody to draw a shape, the first question asked is, "What shape?" No one can draw a shape, because it is an abstract concept (in fact, the `Draw()` method in the `Shape` code following contains no implementation). You must specify a concrete shape. To do this, you provide the actual imple-mentation in `Circle`. Even though `Shape` has a `Draw` method, `Circle` overrides this method and provides its own `Draw()` method. Overriding basically means replacing an implementation of a parent with one from a child.

For example, suppose you have an array of three shapes—`Circle`, `Square`, and `Star`. Even though you treat them all as `Shape` objects, and send a `Draw` message to each `Shape` object, the end result is different for each because `Circle`, `Square`, and `Star` provide the actual implementations. In short, each class is able to respond differently to the same `Draw` method and draw itself. This is what is meant by polymorphism.

Consider the following `Shape` class:

```
public abstract class Shape{

    private double area;

    public abstract double getArea();

}
```

The `Shape` class has an attribute called `area` that holds the value for the area of the shape. The method `getArea()` includes an identifier called `abstract`. When a method is defined as `abstract`, a subclass must provide the implementation for this method; in this case, `Shape` is requiring subclasses to provide a `getArea()` implementation. Now let's create a class called `Circle` that inherits from `Shape` (the `extends` keyword specifies that `Circle` inherits from `Shape`):

```
public class Circle extends Shape{

    double radius;

    public Circle(double r) {

        radius = r;

    }

    public double getArea() {

        area = 3.14*(radius*radius);
        return (area);

    }
}
```

We introduce a new concept here called a *constructor*. The `Circle` class has a method with the same name, `Circle`. When a method name is the same as the class and no return type is provided, the method is a special method, called a constructor. Consider a constructor as the entry point for the class, where the object is built; the constructor is a good place to perform initializations and start-up tasks.

The `Circle` constructor accepts a single parameter, representing the radius, and assigns it to the `radius` attribute of the `Circle` class.

The `Circle` class also provides the implementation for the `getArea` method, originally defined as abstract in the `Shape` class.

We can create a similar class, called `Rectangle`:

```
public class Rectangle extends Shape{

    double length;
    double width;

    public Rectangle(double l, double w){
        length = l;
        width = w;
    }

    public double getArea() {
        area = length*width;
        return (area);
    }

}
```

Now we can create any number of rectangles, circles, and so on and invoke their `getArea()` method. This is because we know that all rectangles and circles inherit from `Shape`, and all `Shape` classes have a `getArea()` method. If a subclass inherits an abstract method from a superclass, it must provide a concrete implementation of that method, or else it will be an abstract class itself (see Figure 1.18 for a UML diagram). This approach also provides the mechanism to create other, new classes quite easily.

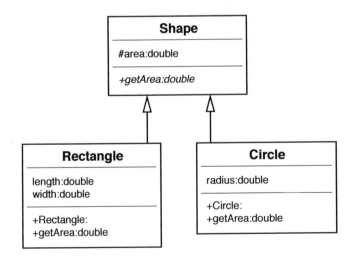

Figure 1.18   Shape UML diagram.

Thus, we can instantiate the `Shape` classes in this way:

```
Circle circle = new Circle(5);
Rectangle rectangle = new Rectangle(4,5);
```

Then, using a construct such as a stack, we can add these `Shape` classes to the stack:

```
stack.push(circle);
stack.push(rectangle);
```

What Is a Stack?

A stack is a data structure that is a last-in, first-out system. It is like a coin changer, where you insert coins at the top of the cylinder and, when you need a coin, you take one off the top, which is the last one you inserted. Pushing an item onto the stack means that you are adding an item to the top (like inserting another coin into the changer). Popping an item off the stack means that you are taking the last item off the stack (like taking the coin off the top).

Now comes the fun part. We can empty the stack, and we do not have to worry about what kind of `Shape` classes are in it (we just know they are shapes):

```
while (  !stack.empty()) {
    Shape shape = (Shape) stack.pop();
    System.out.println ("Area = " + shape.getArea());
}
```

In reality, we are sending the same message to all the shapes:

```
shape.getArea()
```

However, the actual behavior that takes place depends on the type of shape. For example, `Circle` calculates the area for a circle, and `Rectangle` calculates the area of a rectangle. In effect (and here is the key concept), we are sending a message to the `Shape` classes and experiencing different behavior depending on what subclass of `Shape` is being used.

This approach is meant to provide standardization the interface across classes, as well as applications. Consider an office suite application that includes a word processing and a spreadsheet application. Let's assume that both have a class called Office which contains an interface called `print()`. This `print()` interface is required for all classes that are part of the office suite. The interesting thing here is that although both the word processor and spreadsheet invoke the print() interface, they do different things—one prints a word processing document and the other a spreadsheet document.

Composition

It is natural to think of objects as containing other objects. A television set contains a tuner and video display. A computer contains video cards, keyboards, and drives. Although the computer can be considered an object unto itself, the drive is also considered a valid object.

In fact, you could open up the computer and remove the drive and hold it in your hand. Both the computer and the drive are considered objects. It is just that the computer contains other objects—such as drives.

In this way, objects are often built, or composed, from other objects: This is composition.

Abstraction

Just as with inheritance, composition provides a mechanism for building objects. In fact, I would argue that there are only two ways to build classes from other classes: *inheritance* and *composition*. As we have seen, inheritance allows one class to inherit from another class. We can thus abstract out attributes and behaviors for common classes. For example, dogs and cats are both mammals because a dog *is-a* mammal and a cat *is-a* mammal. With composition, we can also build classes by embedding classes in other classes.

Consider the relationship between a car and an engine. The benefits of separating the engine from the car are evident. By building the engine separately, we can use the engine in various cars—not to mention other advantages. But we can't say that an engine *is-a* car. This just doesn't sound right when it rolls off the tongue (and because we are modeling real-world systems, this is the effect we want). Rather, we use the term *has-a* to describe composition relationships. A car *has-a(n)* engine.

Has-a Relationships

Although an inheritance relationship is considered an *is-a* relationship for reasons already discussed, a composition relationship is termed a *has-a relationship*. Using the example in the previous section, a television *has-a* tuner and *has-a* video display. A television is obviously not a tuner, so there is no inheritance relationship. In the same vein, a computer *has-a* video card, *has-a* keyboard, and *has-a* disk drive. The topics of inheritance, composition, and how they relate to each other are covered in great detail in Chapter 7, "Mastering Inheritance and Composition."

Conclusion

There is a lot to cover when discussing OO technologies. However, you should leave this chapter with a good understanding of the following topics:

- **Encapsulation**—Encapsulating the data and behavior into a single object is of primary importance in OO development. A single object contains both its data and behaviors and can hide what it wants from other objects.

- **Inheritance**—A class can inherit from another class and take advantage of the attributes and methods defined by the superclass.

- **Polymorphism**—Polymorphism means that similar objects can respond to the same message in different ways. For example, you might have a system with many shapes.

However, a circle, a square, and a star are each drawn differently. Using polymorphism, you can send each of these shapes the same message (for example, Draw), and each shape is responsible for drawing itself.

- **Composition**—Composition means that an object is built from other objects.

This chapter covers the fundamental OO concepts, of which by now you should have a good grasp.

Example Code Used in This Chapter

The following code is presented in C# .NET. Code for other languages, such as VB .NET and Objective-C, are available electronically on the publisher's web site. These examples correspond to the Java code that is listed inside the chapter itself.

The TestPerson Example: C# .NET

```csharp
using System;

namespace ConsoleApplication1
{
    class TestPerson
    {
        static void Main(string[] args)
        {

            Person joe = new Person();

            joe.Name = "joe";

            Console.WriteLine(joe.Name);

            Console.ReadLine();
        }
    }

    public class Person
    {

        //Attributes
        private String strName;
        private String strAddress;

        //Methods
        public String Name
```

```
        {
            get { return strName; }
            set { strName = value; }
        }

        public String Address
        {
            get { return strAddress; }
            set { strAddress = value; }
        }

    }
}
```

The `TestShape` Example: C# .NET

```
using System;

namespace TestShape
{
    class TestShape
    {
        public static void Main()
        {

            Circle circle = new Circle(5);
            Console.WriteLine(circle.calcArea());

            Rectangle rectangle = new Rectangle(4, 5);
            Console.WriteLine(rectangle.calcArea());

            Console.ReadLine();

        }
    }
    public abstract class Shape
    {

        protected double area;

        public abstract double calcArea();

    }
    public class Circle : Shape
    {
```

```
    private double radius;

    public Circle(double r)
    {

        radius = r;

    }

    public override double calcArea()
    {

        area = 3.14 * (radius * radius);
        return (area);

    }
}
public class Rectangle : Shape
{

    private double length;
    private double width;

    public Rectangle(double l, double w)
    {
        length = l;
        width = w;
    }

    public override double calcArea()
    {
        area = length * width;
        return (area);
    }
}
}
```

2

How to Think in Terms of Objects

In Chapter 1, "Introduction to Object-Oriented Concepts," you learned the fundamental object-oriented (OO) concepts. The rest of the book delves more deeply into these concepts and introduces several others. Many factors go into a good design, whether it is an OO design or not. The fundamental unit of OO design is the class. The desired end result of OO design is a robust and functional object model—in other words, a complete system.

As with most things in life, there is no single right or wrong way to approach a problem. There are usually many ways to tackle the same problem. So when attempting to design an OO solution, don't get hung up in trying to do a perfect design the first time (there will always be room for improvement). What you really need to do is brainstorm and let your thought process go in different directions. Do not try to conform to any standards or conventions when trying to solve a problem because the whole idea is to be creative.

In fact, at the start of the process, don't even begin to consider a specific programming language. The first order of business is to identify and solve business problems. Work on the conceptual analysis and design first. Think about specific technologies only when they are fundamental to the business problem. For example, you can't design a wireless network without wireless technology. However, it is often the case that you will have more than one software solution to consider.

Thus, before you start to design a system, or even a class, think the problem through and have some fun! In this chapter, we explore the fine art and science of OO thinking.

Any fundamental change in thinking is not trivial. As a case in point, a lot has been mentioned about the move from structured to OO development. As was mentioned earlier, one side-effect of this debate is the misconception that structured and object-oriented development are mutually exclusive. This is not the case. As we know from our discussion on wrappers, structured and object-oriented development coexist. In fact, when you write an OO application, you are using structured constructs everywhere. I have never seen a program, OO or otherwise, that does not use loops, if-statements, and so on. Yet making the switch to OO design does require a different type of investment.

Changing from FORTRAN to COBOL, or even from C, requires that you learn a new language; however, making the move from COBOL to C++, C# .NET, Visual Basic .NET, Objective-C, or Java requires that you learn a new thought process. This is where the overused phrase *OO paradigm* rears its ugly head. When moving to an OO language, you must first go through the investment of learning OO concepts and the corresponding thought process. If this paradigm shift does not take place, one of two things will happen: Either the project will not truly be OO in nature (for example, it will use C++ without using OO constructs), or the project will be a complete object-disoriented mess.

Three important things you can do to develop a good sense of the OO thought process are covered in this chapter:

- Knowing the difference between the interface and implementation

- Thinking more abstractly

- Giving the user the minimal interface possible

We have already touched on some of these concepts in Chapter 1, and we now go into much more detail.

Knowing the Difference Between the Interface and the Implementation

As we saw in Chapter 1, one of the keys to building a strong OO design is to understand the difference between the interface and the implementation. Thus, when designing a class, what the user needs to know and what the user does not need to know are of vital importance. The data hiding mechanism inherent with encapsulation is the means by which nonessential data is hidden from the user.

> **Caution**
>
> Do not confuse the concept of the interface with terms like *graphical user interface (GUI)*. Although a GUI is, as its name implies, an interface, the term *interfaces*, as used here, is more general in nature and is not restricted to a graphical interface.

Remember the toaster example in Chapter 1? The toaster, or any appliance for that matter, is plugged into the interface, which is the electrical outlet—see Figure 2.1. All appliances gain access to the required electricity by complying with the correct interface: the electrical outlet. The toaster doesn't need to know anything about the implementation or how the electricity is produced. For all the toaster cares, a coal plant or a nuclear plant could produce the electricity—the appliance does not care which, as long as the interface works as specified, correctly and safely.

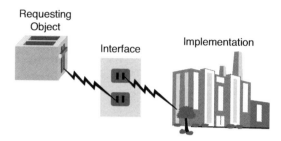

Figure 2.1   Power plant revisited.

As another example, consider an automobile. The interface between you and the car includes components such as the steering wheel, gas pedal, brake, and ignition switch. For most people, aesthetic issues aside, the main concern when driving a car is that the car starts, accelerates, stops, steers, and so on. The implementation, basically the stuff that you don't see, is of little concern to the average driver. In fact, most people would not even be able to identify certain components, such as the catalytic converter and gasket. However, any driver would recognize and know how to use the steering wheel because this is a common interface. By installing a standard steering wheel in the car, manufacturers are assured that the people in their target market will be able to use the system.

If, however, a manufacturer decided to install a joystick in place of the steering wheel, most drivers would balk at this, and the automobile might not be a big seller (except for some eclectic people who love bucking the trends). On the other hand, as long as the performance and aesthetics didn't change, the average driver would not notice if the manufacturer changed the engine (part of the implementation) of the automobile.

It must be stressed that the interchangeable engines must be identical in every way—as far as the interface goes. Replacing a four-cylinder engine with an eight-cylinder engine would change the rules and likely would not work with other components that interface with the engine, just as changing the current from AC to DC would affect the rules in the power plant example.

The engine is part of the implementation, and the steering wheel is part of the interface. A change in the implementation should have no impact on the driver, whereas a change to the interface might. The driver would notice an aesthetic change to the steering wheel, even if it performs in a similar manner. It must be stressed that a change to the engine that *is* noticeable by the driver breaks this rule. For example, a change that would result in noticeable loss of power is actually changing the interface.

What Users See

Interfaces also relate directly to classes. End users do not normally see any classes—they see the GUI or command line. However, programmers *would* see the class interfaces. Class reuse means that someone has already written a class. Thus, a programmer who uses a class must know how to get the class to work properly. This programmer will combine many classes to create a system. The programmer is the one who needs to understand the interfaces of a class. Therefore, when we talk about users in this chapter, we primarily mean designers and developers—not necessarily end users. Thus, when we talk about interfaces in this context, we are talking about class interfaces, not GUIs.

Properly constructed classes are designed in two parts—the interface and the implementation.

The Interface

The services presented to an end user compose the interface. In the best case, *only* the services the end user needs are presented. Of course, which services the user needs might be a matter of opinion. If you put 10 people in a room and ask each of them to do an independent design, you might receive 10 totally different designs—and there is nothing wrong with that. However, as a general rule, the interface to a class should contain only what the user needs to know. In the toaster example, the user needs to know only that the toaster must be plugged into the interface (which in this case is the electrical outlet) and how to operate the toaster itself.

> Identifying the User
>
> Perhaps the most important consideration when designing a class is identifying the audience, or users, of the class.

The Implementation

The implementation details are hidden from the user. One goal regarding the implementation should be kept in mind: A change to the implementation *should not* require a change to the user's code. This might seem a bit confusing, but this goal is at the heart of the design issue. If the interface is designed properly, a change to the implementation should not require a change to the user's code. Remember that the interface includes the syntax to call a method and return a value. If this interface does not change, the user does not care whether the implementation is changed. As long as the programmer can use the same syntax and retrieve the same value, that's all that matters.

We see this all the time when using a cell phone. To make a call, the interface is simple—we either dial a number or select an entry in the address book. Yet, if the provider updates the software, it doesn't change the way you make a call. The interface stays the same regardless of how the implementation changes. However, I can think of one situation when the provider did change the interface—when my area code changed. Fundamental interface changes, like an area code change, do require the users to change behavior. Businesses try to keep these types of changes to a minimum, for some customers will not like the change or perhaps not put up with the hassle.

Recall that in the toaster example, although the interface is always the electric outlet, the implementation could change from a coal power plant to a nuclear power plant without affecting the toaster. One very important caveat should be made here: The coal or nuclear plant must also conform to the interface specification. If the coal plant produces AC power, but the nuclear plant produces DC power, a problem exists. The bottom line is that both the user and the implementation must conform to the interface specification.

An Interface/Implementation Example

Let's create a simple (if not very functional) database reader class. We'll write some Java code that will retrieve records from the database. As we've discussed, knowing your end users is always the most important issue when doing any kind of design. You should do some analysis of the situation and conduct interviews with end users, and then list the requirements for the project. The following are some requirements we might want to use for the database reader:

- We must be able to open a connection to the database.

- We must be able to close the connection to the database.

- We must be able to position the cursor on the first record in the database.

- We must be able to position the cursor on the last record in the database.

- We must be able to find the number of records in the database.

- We must be able to determine whether there are more records in the database (that is, if we are at the end).

- We must be able to position the cursor at a specific record by supplying the key.

- We must be able to retrieve a record by supplying a key.

- We must be able to get the next record, based on the position of the cursor.

With these requirements in mind, we can make an initial attempt to design the database reader class by creating possible interfaces for these end users.

In this case, the database reader class is intended for programmers who require use of a database. Thus, the interface is essentially the application-programming interface (API) that the programmer will use. These methods are, in effect, wrappers that enclose the functionality provided by the database system. Why would we do this? We explore this question in much greater detail later in the chapter; the short answer is that we might need to customize some database functionality. For example, we might need to process the objects so that we can write them to a relational database. Writing this *middleware* is not trivial as far as design and coding go, but it is a real-life example of wrapping functionality. More important, we may want to change the database engine itself without having to change the code.

Figure 2.2 shows a class diagram representing a possible interface to the `DataBaseReader` class.

Note that the methods in this class are all public (remember that there are plus signs next to the names of methods that are public interfaces). Also note that only the interface is represented; the implementation is not shown. Take a minute to determine whether this class diagram generally satisfies the requirements outlined earlier for the project. If you find out later that the diagram does not meet all the requirements, that's okay; remember that OO design is an iterative process, so you do not have to get it exactly right the first time.

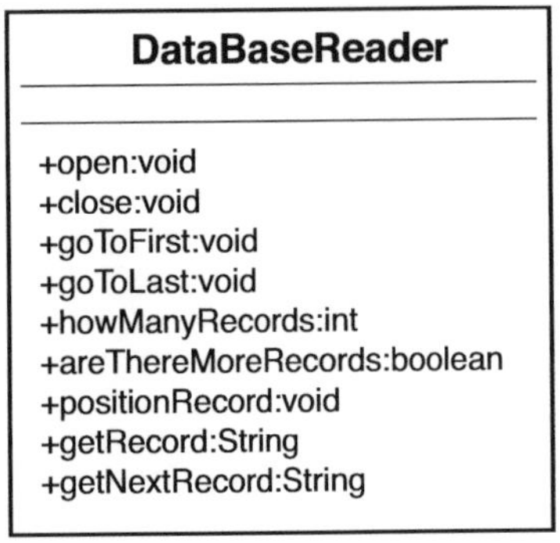

```
 ┌─────────────────────────────────────┐
 │         DataBaseReader              │
 ├─────────────────────────────────────┤
 ├─────────────────────────────────────┤
 │  +open:void                         │
 │  +close:void                        │
 │  +goToFirst:void                    │
 │  +goToLast:void                     │
 │  +howManyRecords:int                │
 │  +areThereMoreRecords:boolean       │
 │  +positionRecord:void               │
 │  +getRecord:String                  │
 │  +getNextRecord:String              │
 └─────────────────────────────────────┘
```

Figure 2.2   A Unified Modeling Language class diagram for the `DataBaseReader` class.

Public Interface

Remember that if a method is public, an application programmer can access it, and thus, it is considered part of the class interface. Do not confuse the term interface with the keyword interface used in Java and .NET—which is discussed in later chapters.

For each of the requirements we listed, we need a corresponding method that provides the functionality we want. Now you need to ask a few questions:

- To effectively use this class, do you, as a programmer, need to know anything else about it?
- Do you need to know how the internal database code opens the database?
- Do you need to know how the internal database code physically positions itself over a specific record?
- Do you need to know how the internal database code determines whether any more records are left?

On all counts, the answer is a resounding *no!* You don't need to know any of this information. All you care about is that you get the proper return values and that the operations are performed correctly. In fact, the application programmer will most likely be at least one more abstract level away from the implementation. The application will use your classes to open the database, which in turn will invoke the proper database API.

Minimal Interface

Although perhaps extreme, one way to determine the minimalist interface is to initially provide the user with no public interfaces. Of course, the class will be useless; however, this forces the user to come back to you and say, "Hey, I need this functionality." Then you can negotiate. Thus, you add interfaces only when it is requested. Never assume that the user needs something.

Creating wrappers might seem like overkill, but there are many advantages to writing them. To illustrate, there are many middleware products on the market today. Consider the problem of mapping objects to a relational database. Some OO databases may be perfect for OO applications. However, one small problem exists: Most companies have years of data in legacy relational database systems. How can a company embrace OO technologies and stay on the cutting edge while retaining its data in a relational database?

First, you can convert all your legacy, relational data to a brand-new OO database. However, anyone who has suffered the acute (and chronic) pain of any data conversion knows that this is to be avoided at all costs. Although these conversions can take large amounts of time and effort, all too often they never work properly.

Second, you can use a middleware product to seamlessly map the objects in your application code to a relational model. This is a much better solution as long as relational databases are so prevalent. Some might argue that OO databases are much more efficient for object persistence than relational databases. In fact, many development systems seamlessly provide this service.

Object Persistence

Object persistence refers to the concept of saving the state of an object so that it can be restored and used at a later time. An object that does not persist basically dies when it goes out of scope. For example, the state of an object can be saved in a database.

However, in the current business environment, relational-to-object mapping is a great solution. Many companies have integrated these technologies. It is common for a company to have a website front-end interface with data on a mainframe.

If you create a totally OO system, an OO database might be a viable (and better performing) option; however, OO databases have not experienced anywhere near the growth that OO languages have.

Standalone Application

Even when creating a new OO application from scratch, it might not be easy to avoid legacy data. Even a newly created OO application is most likely not a standalone application and might need to exchange information stored in relational databases (or any other data storage device, for that matter).

Let's return to the database example. Figure 2.2 shows the public interface to the class, and nothing else. When this class is complete, it will probably contain more methods, and it will certainly contain attributes. However, as a programmer using this class, you do not need to know anything about these private methods and attributes. You certainly don't need to know what the code looks like within the public methods. You simply need to know how to interact with the interfaces.

What would the code for this public interface look like (assume that we start with a Oracle database example)? Let's look at the open() method:

```
public void open(String Name){

        /* Some application-specific processing */

        /* call the Oracle API to open the database */

        /* Some more application-specific processing */

};
```

In this case, you, wearing your programmer's hat, realize that the open method requires String as a parameter. Name, which represents a database file, is passed in, but it's not important to explain how Name is mapped to a specific database for this example. That's all we need to know. Now comes the fun stuff—what really makes interfaces so great!

Just to annoy our users, let's change the database implementation. Last night we translated all the data from an Oracle database to an SQLAnywhere database (we endured the acute and chronic pain). It took us hours—but we did it.

Now the code looks like this:

```
public void open(String Name){

        /* Some application-specific processing

        /* call the SQLAnywhere API to open the database */

        /* Some more application-specific processing */

};
```

To our great chagrin, this morning not one user complained. This is because even though the implementation changed, the interface did not! As far as the user is concerned, the calls are still the same. The code change for the implementation might have required quite a bit of work (and the module with the one-line code change would have to be rebuilt), but not one line of application code that uses this DataBaseReader class needed to change.

Code Recompilation
Dynamically loaded classes are loaded at runtime—not statically linked into an executable file. When using dynamically loaded classes, like Java and .NET do, no user classes would have to be recompiled. However, in statically linked languages such as C++, a link is required to bring in the new class.

By separating the user interface from the implementation, we can save a lot of headaches down the road. In Figure 2.3, the database implementations are transparent to the end users, who see only the interface.

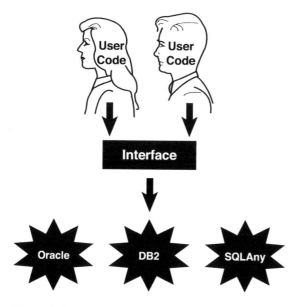

Figure 2.3   The interface.

Using Abstract Thinking When Designing Interfaces

One of the main advantages of OO programming is that classes can be reused. In general, reusable classes tend to have interfaces that are more abstract than concrete. Concrete interfaces tend to be very specific, whereas abstract interfaces are more general. However, simply stating that a highly abstract interface is more useful than a highly concrete interface, although often true, is not always the case.

It is possible to write a very useful, concrete class that is not at all reusable. This happens all the time, and nothing is wrong with it in some situations. However, we are now in the design business and want to take advantage of what OO offers us. So our goal is to design abstract, highly reusable classes—and to do this, we will design highly abstract user interfaces. To illustrate the difference between an abstract and a concrete interface, let's create a taxi object. It is much more useful to have an interface such as "drive me to the airport" than to have separate interfaces such as "turn right," "turn left," "start," "stop," and so on, because as illustrated in Figure 2.4, all the user wants to do is get to the airport.

Abstract

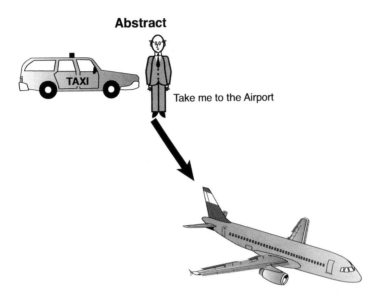

Take me to the Airport

Figure 2.4   An abstract interface.

When you emerge from your hotel, throw your bags into the back seat of the taxi, and get in, the cabbie will turn to you and ask, "Where do you want to go?" You reply, "Please take me to the airport." (This assumes, of course, that there is only one major airport in the city. In Chicago, you would have to say, "Please take me to Midway Airport" or "Please take me to O'Hare.") You might not even know how to get to the airport yourself, and even if you did, you wouldn't want to have to tell the cabbie when to turn and which direction to turn, as illustrated in Figure 2.5. How the cabbie implements the actual drive is of no concern to you, the passenger. (However, the fare might become an issue at some point, if the cabbie cheats and takes you the long way to the airport.)

Now, where does the connection between abstract and reuse come in? Ask yourself which of these two scenarios is more reusable, the abstract or the not-so-abstract? To put it more simply, which phrase is more reusable: "Take me to the airport," or "Turn right, then right, then left, then left, then left"? Obviously, the first phrase is more reusable. You can use it in any city, whenever you get into a taxi and want to go to the airport. The second phrase will work only in a specific case. Thus, the abstract interface "Take me to the airport" is generally the way to go for a good, reusable OO design whose implementation would be different in Chicago, New York, or Cleveland.

Not So Abstract

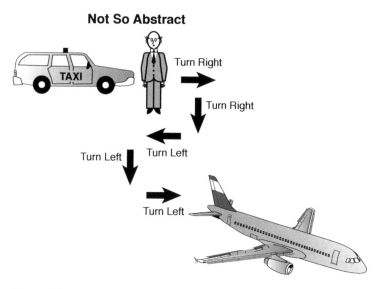

Figure 2.5   A not-so-abstract interface.

Providing the Absolute Minimal User Interface Possible

When designing a class, the general rule is to always provide the user with as little knowledge of the inner workings of the class as possible. To accomplish this, follow these simple rules:

- Give the users only what they absolutely need. In effect, this means the class has as few interfaces as possible. When you start designing a class, start with a minimal interface. The design of a class is iterative, so you will soon discover that the minimal set of interfaces might not suffice. This is fine.

  It is better to have to add interfaces because users really need it than to give the users more interfaces than they need. At times it is problematic for the user to have certain interfaces. For example, you don't want an interface that provides salary information to all users—only the ones who need to know.

  For the moment, let's use a hardware example to illustrate our software example. Imagine handing a user a PC box without a monitor or a keyboard. Obviously, the PC would be of little use. You have just provided the user with the minimal set of interfaces to the PC. However, this minimal set is insufficient, and it immediately becomes necessary to add interfaces.

- Public interfaces define what the users can access. If you initially hide the entire class from the user by making the interfaces private, when programmers start using the class, you will be forced to make certain methods public—these methods thus become the public interface.

- It is vital to design classes from a user's perspective and not from an information systems viewpoint. Too often designers of classes (not to mention any other kind of software) design the class to make it fit into a specific technological model. Even if the designer takes a user's perspective, it is still probably a technician user's perspective, and the class is designed with an eye on getting it to work from a technology standpoint and not from ease of use for the user.

- Make sure when you are designing a class that you go over the requirements and the design with the people who will actually use it—not just developers. The class will most likely evolve and need to be updated when a prototype of the system is built.

Determining the Users

Let's look again at the taxi example. We have already decided that the users are the ones who will actually use the system. This said, the obvious question is who are the users?

The first impulse is to say the *customers*. This is only about half right. Although the customers are certainly users, the cabbie must be able to successfully provide the service to the customers. In other words, providing an interface that would, no doubt, please the customer, such as "Take me to the airport for free," is not going to go over well with the cabbie. Thus, in reality, to build a realistic and usable interface, *both* the customer and the cabbie must be considered users.

For a software analogy, consider that users might want a programmer to provide a certain function. However, if the programmer finds the request technically impossible, the request can't be satisfied, no matter how much the programmer wants to help.

In short, any object that sends a message to the taxi object is considered a user (and yes, the users are objects, too). Figure 2.6 shows how the cabbie provides a service.

> **Looking Ahead**
> The cabbie is most likely an object as well.

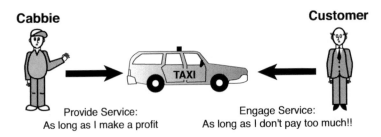

Figure 2.6   Providing services.

Object Behavior

Identifying the users is only a part of the exercise. After the users are identified, you must determine the behaviors of the objects. From the viewpoint of all the users, begin identifying the purpose of each object and what it must do to perform properly. Note that many of the initial choices will not survive the final cut of the public interface. These choices are identified by gathering requirements using various methods such as UML UseCases.

Environmental Constraints

In their book *Object-Oriented Design in Java*, Gilbert and McCarty point out that the environment often imposes limitations on what an object can do. In fact, environmental constraints are almost always a factor. Computer hardware might limit software functionality. For example, a system might not be connected to a network, or a company might use a specific type of printer. In the taxi example, the cab cannot drive on a road if a bridge is out, even if it provides a quicker way to the airport.

Identifying the Public Interfaces

With all the information gathered about the users, the object behaviors, and the environment, you need to determine the public interfaces for each user object. So, think about how you would use the taxi object:

- Get into the taxi.
- Tell the cabbie where you want to go.
- Pay the cabbie.
- Give the cabbie a tip.
- Get out of the taxi.

What do you need to do to use the taxi object?

- Have a place to go.
- Hail a taxi.
- Pay the cabbie money.

Initially, you think about how the object is used and not how it is built. You might discover that the object needs more interfaces, such as "Put luggage in the trunk" or "Enter into a mindless conversation with the cabbie." Figure 2.7 provides a class diagram that lists possible methods for the Cabbie class.

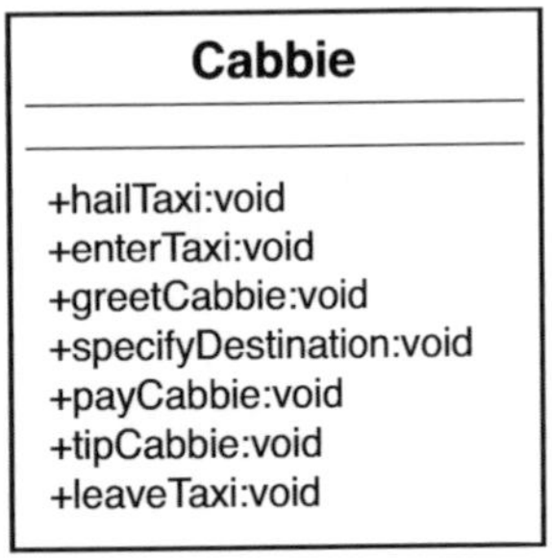

```
┌─────────────────────────────────┐
│            Cabbie               │
│─────────────────────────────────│
│                                 │
│─────────────────────────────────│
│  +hailTaxi:void                 │
│  +enterTaxi:void                │
│  +greetCabbie:void              │
│  +specifyDestination:void       │
│  +payCabbie:void                │
│  +tipCabbie:void                │
│  +leaveTaxi:void                │
└─────────────────────────────────┘
```

Figure 2.7   The methods in a cabbie class.

As is always the case, nailing down the final interface is an iterative process. For each interface, you must determine whether the interface contributes to the operation of the object. If it does not, perhaps it is not necessary. Many OO texts recommend that each interface model only one behavior. This returns us to the question of how abstract we want to get with the design. If we have an interface called enterTaxi(), we certainly do not want enterTaxi() to have logic in it to pay the cabbie. If we do this, not only is the design somewhat illogical, but there is virtually no way that a user of the class can tell what has to be done to pay the cabbie.

Identifying the Implementation

After the public interfaces are chosen, you need to identify the implementation. After the class is designed and all the methods required to operate the class properly are in place, the specifics of how to get the class to work are considered.

Technically, anything that is not a public interface can be considered the implementation. This means that the user will never see any of the methods that are considered part of the implementation, including the method's signature (which includes the name of the method and the parameter list), as well as the actual code inside the method.

It is possible to have a private method that is used internally by the class. Any private method is considered part of the implementation given that the user will never see it and thus will not have access to it. For example, a class may have a changePassword() method; however, the same class may have a private method that encrypts the password. This method would be hidden from the user and called only from inside the changePassword() method.

The implementation is totally hidden from the user. The code within public methods is a part of the implementation because the user cannot see it. (The user should see only the calling structure of an interface—not the code inside it.)

This means that, theoretically, anything that is considered the implementation might change without affecting how the user interfaces with the class. This assumes, of course, that the implementation is providing the answers the user expects.

Whereas the interface represents how the user sees the object, the implementation is really the nuts and bolts of the object. The implementation contains the code that represents that state of an object.

Conclusion

In this chapter, we have explored three areas that can get you started on the path to thinking in an OO way. Remember that there is no firm list of issues pertaining to the OO thought process. Doing things in an OO way is more of an art than a science. Try to think of your own ways to describe OO thinking.

In Chapter 3, "Advanced Object-Oriented Concepts," we discuss the object life cycle: it is born, it lives, and it dies. While it is alive, it might transition through many states. For example, a `DataBaseReader` object is in one state if the database is open and another state if the database is closed. How this is represented depends on the design of the class.

References

- Meyers, Scott. 2005. *Effective C++*, 3rd edition. Boston, MA: Addison-Wesley Professional.

- Fowler, Martin. 2003. *UML Distilled*, 3rd edition. Boston, MA: Addison-Wesley Professional.

- Gilbert, Stephen, and Bill McCarty. 1998. *Object-Oriented Design in Java*. Berkeley, CA: The Waite Group Press (Pearson Education).

Advanced Object-Oriented Concepts

Chapter 1, "Introduction to Object-Oriented Concepts," and Chapter 2, "How to Think in Terms of Objects," cover the basics of object-oriented (OO) concepts. Before we embark on our journey to learn some of the finer design issues relating to building an OO system, we need to cover a few more advanced OO concepts, such as constructors, operator overloading, and multiple inheritance. We also will consider error-handling techniques and the importance of understudying how scope applies to object-oriented design.

Some of these concepts might not be vital to understanding an OO design at a higher level, but they are necessary to anyone involved in the design and implementation of an OO system.

Constructors

Constructors may be a new concept for structured programmers. Although constructors are not normally used in non-OO languages such as COBOL, C, and Basic, the *struct*, which is part of C/C++, does include constructors. In the first two chapters, we alluded to these special methods that are used to *construct* objects. In some OO languages, such as Java and C#, constructors are methods that share the same name as the class. Visual Basic .NET uses the designation *New* and Objective-C uses the *init* keyword. As usual, we will focus on the concepts of constructors and not cover the specific syntax of all the languages. Let's take a look at some Java code that implements a constructor.

For example, a constructor for the `Cabbie` class we covered in Chapter 2 would look like this:

```
public Cabbie(){
    /* code to construct the object */
}
```

The compiler will recognize that the method name is identical to the class name and consider the method a constructor.

> **Caution**
>
> Note that in this Java code (as with C# and C++), a constructor does not have a return value. If you provide a return value, the compiler will not treat the method as a constructor.

For example, if you include the following code in the class, the compiler will not consider this a constructor because it has a return value—in this case, an integer:

```
public int Cabbie(){
    /* code to construct the object */
}
```

This syntax requirement can cause problems because this code will compile but will not behave as expected.

When Is a Constructor Called?

When a new object is created, one of the first things that happens is that the constructor is called. Check out the following code:

```
Cabbie myCabbie = new Cabbie();
```

The new keyword creates a new instance of the Cabbie class, thus allocating the required memory. Then the constructor itself is called, passing the arguments in the parameter list. The constructor provides the developer the opportunity to attend to the appropriate initialization.

Thus, the code new Cabbie() will instantiate a Cabbie object and call the Cabbie method, which is the constructor.

What's Inside a Constructor?

Perhaps the most important function of a constructor is to initialize the memory allocated when the new keyword is encountered. In short, code included inside a constructor should set the newly created object to its initial, stable, safe state.

For example, if you have a counter object with an attribute called count, you need to set count to zero in the constructor:

```
count = 0;
```

> **Initializing Attributes**
>
> In structured programming, a routine named housekeeping (or initialization) is often used for initialization purposes. Initializing attributes is a common function performed within a constructor.

The Default Constructor

If you write a class and do not include a constructor, the class will still compile, and you can still use it. If the class provides no explicit constructor, a default constructor will be provided. It is important to understand that at least one constructor always exists, regardless of whether you write a constructor yourself. If you do not provide a constructor, the system will provide a default constructor for you.

Besides the creation of the object itself, the only action that a default constructor takes is to call the constructor of its superclass. In many cases, the superclass will be part of the language framework, like the `Object` class in Java. For example, if a constructor is not provided for the `Cabbie` class, the following default constructor is inserted:

```
public Cabbie(){
    super();
}
```

If you were to decompile the bytecode produced by the compiler, you would see this code. The compiler actually inserts it.

In this case, if `Cabbie` does not explicitly inherit from another class, the `Object` class will be the parent class. Perhaps the default constructor might be sufficient in some cases; however, in most cases, some sort of memory initialization should be performed. Regardless of the situation, it is good programming practice to always include at least one constructor in a class. If there are attributes in the class, it is always good practice to initialize them. Moreover, initializing variables is always a good practice when writing code, object-oriented or not.

Providing a Constructor

The general rule is that you should *always* provide a constructor, even if you do not plan to do anything inside it. You can provide a constructor with nothing in it and then add to it later. Although there is technically nothing wrong with using the default constructor provided by the compiler, for documentation and maintenance purposes, it is always nice to know exactly what your code looks like.

It is not surprising that maintenance becomes an issue here. If you depend on the default constructor and then subsequent maintenance adds another constructor, the default constructor is no longer created. In short, the default constructor is added only if you don't include any constructors. As soon as you include just one, the default constructor is not provided.

Using Multiple Constructors

In many cases, an object can be constructed in more than one way. To accommodate this situation, you need to provide more than one constructor. For example, let's consider the `Count` class presented here:

```
public class Count {

    int count;
```

```
    public Count(){
        count = 0;
    }
}
```

On the one hand, we want to initialize the attribute count to count to zero: We can easily accomplish this by having a constructor initialize count to zero as follows:

```
public Count(){
    count = 0;
}
```

On the other hand, we might want to pass an initialization parameter that allows count to be set to various numbers:

```
public Count (int number){
    count = number;
}
```

This is called *overloading a method* (overloading pertains to all methods, not just constructors). Most OO languages provide functionality for overloading a method.

Overloading Methods

Overloading allows a programmer to use the same method name over and over, as long as the signature of the method is different each time. The signature consists of the method name and a parameter list (see Figure 3.1).

Thus, the following methods *all* have different signatures:

```
public void getCab();


// different parameter list
public void getCab (String cabbieName);

// different parameter list
public void getCab (int numberOfPassengers);
```

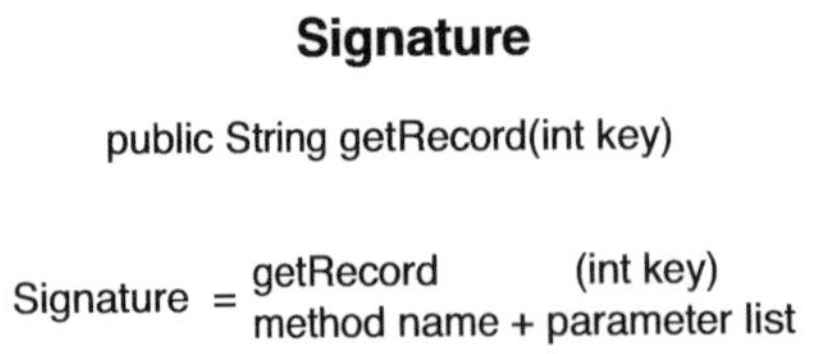

Signature

public String getRecord(int key)

Signature = getRecord   (int key)
            method name + parameter list

Figure 3.1   The components of a signature.

Signatures

Depending on the language, the signature may or may not include the return type. In Java and C#, the return type is not part of the signature. For example, the following methods would conflict even though the return types are different:

```
public void getCab (String cabbieName);
public int getCab (String cabbieName);
```

The best way to understand signatures is to write some code and run it through the compiler.

By using different signatures, you can construct objects differently depending on the constructor used. This functionality is very helpful when you don't always know ahead of time how much information you have available. For example, when creating a shopping cart, customers may already be logged in to their account (and you will have all of their information). On the other hand, a totally new customer may be placing items in the cart with no account information available at all. In each case, the constructor would initialize differently.

Using UML to Model Classes

Let's return to the database reader example we used earlier in Chapter 2. Consider that we have two ways we can construct a database reader:

- Pass the name of the database and position the cursor at the beginning of the database.
- Pass the name of the database and the position within the database where we want the cursor to position itself.

Figure 3.2 shows a class diagram for the DataBaseReader class. Note that the diagram lists two constructors for the class. Although the diagram shows the two constructors, without the parameter list, there is no way to know which constructor is which. To distinguish the constructors, you can look at the corresponding code in the DataBaseReader class listed next.

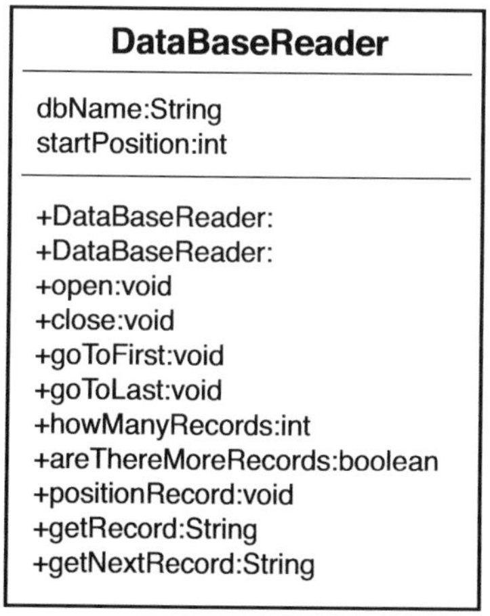

```
DataBaseReader

dbName:String
startPosition:int

+DataBaseReader:
+DataBaseReader:
+open:void
+close:void
+goToFirst:void
+goToLast:void
+howManyRecords:int
+areThereMoreRecords:boolean
+positionRecord:void
+getRecord:String
+getNextRecord:String
```

Figure 3.2   The DataBaseReader class diagram.

No Return Type

Notice that in this class diagram, the constructors do not have a return type. All other methods besides constructors must have return types.

Here is a code segment of the class that shows its constructors and the attributes that the constructors initialize (see Figure 3.3):

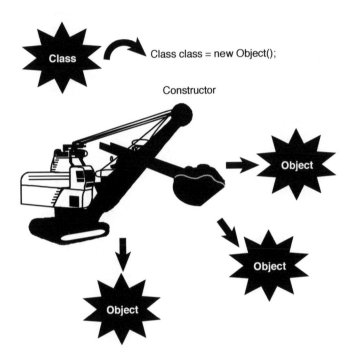

Class class = new Object();

Figure 3.3   Creating a new object.

```
public class DataBaseReader {

    String dbName;
    int startPosition;

    // initialize just the name
    public DataBaseReader (String name){
        dbName = name;
      startPosition = 0;
    };

    // initialize the name and the position
    public DataBaseReader (String name, int pos){
```

```
        dbName = name;
        startPosition = pos;
    };

    .. // rest of class
}
```

Note how startPosition is initialized in both cases. If the constructor is not passed the information via the parameter list, it is initialized to a default value, such as 0.

How the Superclass Is Constructed

When using inheritance, you must know how the parent class is constructed. Remember that when you use inheritance, you are inheriting everything about the parent. Thus, you must become intimately aware of all the parent's data and behavior. The inheritance of an attribute is fairly obvious. However, how a constructor is inherited is not as obvious. After the new keyword is encountered and the object is allocated, the following steps occur (see Figure 3.4):

1. Inside the constructor, the constructor of the class's superclass is called. If there is no explicit call to the superclass constructor, the default is called automatically; however, you can see the code in the bytecodes.

2. Each class attribute of the object is initialized. These are the attributes that are part of the class definition (instance variables), not the attributes inside the constructor or any other method (local variables). In the DataBaseReader code presented earlier, the integer startPosition is an instance variable of the class.

3. The rest of the code in the constructor executes.

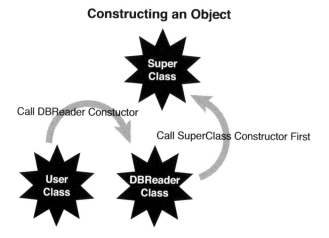

Constructing an Object

Call DBReader Constuctor

Call SuperClass Constructor First

Super Class

User Class

DBReader Class

Figure 3.4   Constructing an object.

The Design of Constructors

As we have already seen, when designing a class, it is good practice to initialize all the attributes. In some languages, the compiler provides some sort of initialization. As always, don't count on the compiler to initialize attributes! In Java, you cannot use an attribute until it is initialized. If the attribute is first set in the code, make sure that you initialize the attribute to some valid condition—for example, set an integer to zero.

Constructors are used to ensure that the application is in a stable state (I like to call it a "safe" state). For example, initializing an attribute to zero, when it is intended for use as a denominator in a division operation, might lead to an unstable application. You must take into consideration that a division by zero is an illegal operation. Initializing to zero is not always the best policy.

During the design, it is good practice to identify a stable state for all attributes and then initialize them to this stable state in the constructor.

Error Handling

It is extremely rare for a class to be written perfectly the first time. In most, if not all, situations, things *will* go wrong. Any developer who does not plan for problems is courting danger.

Assuming that your code has the capability to detect and trap an error condition, you can handle the error in several ways: On page 223 of their book *Java Primer Plus*, Tyma, Torok, and Downing (9781571690623) state that there are three basic solutions to handling problems that are detected in a program: fix it, ignore the problem by squelching it, or exit the runtime in some graceful manner. On page 139 of their book *Object-Oriented Design in Java* (978-1571691347), Gilbert and McCarty expand on this theme by adding the choice of throwing an exception:

- Ignore the problem—not a good idea!
- Check for potential problems and abort the program when you find a problem.
- Check for potential problems, catch the mistake, and attempt to fix the problem.
- Throw an exception. (Often this is the preferred way to handle the situation.)

These strategies are discussed in the following sections.

Ignoring the Problem

Simply ignoring a potential problem is a recipe for disaster. And if you are going to ignore the problem, why bother detecting it in the first place? It is obvious that you should not ignore any known problem. The primary directive for all applications is that the application should never crash. If you do not handle your errors, the application will eventually terminate ungracefully or continue in a mode that can be considered an unstable state. In the latter case, you might not even know you are getting incorrect results, and that can be much worse than a program crash.

Checking for Problems and Aborting the Application

If you choose to check for potential problems and abort the application when a problem is detected, the application can display a message indicating that a problem exists. In this case, the application gracefully exits, and the user is left staring at the computer screen, shaking her head and wondering what just happened. Although this is a far superior option to ignoring the problem, it is by no means optimal. However, this does allow the system to clean up things and put itself in a more stable state, such as closing files and forcing a system restart.

Checking for Problems and Attempting to Recover

Checking for potential problems, catching the mistake, and attempting to recover is a far superior solution than simply checking for problems and aborting. In this case, the problem is detected by the code, and the application attempts to fix itself. This works well in certain situations. For example, consider the following code:

```
if (a == 0)
    a=1;

c = b/a;
```

It is obvious that if the conditional statement is not included in the code, and a zero makes its way to the divide statement, you will get a system exception because you cannot divide by zero. By catching the exception and setting the variable a to 1, at least the system will not crash. However, setting a to 1 might not be a proper solution because the result would be incorrect. The better solution would be to prompt the user to reenter the proper input value.

> ### A Mix of Error-Handling Techniques
>
> Despite the fact that this type of error handling is not necessarily object-oriented in nature, I believe that it has a valid place in OO design. Throwing an exception (discussed in the next section) can be expensive in terms of overhead. Thus, although exceptions may be a valid design choice, you will still want to consider other error-handling techniques (even tried-and-true structured techniques), depending on your design and performance needs.

Although the error-checking techniques mentioned previously are preferable to doing nothing, they still have a few problems. It is not always easy to determine where a problem first appears. And it might take a while for the problem to be detected. In any event, it is beyond the scope of this book to explain error handling in great detail. However, it is important to design error handling into the class right from the start, and often the operating system itself can alert you to problems that it detects.

Throwing an Exception

Most OO languages provide a feature called *exceptions*. In the most basic sense, exceptions are unexpected events that occur within a system. Exceptions provide a way to detect problems and then handle them. In Java, C#, C++, Objective-C, and Visual Basic, exceptions are handled by the keywords `catch` and `throw`. This might sound like a baseball game, but the key concept here is that a specific block of code is written to handle a specific exception. This solves the problem of trying to figure out where the problem started and unwinding the code to the proper point.

Here is the structure for a Java `try`/`catch` block:

```
try {

    // possible nasty code

} catch(Exception e) {

    // code to handle the exception
}
```

If an exception is thrown within the `try` block, the `catch` block will handle it. When an exception is thrown while the block is executing, the following occurs:

1. The execution of the `try` block is terminated.

2. The `catch` clauses are checked to determine whether an appropriate `catch` block for the offending exception was included. (There might be more than one `catch` clause per `try` block.)

3. If none of the `catch` clauses handles the offending exception, it is passed to the next higher-level `try` block. (If the exception is not caught in the code, the system ultimately catches it, and the results are unpredictable—that is, an application crash.)

4. If a `catch` clause is matched (the first match encountered), the statements in the `catch` clause are executed.

5. Execution then resumes with the statement following the `try` block.

Suffice it to say that exceptions are an important advantage for OO programming languages. Here is an example of how an exception is caught in Java:

```
try {

    // possible nasty code
    count = 0;
    count = 5/count;

} catch(ArithmeticException e) {

    // code to handle the exception
    System.out.println(e.getMessage());
    count = 1;

}
System.out.println("The exception is handled.");
```

Exception Granularity

You can catch exceptions at various levels of granularity. You can catch all exceptions or check for specific exceptions, such as arithmetic exceptions. If your code does not catch an exception, the Java runtime will—and it won't be happy about it!

In this example, the division by zero (because count is equal to 0) within the try block will cause an arithmetic exception. If the exception was generated (thrown) outside a try block, the program would most likely have been terminated (crashed). However, because the exception was thrown within a try block, the catch block is checked to see whether the specific exception (in this case, an arithmetic exception) was planned for. Because the catch block contains a check for the arithmetic exception, the code within the catch block is executed, thus setting count to 1. After the catch block executes, the try/catch block is exited, and the message The exception is handled. appears on the Java console. The logical flow of this process is illustrated in Figure 3.5.

Figure 3.5   Catching an exception.

If you had not put ArithmeticException in the catch block, the program would likely have crashed. You can catch all exceptions by using the following code:

```
try {

    // possible nasty code

} catch(Exception e) {

    // code to handle the exception
}
```

The Exception parameter in the catch block is used to catch any exception that might be generated within a try block.

Bulletproof Code

It's a good idea to use a combination of the methods described here to make your program as bulletproof to your user as possible.

The Importance of Scope

Multiple objects can be instantiated from a single class. Each of these objects has a unique identity and state. This is an important point. Each object is constructed separately and is allocated its own separate memory. However, some attributes and methods may, if properly declared, be shared by all the objects instantiated from the same class, thus sharing the memory allocated for these class attributes and methods.

A Shared Method

A constructor is a good example of a method that is shared by all instances of a class.

Methods represent the behaviors of an object; the state of the object is represented by attributes. There are three types of attributes:

- Local attributes
- Object attributes
- Class attributes

Local Attributes

Local attributes are owned by a specific method. Consider the following code:

```
public class Number {

    public method1() {
        int count;

    }

    public method2() {

    }

}
```

The method method1 contains a local variable called count. This integer is accessible only inside method1. The method method2 has no idea that the integer count even exists.

At this point, we introduce a very important concept: scope. Attributes (and methods) exist within a particular scope. In this case, the integer count exists within the scope of method1. In Java, C#, C++ and Objective-C, scope is delineated by curly braces ({}). In the Number class, there are several possible scopes—just start matching the curly braces.

The class itself has its own scope. Each instance of the class (that is, each object) has its own scope. Both method1 and method2 have their own scopes as well. Because count lives within method1's curly braces, when method1 is invoked, a copy of count is created. When method1 terminates, the copy of count is removed.

For some more fun, look at this code:

```
public class Number {

    public method1() {
        int count;
    }

    public method2() {
        int count;
    }

}
```

This example has two copies of an integer count in this class. Remember that method1 and method2 each has its own scope. Thus, the compiler can tell which copy of count to access simply by recognizing which method it is in. You can think of it in these terms:

```
method1.count;
```

```
method2.count;
```

As far as the compiler is concerned, the two attributes are easily differentiated, even though they have the same name. It is almost like two people having the same last name, but based on the context of their first names, you know that they are two separate individuals.

Object Attributes

In many design situations, an attribute must be shared by several methods within the same object. In Figure 3.6, for example, three objects have been constructed from a single class. Consider the following code:

```
public class Number {

    int count;     // available to both method1 and method2

    public method1() {
        count = 1;
    }

    public method2() {
        count = 2;
    }

}
```

Object Attributes

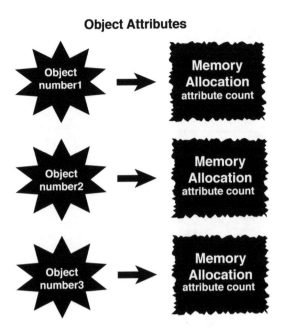

Figure 3.6   Object attributes.

Note here that the class attribute count is declared outside the scope of both `method1` and `method2`. However, it is within the scope of the class. Thus, `count` is available to both `method1` and `method2`. (Basically, all methods in the class have access to this attribute.) Notice that the code for both methods is setting `count` to a specific value. There is only one copy of `count` for the entire object, so both assignments operate on the same copy in memory. However, this copy of `count` is not shared between different objects.

To illustrate, let's create three copies of the `Number` class:

```
Number number1 = new Number();
Number number2 = new Number();
Number number3 = new Number();
```

Each of these objects—`number1`, `number2`, and `number3`—is constructed separately and is allocated its own resources. There are three separate instances of the integer `count`. When `number1` changes its attribute `count`, this in no way affects the copy of `count` in object `number2` or object `number3`. In this case, integer `count` is an *object attribute*.

You can play some interesting games with scope. Consider the following code:

```
public class Number {

    int count;
```

```
    public method1() {
        int count;
    }

    public method2() {
        int count;
    }

}
```

In this case, three totally separate memory locations have the name of count for each object. The object owns one copy, and method1() and method2() each have their own copy.

To access the object variable from within one of the methods, say method1(), you can use a pointer called this in the C-based languages:

```
public method1() {
        int count;

        this.count = 1;
}
```

Notice that some code looks a bit curious:

```
this.count = 1;
```

The selection of the word this as a keyword is perhaps unfortunate. However, we must live with it. The use of the this keyword directs the compiler to access the object variable count and not the local variables within the method bodies.

> **Note**
>
> The keyword this is a reference to the current object.

Class Attributes

As mentioned earlier, it is possible for two or more objects to share attributes. In Java, C#, C++ and Objective-C, you do this by making the attribute *static*:

```
public class Number {

    static int count;

    public method1() {
    }

}
```

By declaring `count` as static, this attribute is allocated a single piece of memory for all objects instantiated from the class. Thus, all objects of the class use the same memory location for `count`. Essentially, each class has a single copy, which is shared by all objects of that class (see Figure 3.7). This is about as close to global data as we get in OO design.

Class Attribute

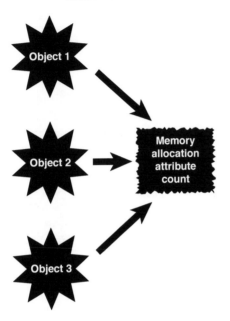

Figure 3.7   Class attributes.

There are many valid uses for class attributes; however, you must be aware of potential synchronization problems. Let's instantiate two `Count` objects:

```
Count Count1 = new Count();
Count Count2 = new Count();
```

For the sake of argument, let's say that the object `Count1` is going merrily about its way and is using `count` as a means to keep track of the pixels on a computer screen. This is not a problem until the object `Count2` decides to use attribute `count` to keep track of sheep. The instant that `Count2` records its first sheep, the data that `Count1` was saving is lost.

Operator Overloading

Some OO languages allow you to overload an operator. C++ is an example of one such language. Operator overloading allows you to change the meaning of an operator. For example, when most people see a plus sign, they assume it represents addition. If you see the equation

```
X = 5 + 6;
```

you expect that X would contain the value 11. And in this case, you would be correct.

However, at times a plus sign could represent something else. For example, in the following code:

```
String firstName = "Joe", lastName = "Smith";

String Name = firstName + " " + lastName;
```

You would expect that Name would contain Joe Smith. The plus sign here has been overloaded to perform string concatenation.

> **String Concatenation**
>
> *String concatenation* occurs when two separate strings are combined to create a new, single string.

In the context of strings, the plus sign does not mean addition of integers or floats, but concatenation of strings.

What about matrix addition? You could have code like this:

```
Matrix a, b, c;

c = a + b;
```

Thus, the plus sign now performs matrix addition, not addition of integers or floats.

Overloading is a powerful mechanism. However, it can be downright confusing for people who read and maintain code. In fact, developers can confuse themselves. To take this to an extreme, it would be possible to change the operation of addition to perform subtraction. Why not? Operator overloading allows you to change the meaning of an operator. Thus, if the plus sign were changed to perform subtraction, the following code would result in an X value of -1:

```
x = 5 + 6;
```

More recent OO languages like Java, .NET, and Objective-C do not allow operator overloading.

Although these languages do not allow the option of overloading operators, the languages themselves do overload the plus sign for string concatenation, but that's about it. The designers of Java must have decided that operator overloading was more of a problem than it was worth. If you must use operator overloading in C++, take care by documenting and commenting properly not to confuse the people who will use the class.

Multiple Inheritance

We cover inheritance in much more detail in Chapter 7, "Mastering Inheritance and Composition." However, this is a good place to begin discussing multiple inheritance, which is one of the more powerful and challenging aspects of class design.

As the name implies, *multiple inheritance* allows a class to inherit from more than one class. In practice, this seems like a great idea. Objects are supposed to model the real world, are they not? And many real-world examples of multiple inheritance exist. Parents are a good example of multiple inheritance. Each child has two parents—that's just the way it is. So it makes sense that you can design classes by using multiple inheritance. In some OO languages, such as C++, you can.

However, this situation falls into a category similar to operator overloading. Multiple inheritance is a very powerful technique, and in fact, some problems are quite difficult to solve without it. Multiple inheritance can even solve some problems quite elegantly. However, multiple inheritance can significantly increase the complexity of a system, both for the programmer and the compiler writers.

As with operator overloading, the designers of Java, .NET, and Objective-C decided that the increased complexity of allowing multiple inheritance far outweighed its advantages, so they eliminated it from the language. In some ways, the Java, .NET, and Objective-C language construct of interfaces compensates for this; however, the bottom line is that Java, .NET, and Objective-C do not allow conventional multiple inheritance.

Behavioral and Implementation Inheritance

Interfaces are a mechanism for behavioral inheritance, whereas abstract classes are used for implementation inheritance. The bottom line is that interface language constructs provide behavioral interfaces, but no implementation, whereas abstract classes may provide both interfaces and implementation. This topic is covered in great detail in Chapter 8, "Frameworks and Reuse: Designing with Interfaces and Abstract Classes."

Object Operations

Some of the most basic operations in programming become more complicated when you're dealing with complex data structures and objects. For example, when you want to copy or compare primitive data types, the process is quite straightforward. However, copying and comparing objects is not quite as simple. On page 34 of his book *Effective C++*, Scott Meyers devotes an entire section to copying and assigning objects.

Classes and References

The problem with complex data structures and objects is that they might contain references. Simply making a copy of the reference does not copy the data structures or the object that it references. In the same vein, when comparing objects, simply comparing a pointer to another pointer only compares the references—not what they point to.

The problems arise when comparisons and copies are performed on objects. Specifically, the question boils down to whether you follow the pointers. Regardless, there should be a way to copy an object. Again, this is not as simple as it might seem. Because objects can contain references, these reference trees must be followed to do a valid copy (if you truly want to do a deep copy).

Deep Versus Shallow Copies

A *deep copy* occurs when all the references are followed and new copies are created for all referenced objects. Many levels might be involved in a deep copy. For objects with references to many objects, which in turn might have references to even more objects, the copy itself can create significant overhead. A *shallow copy* would simply copy the reference and not follow the levels. Gilbert and McCarty have a good discussion about what shallow and deep hierarchies are on page 265 of *Object-Oriented Design in Java* in a section called "Prefer a Tree to a Forest."

To illustrate, in Figure 3.8, if you do a simple copy of the object (called a *bitwise copy*), only the references are copied—not any of the actual objects. Thus, both objects (the original and the copy) will reference (point to) the same objects. To perform a complete copy, in which all reference objects are copied, you must write code to create all the subobjects.

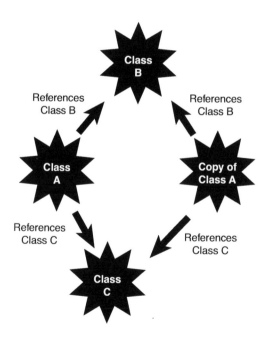

Figure 3.8   Following object references.

This problem also manifests itself when comparing objects. As with the copy function, this is not as simple as it might seem. Because objects contain references, these reference trees must be followed to do a valid comparison of objects. In most cases, languages provide a default mechanism to compare objects. As is usually the case, do not count on the default mechanism. When designing a class, you should consider providing a comparison function in your class that you know will behave as you want it to.

Conclusion

This chapter covered a number of advanced OO concepts that, although perhaps not vital to a general understanding of OO concepts, are quite necessary in higher-level OO tasks, such as designing a class. In Chapter 4, "The Anatomy of a Class," we start looking specifically at how to design and build a class.

References

- Meyers, Scott. 2005. *Effective C++*, 3rd edition. Boston, MA: Addison-Wesley Professional.
- Gilbert, Stephen, and Bill McCarty. 1998. *Object-Oriented Design in Java*. Berkeley, CA: The Waite Group Press.
- Tyma, Paul, Gabriel Torok, and Troy Downing. 1996. *Java Primer Plus*. Berkeley, CA: The Waite Group.

Example Code Used in This Chapter

The following code is presented in C# .NET. Code for other languages, such as VB .NET and Objective-C, are available electronically on the publisher's website. These examples correspond to the Java code that is listed inside the chapter itself.

The `TestNumber` Example: C# .NET

```
using System;

namespace TestNumber
{
    class Program
    {
        public static void Main()
        {

            Number number1 = new Number();
            Number number2 = new Number();
            Number number3 = new Number();
```

```
        }
    }

    public class Number
    {

        int count = 0;      // available to both method1 and method2

        public void method1()
        {
            count = 1;
        }

        public void method2()
        {
            count = 2;
        }

    }
}
```

4

The Anatomy of a Class

In previous chapters, we have covered the fundamental object-oriented (OO) concepts and determined the difference between the interface and the implementation. No matter how well you think out the problem of what should be part of the interface and what should be part of the implementation, the bottom line always comes down to how useful the class is and how it interacts with other classes. A class should never be designed in a vacuum, for as might be said, no class is an island. When objects are instantiated, they almost always interact with other objects. An object can also be part of another object or be part of an inheritance hierarchy.

This chapter examines a simple class and then takes it apart piece by piece along with guidelines that you should consider when designing classes. We will continue using the cabbie example presented in Chapter 2, "How to Think in Terms of Objects."

Each of the following sections covers a particular aspect of a class. Although not all components are necessary in every class, it is important to understand how a class is designed and constructed.

> **Note**
>
> This class is meant for illustration purposes only. Some of the methods are not fleshed out (meaning that there is no implementation) and simply present the interface—primarily to emphasize that the interface is the focus of the initial design.

The Name of the Class

The name of the class is important for several reasons. The obvious reason is to identify the class itself. Beyond simple identification, the name must be descriptive. The choice of a name is important because it provides information about what the class does and how it interacts within larger systems.

The name is also important when considering language constraints. For example, in Java, the public class name must be the same as the filename. If these names do not match, the application won't work.

Figure 4.1 shows the class that will be examined. Plain and simple, the name of the class in our example, Cabbie, is the name located after the keyword class:

```
public class Cabbie {


}
```

Comments
```
/*
   This class defines a cabbie and assigns a cab
*/
public class Cabbie{      ◀◼◼  Class Name

         //Place name of Company Here
         private static String companyName = "Blue Cab Company";
                                                                      Attributes
         //.Name of the Cabbie
         private String Name;

         //Car assigned to Cabbie
         private Cab myCab;

         // Default Constructor for the Cabbie
         public Cabbie() {

            name = null;
            myCab = null;


         }
                        // Name Initializing Constructor for the Cabbie
                        public Cabbie(String iName, String serialNumber){

                           Name = iName;
                           myCab = new Cab(serialNumber);
                        }

         // Set the Name of the Cabbie
         public void setName(String iName) {
            Name = iName;
         }

         // Get the Name of the Company            Accessor Methods (Public Interfaces)
         public static string getName(){
            return Name;
         }

         // Get the Name of the Cabbie
           public static String getCompanyName(){
             return companyName;
           }

         public void giveDestination(){
         }

         private void turnRight(){
         }                               Private Implementation
         private void turnLeft(){
         }

      }
```

Constructors

A Public Interface

Figure 4.1   Our sample class.

Using Java Syntax

Remember that the convention for this book is to use Java syntax. The syntax will be similar but somewhat different in C#, .NET, VB .NET, Objective-C, or C++, and totally different in other OO languages such as Smalltalk.

The class Cabbie name is used whenever this class is instantiated.

Comments

Regardless of the syntax of the comments used, they are vital to understanding the function of a class. In Java, C# .NET, Objective-C, and C++, there are two kinds of comments.

The Extra Java and C# Comment Style

In Java and C#, there are three types of comments. In Java, the third comment type (/** */) relates to a form of documentation that Java provides. We do not cover this type of comment in this book. C# provides similar syntax to create XML documents.

The first comment is the old C-style comment, which uses /* (slash-asterisk) to open the comment and */ (asterisk-slash) to close the comment. This type of comment can span more than one line, and it's important not to forget to use the pair of open and close comment symbols for each comment. If you miss the closing comment (*/), some of your code might be tagged as a comment and ignored by the compiler. Here is an example of this type of comment used with the Cabbie class:

```
/*

   This class defines a cabbie and assigns a cab

*/
```

The second type of comment is the // (slash-slash), which renders everything after it, to the end of the line, a comment. This type of comment spans only one line, so you don't need to remember to use a close comment symbol, but you do need to remember to confine the comment to just one line and not include any live code after the comment. Here is an example of this type of comment used with the Cabbie class:

```
// Name of the cabbie
```

Attributes

Attributes represent the state of the object because they store the information about the object. For our example, the Cabbie class has attributes that store the name of the company, the name of the cabbie, and the cab assigned to the cabbie. For example, the first attribute stores the name of the company:

```
private static String companyName = "Blue Cab Company";
```

Note here the two keywords `private` and `static`. The keyword `private` signifies that a method or variable can be accessed only within the declaring object.

Hiding as Much Data as Possible

All the attributes in this example are private. This is in keeping with the design principle of keeping the interface design as minimal as possible. The only way to access these attributes is through the method interfaces provided (which we explore later in this chapter).

The `static` keyword signifies that there will be only one copy of this attribute for all the objects instantiated by this class. Basically, this is a class attribute. (See Chapter 3, "Advanced Object-Oriented Concepts," for more discussion on class attributes.) Thus, even if 500 objects are instantiated from the `Cabbie` class, only one copy will be in memory of the `companyName` attribute (see Figure 4.2).

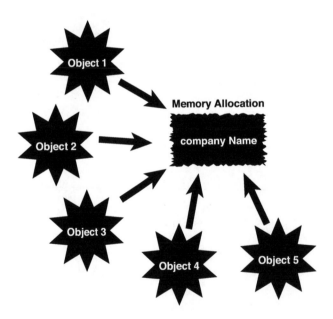

Figure 4.2   Object memory allocation.

The second attribute, `name`, is a string that stores the name of the cabbie:

```
private String name;
```

This attribute is also private so that other objects cannot access it directly. They must use the interface methods.

The `myCab` attribute is a reference to another object. The class, called `Cab`, holds information about the cab, such as its serial number and maintenance records:

```
private Cab myCab;
```

Passing a Reference

It is likely that the `Cab` object was created by another object. Thus, the object reference would be passed to the `Cabbie` object. However, for the sake of this example, the `Cab` is created within the `Cabbie` object. As a result, we are not really interested in the internals of the `Cab` object.

Note that at this point, only a reference to a `Cab` object is created; there is no memory allocated by this definition.

Constructors

This `Cabbie` class contains two constructors. We know they are constructors because they have the same name as the class: `Cabbie`. The first constructor is the default constructor:

```
public Cabbie() {

        name = null;
        myCab = null;

}
```

Technically, this is not a default constructor provided by the system. Recall that the compiler will provide a default constructor if you do not specify any constructor for a class. By definition, the reason it is called a default constructor here is because it is a constructor with no arguments, which, in effect, overrides the compiler's default constructor.

If you provide a constructor with arguments, the system will not provide a default constructor. Although this can seem complicated, the rule is that the compiler's default constructor is included only if you provide *no* constructors in your code.

In this constructor, the attributes `Name` and `myCab` are set to `null`:

```
name = null;
myCab = null;
```

The Nothingness of Null

In many programming languages, the value `null` represents a value of nothing. This might seem like an esoteric concept, but setting an attribute to nothing is a useful programming technique. Checking a variable for `null` can identify whether a value has been properly initialized. For example, you might want to declare an attribute that will later require user input. Thus, you can initialize the attribute to `null` before the user is given the opportunity to enter the data. By setting the attribute to `null` (which is a valid condition), you can check whether an attribute has been properly set. Note that in some languages, this is not allowed with the string type. In .NET, for example, it is required to use name = string.empty;.

As we know, it is always a good idea to initialize attributes in the constructors. In the same vein, it's a good programming practice to then test the value of an attribute to see whether it is `null`. This can save you a lot of headaches later if the attribute or object was not set properly. For example, if you use the `myCab` reference before a real object is assigned to it, you will most likely have a problem. If you set the `myCab` reference to `null` in the constructor, you can later check to see whether `myCab` is still `null` when you attempt to use it. An exception might be generated if you treat an uninitialized reference as if it were properly initialized.

Consider another example: If you have an Employee class that includes a spouse attribute (perhaps for insurance purposes), you better make provisions for the situation when an employee is not married. By initially setting the attribute to null, you can then check for this status.

The second constructor provides a way for the user of the class to initialize the `Name` and `myCab` attributes:

```
public Cabbie(String iName, String serialNumber) {

    name = iName;
    myCab = new Cab(serialNumber);

}
```

In this case, the user would provide two strings in the parameter list of the constructor to properly initialize attributes. Notice that the `myCab` object is instantiated in this constructor:

```
myCab = new Cab(serialNumber);
```

As a result of executing this line of code, the storage for a `Cab` object is allocated. Figure 4.3 illustrates how a new instance of a `Cab` object is referenced by the attribute `myCab`. Using two constructors in this example demonstrates a common use of method overloading. Notice that the constructors are all defined as `public`. This makes sense because in this case, the constructors are obvious members of the class interface. If the constructors were private, other objects couldn't access them—thus, other objects could not instantiate a `Cab` object.

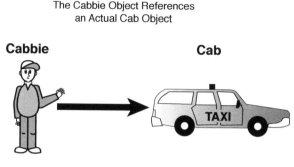

The Cabbie Object References
an Actual Cab Object

Cabbie   **Cab**

TAXI

myCab = new Cab (serialNumber);

Figure 4.3   The `Cabbie` object referencing a cab object.

Accessors

In most, if not all, examples in this book, the attributes are defined as `private` so that any other objects cannot access the attributes directly. It would be ridiculous to create an object in isolation that does not interact with other objects—for we want to share appropriate information. Isn't it necessary to inspect and sometimes change another class's attribute? The answer is, of course, yes. There are many times when an object needs to access another object's attributes; however, it does not need to do it directly.

A class should be very protective of its attributes. For example, you do not want object A to have the capability to inspect or change the attributes of object B without object B having control. There are several reasons for this; the most important reasons boil down to data integrity and efficient debugging.

Assume that a bug exists in the `Cab` class. You have tracked the problem to the `Name` attribute. Somehow it is getting overwritten, and garbage is turning up in some name queries. If `Name` were `public` and any class could change it, you would have to go searching through all the possible code, trying to find places that reference and change `Name`. However, if you let only a `Cabbie` object change `Name`, you'd have to look only in the `Cabbie` class. This access is provided by a type of method called an *accessor*. Sometimes accessors are referred to as getters and setters, and sometimes they're simply called `get()` and `set()`. By convention, in this book, we name the methods with the `set` and `get` prefixes, as in the following:

```
// Set the Name of the Cabbie
public void setName(String iName) {
    name = iName;
}

// Get the Name of the Cabbie
```

```
public String getName() {
    return name;
}
```

In this code snippet, a `Supervisor` object must ask the `Cabbie` object to return its name (see Figure 4.4). The important point here is that the `Supervisor` object can't retrieve the information on its own; it must ask the `Cabbie` object for the information. This concept is important at many levels. For example, you might have a `setAge()` method that checks to see whether the age entered was 0 or below. If the age is less than 0, the `setAge()` method can refuse to set this incorrect value. In general, the setters are used to ensure a level of data integrity.

This is also an issue of security. You may have sensitive data, such as passwords or payroll information that you want to control access to. Thus, accessing data via getters and setters provides the capability to use mechanisms like password checks and other validation techniques. This greatly increases the integrity of the data.

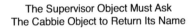

The Supervisor Object Must Ask
The Cabbie Object to Return Its Name

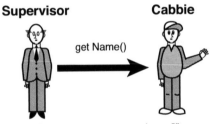

Supervisor   **Cabbie**

get Name()

"Can I have your name please?"

Figure 4.4   Asking for information.

Notice that the `getCompanyName` method is declared as `static`, as a class method; class methods are described in more detail in Chapter 3. Remember that the attribute `companyName` is also declared as `static`. A method, like an attribute, can be declared `static` to indicate that there is only one copy of the method for the entire class.

Objects

Actually, there isn't a physical copy of each nonstatic method for each object. Each object would point to the same physical code. However, from a conceptual level, you can think of objects as being wholly independent and having their own attributes and methods.

The following code fragment illustrates how to define a static method, and Figure 4.5 shows how more than one object points to the same code.

> ### Static Attributes
>
> If an attribute is static, and the class provides a setter for that attribute, any object that invokes the setter will change the single copy. Thus, the value for the attribute will change for all objects.

```
// Get the Name of the Cabbie
public static String getCompanyName() {
    return companyName;
}
```

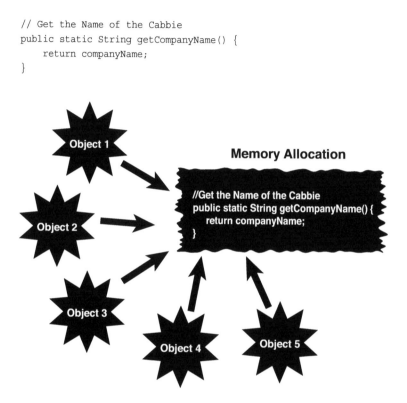

Figure 4.5   Method memory allocation.

Public Interface Methods

Both the constructors and the accessor methods are declared as public and are part of the public interface. They are singled out because of their specific importance to the construction of the class. However, much of the *real* work is provided in other methods. As mentioned in Chapter 2, the public interface methods tend to be very abstract, and the implementation tends to be more concrete. For this class, we provide a method called giveDestination that is the public interface for the user to describe where she wants to go:

```
public void giveDestination (){

}
```

What is inside of this method is not important at this time. The main point is that this is a public method, and it is part of the public interface to the class.

Private Implementation Methods

Although all the methods discussed so far in this chapter are defined as `public`, not all the methods in a class are part of the public interface. It is common for methods in a class to be hidden from other classes. These methods are declared as `private`:

```
private void turnRight(){
}

private void turnLeft() {
}
```

These private methods are meant to be part of the implementation and not the public interface. You might ask who invokes these methods, if no other class can. The answer is simple—you might have already surmised that these methods are called internally from the class itself. For example, these methods could be called from within the method `giveDestination`:

```
public void giveDestination (){

    .. some code

    turnRight();
    turnLeft();

    .. some more code

}
```

As another example, you may have an internal method that provides encryption that you will use only from within the class itself. In short, this encryption method can't be called from outside the instantiated object itself.

The point here is that private methods are strictly part of the implementation and are not accessible by other classes.

Conclusion

In this chapter, we have gotten inside a class and described the fundamental concepts necessary for understanding how a class is built. Although this chapter takes a practical approach to discussing classes, Chapter 5, "Class Design Guidelines," covers the class from a general design perspective.

References

- Fowler, Martin. 2003. *UML Distilled,* 3rd edition. Boston, MA: Addison-Wesley Professional.

- Gilbert, Stephen, and Bill McCarty. 1998. *Object-Oriented Design in Java.* Berkeley, CA: The Waite Group Press.

- Tyma, Paul, Gabriel Torok, and Troy Downing. 1996. *Java Primer Plus.* Berkeley, CA: The Waite Group.

Example Code Used in This Chapter

The following code is presented in C# .NET. Code for other languages, such as VB .NET and Objective-C, are available electronically on the publisher's website. These examples correspond to the Java code that is listed inside the chapter itself.

The `TestCab` Example: C# .NET

```
using System;

namespace ConsoleApplication1
{
    class TestPerson
    {
        public static void Main()
        {
            Cabbie joe = new Cabbie("Joe", "1234");

            Console.WriteLine(joe.Name);
            Console.ReadLine();
        }
    }

    public class Cabbie
    {

            private string _Name;
            private Cab _Cab;

            public Cabbie() {

             _Name = null;
             _Cab = null;

            }
```

```
        public Cabbie(string name, string serialNumber) {

        _Name = name;
           _Cab = new Cab(serialNumber);

          }

    //Methods
    public String Name
    {
        get { return _Name; }
        set { _Name = value; }
    }

  }

  public class Cab
  {

          public Cab (string serialNumber) {

          SerialNumber = serialNumber;

          }

    //The property is public to get, but private to set
    public string SerialNumber { get; private set; }

  }
}
```

5

Class Design Guidelines

As we have already discussed, OO programming supports the idea of creating classes that are complete packages, encapsulating the data and behavior of a single entity. So, a class should represent a logical component, such as a taxicab.

This chapter presents several suggestions for designing solid classes. Obviously, no list such as this can be considered complete. You will undoubtedly add many guidelines to your personal list and incorporate useful guidelines from other developers.

Modeling Real-World Systems

One of the primary goals of object-oriented (OO) programming is to model real-world systems in ways similar to the ways in which people actually think. Designing classes is the object-oriented way to create these models. Rather than using a structured, or *top-down*, approach, where data and behavior are logically separate entities, the OO approach encapsulates the data and behavior into objects that interact with each other. We no longer think of a problem as a sequence of events or routines operating on separate data files. The elegance of this mindset is that classes literally model real-world objects and how these objects interact with other real-world objects.

These interactions occur in a way similar to the interactions between real-world objects, such as people. Thus, when creating classes, you should design them in a way that represents the true behavior of the object. Let's use the cabbie example from previous chapters. The Cab class and the Cabbie class model a real-world entity. As illustrated in Figure 5.1, the Cab and the Cabbie objects encapsulate their data and behavior, and they interact through each other's public interfaces.

When moving to OO development for the first time, many people tend to still think in a structured way. One of the primary mistakes is to create a class that has behavior but no class data. In effect, they are creating a set of functions or subroutines in the structured model. This is not what you want to do because it doesn't take advantage of the power of encapsulation.

Cabbie

Cab

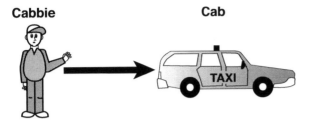

Figure 5.1   A cabbie and a cab are real-world objects.

> **Note**
> One of my favorite books pertaining to class design guidelines and suggestions remains
> *Effective C++: 50 Specific Ways to Improve Your Programs and Designs*, by Scott Meyers. It offers
> important information about program design in a very concise manner.

One of the reasons that Effective C++ interests me so much is that because C++ is backward-compatible with C, the compiler allows you to write structured code in C++ without using OO design principles. This is exactly the reason why following guidelines, such as the ones presented in Effective C++, is so important. As I mentioned earlier, during interviews, some people claim that they are OO programmers simply because they program in C++. This indicates a total misunderstanding of what OO design is all about. Thus, you may have to pay more attention to the OO design issues in languages such as C++ and Objective-C as opposed to Java or .NET.

Identifying the Public Interfaces

It should be clear by now that perhaps the most important issue when designing a class is to keep the public interface to a minimum. The entire purpose of building a class is to provide something useful and concise. On page 109 of their book *Object-Oriented Design in Java*, Gilbert and McCarty state that "the interface of a well-designed object describes the services that the client wants accomplished." If a class does not provide a useful service to a user, it should not have been built in the first place.

The Minimum Public Interface

Providing the minimum public interface makes the class as concise as possible. The goal is to provide the user with the exact interface to do the job right. If the public interface is incomplete (that is, there is missing behavior), the user will not be able to do the complete job. If the public interface is not properly restricted (that is, the user has access to behavior that is unnecessary or even dangerous), problems can result in the need for debugging, and even trouble with system integrity and security can surface.

Creating a class is a business proposition, and as with all steps in the design process, it is very important that the users are involved with the design right from the start and throughout the testing phase. In this way, the utility of the class, as well as the proper interfaces, will be assured.

Even if the public interface of a class is insufficient for a certain application, object technology easily allows the capability to extend and adapt this interface. In short, if designed with inheritance composition in mind, a new class can utilize an existing class and create a new class with an extended interface.

To illustrate, consider the cabbie example again. If other objects in the system need to get the name of a cabbie, the `Cabbie` class must provide a public interface to return its name; this is the `getName()` method. Thus, if a `Supervisor` object needs a name from a `Cabbie` object, it must invoke the `getName()` method from the `Cabbie` object. In effect, the supervisor is asking the cabbie for its name (see Figure 5.2).

Supervisor   **Cabbie**

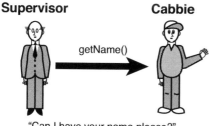

getName()

"Can I have your name please?"

Figure 5.2   The public interface specifies how the objects interact.

Users of your code need to know nothing about its internal workings. All they need to know is how to instantiate and use the object. In short, provide users a way to get there but hide the details.

Hiding the Implementation

The need for hiding the implementation has already been covered in great detail. Whereas identifying the public interface is a design issue that revolves around the users of the class, the implementation should not involve the users at all. The implementation must provide the services that the user needs, but how these services are actually performed should not be made apparent to the user. A class is most useful if the implementation can change without affecting the users. For example, a change to the implementation should not necessitate a change in the user's application code.

In the cabbie example, the `Cabbie` class might contain behavior pertaining to how it eats breakfast. However, the cabbie's supervisor does not need to know what the cabbie has for breakfast. Thus, this behavior is part of the implementation of the `Cabbie` object and should not be available to other objects in this system (see Figure 5.3). Gilbert and McCarty state that the prime directive of encapsulation is that "all fields shall be private." In this way, none of the fields in a class is accessible from other objects.

Supervisor   **Cabbie**

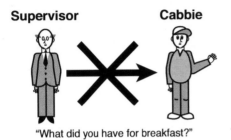

"What did you have for breakfast?"

Figure 5.3   Objects don't need to know some implementation details.

Designing Robust Constructors (and Perhaps Destructors)

When designing a class, one of the most important design issues involves how the class will be constructed. Constructors are discussed in Chapter 3, "Advanced Object-Oriented Concepts." Revisit this discussion if you need a refresher on guidelines for designing constructors.

First and foremost, a constructor should put an object into an initial, safe state. This includes issues such as attribute initialization and memory management. You also need to make sure the object is constructed properly in the default condition. It is normally a good idea to provide a constructor to handle this default situation.

In languages that include destructors, it is of vital importance that the destructors include proper clean-up functions. In most cases, this clean-up pertains to releasing system memory that the object acquired at some point. Java and .NET reclaim memory automatically via a garbage collection mechanism. In languages such as C++, the developer must include code in the destructor to properly free up the memory that the object acquired during its existence. If this function is ignored, a memory leak will result.

> **Memory Leaks**
>
> When an object fails to properly release the memory that it acquired during an object's life cycle, the memory is lost to the entire operating system as long as the application that created the object is executing. For example, suppose multiple objects of the same class are created and then destroyed, perhaps in some sort of loop. If these objects fail to release their memory when they go out of scope, this memory leak slowly depletes the available pool of system memory. At some point, it is possible that enough memory will be consumed that the system will have no available memory left to allocate. This means that any application executing in the system would be unable to acquire any memory. This could put the application in an unsafe state and even lock up the system.

Designing Error Handling into a Class

As with the design of constructors, designing how a class handles errors is of vital importance. Error handling is discussed in detail in Chapter 3.

It is virtually certain that every system will encounter unforeseen problems. Thus, it is not a good idea to ignore potential errors. The developer of a good class (or any code, for that matter) anticipates potential errors and includes code to handle these conditions when they are encountered.

The general rule is that the application should never crash. When an error is encountered, the system should either fix itself and continue, or exit gracefully without losing any data that's important to the user.

Documenting a Class and Using Comments

The topic of comments and documentation comes up in every programming book and article, in every code review, and in every discussion you have about good design. Unfortunately, comments and good documentation are often not taken seriously, or even worse, they are ignored.

Most developers know that they should thoroughly document their code, but they don't usually want to take the time to do it. However, a good design is practically impossible without good documentation practices. At the class level, the scope might be small enough that a developer can get away with shoddy documentation. However, when the class gets passed to someone else to extend and/or maintain, or it becomes part of a larger system (which is what should happen), a lack of proper documentation and comments can undermine the entire system.

Many people have said all this before. One of the most crucial aspects of a good design, whether it's a design for a class or something else, is to carefully document the process. Implementations such as Java and .NET provide special comment syntax to facilitate the documentation process. Check out Chapter 4, "The Anatomy of a Class," for the appropriate syntax.

> **Too Much Documentation**
>
> Be aware that over-commenting can be a problem as well. Too much documentation and/or commenting can become background noise and may defeat the purpose of the documentation in the first place. Just like in good class design, make the documentation and comments straightforward and to the point.

Building Objects with the Intent to Cooperate

We can safely say that almost no class lives in isolation. In most cases, there is no reason to build a class if it is not going to interact with other classes. This is a fact in the life of a class. A class will service other classes; it will request the services of other classes, or both. In later chapters, we discuss various ways that classes interact with each other.

In the cabbie example, the cabbie and the supervisor are not standalone entities; they interact with each other at various levels (see Figure 5.4).

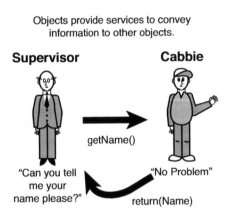

Figure 5.4   Objects should request information.

When designing a class, make sure you are aware of how other objects will interact with it.

Designing with Reuse in Mind

Objects can be reused in different systems, and code should be written with reuse in mind. For example, when a `Cabbie` class is developed and tested, it can be used anywhere you need a cabbie. To make a class usable in various systems, the class must be designed with reuse in mind. This is where much of the thought is required in the design process. Attempting to predict all the possible scenarios in which a `Cabbie` object must operate is not a trivial task—in fact, it is virtually impossible.

Designing with Extensibility in Mind

Adding new features to a class might be as simple as extending an existing class, adding a few new methods, and modifying the behavior of others. It is not necessary to rewrite everything. This is where inheritance comes into play. If you have just written a Person class, you must consider the fact that you might later want to write an Employee class or a Vendor class. Thus, having Employee inherit from Person might be the best strategy; in this case, the Person class is said to be *extensible*. You do not want to design Person so that it contains behavior that prevents it from being extended by classes such as Employee or Vendor (assuming that in your design, you really intend for other classes to extend Person). For example, you would not want to code functionality into an Employee class that is specific to supervisory functions. If you did, and then a class that does not require supervisory functionality inherited from Employee, you would have a problem.

This point touches on the abstraction guideline discussed earlier. Person should contain only the data and behaviors that are specific to a person. Other classes can then subclass it and inherit appropriate data and behaviors.

What Attributes and Methods Can Be Static?

It is important to decide what attributes and methods can be declared as static. Revisit the discussions in Chapter 3 on using the static keyword to understand how to design these into your classes—these attributes and methods are shared by all objects of a class.

Making Names Descriptive

Earlier we discussed the use of proper documentation and comments. Following a naming convention for your classes, attributes, and methods is a similar subject. There are many naming conventions, and the convention you choose is not as important as choosing one and sticking to it. However, when you choose a convention, make sure that when you create classes, attributes, and method names, you not only follow the convention, but also make the names descriptive. When someone reads the name, he should be able to tell from the name what the object represents. These naming conventions are often dictated by the coding standards at various organizations.

Good Naming

Make sure that a naming convention makes sense. Often, people go overboard and create conventions that might make sense to them, but are totally incomprehensible to others. Take care when forcing others to conform to a convention. Make sure that the conventions are sensible and that everyone involved understands the intent behind them.

Making names descriptive is a good development practice that transcends the various development paradigms.

Abstracting Out Nonportable Code

If you are designing a system that must use nonportable (native) code (that is, the code will run only on a specific hardware platform), you should abstract this code out of the class. By abstracting out, we mean isolating the non-portable code in its own class or at least its own method (a method that can be overridden). For example, if you are writing code to access a serial port of particular hardware, you should create a wrapper class to deal with it. Your class should then send a message to the wrapper class to get the information or services it needs. Do not put the system-dependent code into your primary class (see Figure 5.5).

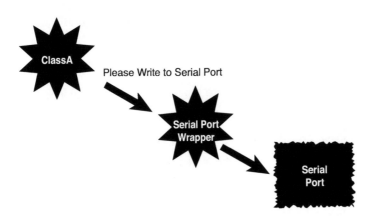

Figure 5.5   A serial port wrapper.

For example, consider the situation when a programmer is interfacing directly with hardware. In these cases, the object code of the various platforms will most likely be quite different and thus code must be written for each platform. However, if the functionality is placed in a 'wrapper' class, then a user of the class can interface directly with the wrapper and not have to worry about the various low-level code. The wrapper class will deal with the differences in these platforms and decide which code to invoke.

Providing a Way to Copy and Compare Objects

Chapter 3 discussed the issue of copying and comparing objects. It is important to understand how objects are copied and compared. You might not want, or expect, a simple bitwise copy or compare operation. You must make sure that your class behaves as expected, and this means you have to spend some time designing how objects are copied and compared.

Keeping the Scope as Small as Possible

Keeping the scope as small as possible goes hand-in-hand with abstraction and hiding the implementation. The idea is to localize attributes and behaviors as much as possible. In this way, maintaining, testing, and extending a class are much easier.

Scope and Global Data

Minimizing the scope of global variables is a good programming style and is not specific to OO programming. Global variables are allowed in structured development, yet they can get dicey. In fact, there is no global data in OO development. Static attributes and methods are shared among objects of the same class; however, they are not available to objects not of the class.

For example, if you have a method that requires a temporary attribute, keep it local. Consider the following code:

```
public class Math {

    int temp=0;

    public int swap (int a, int b) {

        temp = a;
        a=b;
        b=temp;

        return temp;

    }

}
```

What is wrong with this class? The problem is that the attribute `temp` is needed only within the scope of the `swap()` method. There is no reason for it to be at the class level. Thus, you should move `temp` within the scope of the `swap()` method:

```
public class Math {

    public int swap (int a, int b) {

        int temp=0;

        temp = a;
        a=b;
        b=temp;

        return temp;

    }

}
```

This is what is meant by keeping the scope as small as possible.

A Class Should Be Responsible for Itself

In a training class based on their book *Java Primer Plus*, Tyma, Torok, and Downing propose the class design guideline that all objects should be responsible for acting on themselves whenever possible. Consider trying to print a circle.

To illustrate, let's use a non-OO example. In this example, the print command is passed a `Circle` as an argument and prints it (see Figure 5.6):

```
print(circle);
```

Choose a Shape and Print

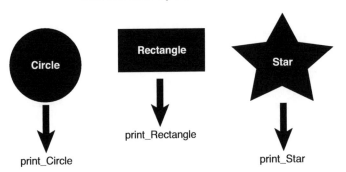

Figure 5.6   A non-OO example of a print scenario.

The functions `print`, `draw`, and others need to have a `case` statement (or something like an `if/else` structure) to determine what to do for the given shape passed. In this case, a separate print routine for each shape could be called:

```
printCircle(circle);
printSquare(square);
```

Every time you add a new shape, all the functions need to add the shape to their `case` statements:

```
switch (shape) {
    case 1:  printCircle(circle); break;
    case 2:  printSquare(square); break;
    case 3:  printTriangle(triangle);  break;
    default: System.out.println("Invalid shape.");break;
}
```

Now let's look at an OO example. By using polymorphism and grouping the `Circle` into a `Shape` category, `Shape` figures out that it is a `Circle` and knows how to print itself (see Figure 5.7):

```
shape.print(); // Shape is actually a Circle
shape.print(); // Shape is actually a Square
```

The important thing to understand here is that the call is identical; the context of the shape dictates how the system reacts.

A Shape Knows How to Print Itself

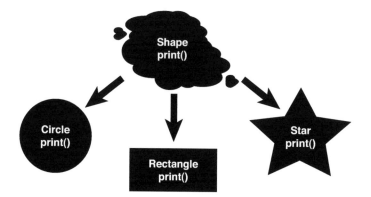

Figure 5.7   An OO example of a print scenario.

Designing with Maintainability in Mind

Designing useful and concise classes promotes a high level of maintainability. Just as you design a class with extensibility in mind, you should also design with future maintenance in mind.

The process of designing classes forces you to organize your code into many (ideally) manageable pieces. Separate pieces of code tend to be more maintainable than larger pieces of code (at least that's the idea). One of the best ways to promote maintainability is to reduce interdependent code—that is, changes in one class have no impact or minimal impact on other classes.

Highly Coupled Classes

Classes that are highly dependent on one another are considered *highly coupled*. Thus, if a change made to one class forces a change to another class, these two classes are considered highly coupled. Classes that have no such dependencies have a very low degree of coupling. For more information on this topic, refer to *The Object Primer,* by Scott Ambler.

If the classes are designed properly in the first place, any changes to the system should be made only to the implementation of an object. Changes to the public interface should be avoided at all costs. Any changes to the public interface will cause ripple effects throughout all the systems that use the interface.

For example, if a change were made to the getName() method of the Cabbie class, every single place in all systems that use this interface must be changed and recompiled. Finding all these method calls is a daunting task, and the likelihood of missing one is pretty high.

To promote a high level of maintainability, keep the coupling level of your classes as low as possible.

Using Iteration in the Development Process

As in most design and programming functions, using an iterative process is recommended. This dovetails well into the concept of providing minimal interfaces. Basically, this means *don't write all the code at once*! Create the code in small increments and then build and test it at each step. A good testing plan quickly uncovers any areas where insufficient interfaces are provided. In this way, the process can iterate until the class has the appropriate interfaces. This testing process is not simply confined to coding. Testing the design with walkthroughs and other design review techniques is very helpful. Testers' lives are more pleasant when iterative processes are used, because they are involved in the process early and are not simply handed a system that is thrown over the wall at the end of the development process.

Testing the Interface

The minimal implementations of the interface are often called *stubs*. (Gilbert and McCarty have a good discussion on stubs in *Object-Oriented Design in Java*.) By using stubs, you can test the interfaces without writing any *real* code. In the following example, rather than connecting to an actual database, stubs are used to verify that the interfaces are working properly (from the user's perspective—remember that interfaces are meant for the user). Thus, the implementation is not necessary at this point. In fact, it might cost valuable time and energy to complete the implementation at this point because the design of the interface will affect the implementation, and the interface is not yet complete.

In Figure 5.8, note that when a user class sends a message to the DataBaseReader class, the information returned to the user class is provided by code stubs and not by the actual database. (In fact, the database most likely does not exist yet.) When the interface is complete and the implementation is under development, the database can then be connected and the stubs disconnected.

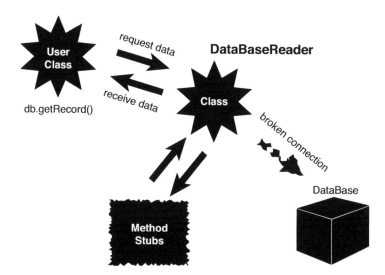

Figure 5.8   Using stubs.

Here is a code example that uses an internal array to simulate a working database (albeit a simple one):

```
public class DataBaseReader {

    private String db[] = { "Record1",
        "Record2",
        "Record3",
        "Record4",
        "Record5"};

    private boolean DBOpen = false;
    private int pos;

    public void open(String Name){
        DBOpen = true;
    }
    public void close(){
        DBOpen = false;
    }
    public void goToFirst(){
        pos = 0;
    }
    public void goToLast(){
        pos = 4;
    }
```

```
public int howManyRecords(){
    int numOfRecords = 5;

    return numOfRecords;
}
public String getRecord(int key){

    /* DB Specific Implementation */
    return db[key];
}
public String getNextRecord(){

    /* DB Specific Implementation */
    return db[pos++];
}

}
```

Notice how the methods simulate the database calls. The strings within the array represent the records that will be written to the database. When the database is successfully integrated into the system, it will be substituted for the array.

Keeping the Stubs Around

When you are done with the stubs, don't delete them. Keep them in the code for possible use later—just make sure the users can't see them. In fact, in a well-designed program, your test stubs should be integrated into the design and kept in the program for later use. In short, design the testing right into the class!

As you find problems with the interface design, make changes and repeat the process until you are satisfied with the result.

Using Object Persistence

Object persistence is another issue that must be addressed in many OO systems. *Persistence* is the concept of maintaining the state of an object. When you run a program, if you don't save the object in some manner, the object dies, never to be recovered. These transient objects might work in some applications, but in most business systems, the state of the object must be saved for later use.

Object Persistence

Although the topic of object persistence and the topics in the next section might not be considered true design guidelines, I believe that they must be addressed when designing classes. I introduce them here to stress that they must be addressed early on when designing classes.

In its simplest form, an object can persist by being serialized and written to a flat file. The state-of-the-art technology is now XML-based. Although it is true that an object theoretically can persist in memory as long as it is not destroyed, we will concentrate on storing persistent objects on some sort of storage device. There are three primary storage devices to consider:

- **Flat file system**—You can store an object in a flat file by serializing the object. This has very limited use.

- **Relational database**—Some sort of middleware is necessary to convert an object to a relational model.

- **OO database**—This may be a more efficient way to make objects persistent, but most companies have all their data in legacy systems and at this point in time are unlikely to convert their relational databases to OO databases.

Serializing and Marshaling Objects

We have already discussed the problem of using objects in environments that were originally designed for structured programming. The middleware example, where we wrote objects to a relational database, is one good example. We also touched on the problem of writing an object to a flat file or sending it over a network.

To send an object over a wire (for example, to a file, over a network), the system must deconstruct the object (flatten it out), send it over the wire, and then reconstruct it on the other end of the wire. This process is called *serializing* an object. The act of sending the object across a wire is called *marshaling* an object. A serialized object, in theory, can be written to a flat file and retrieved later, in the same state in which it was written.

The major issue here is that the serialization and deserialization must use the same specifications. It is sort of like an encryption algorithm. If one object encrypts a string, the object that wants to decrypt it must use the same encryption algorithm. Java provides an interface called `Serializable` that provides this translation.

C# .NET and Visual Basic .NET provide the `ISerializable` interface, where the Microsoft documentation describes it as: *Allows an object to control its own serialization and deserialization.* All classes that are meant to be serialized must implement this interface. The syntax for both C# .NET and Visual Basic .NET are listed in the following:

```
' Visual Basic .NET
Public Interface ISerializable
```

```
// C# .NET
public interface ISerializable
```

One of the problems with serialization is that it is often proprietary. The use of XML, which is discussed in detail later, is nonproprietary.

Conclusion

This chapter presents many guidelines that can help you in designing classes. This is by no means a complete list of guidelines. You will undoubtedly come across additional guidelines as you go about your travels in OO design.

This chapter deals with design issues as they pertain to individual classes. However, we have already seen that a class does not live in isolation. Classes must be designed to interact with other classes. A group of classes that interact with each other is part of a system. Ultimately, these systems provide value to end users. Chapter 6, "Designing with Objects," covers the topic of designing complete systems.

References

- Meyers, Scott. 2005. *Effective C++*, 3rd edition. Boston, MA: Addison-Wesley Professional.

- Ambler, Scott. 2004. *The Object Primer*, 3rd edition. Cambridge, United Kingdom: Cambridge University Press.

- Jaworski, Jamie. 1999. *Java 2 Platform Unleashed*. Indianapolis, IN: Sams Publishing.

- Gilbert, Stephen, and Bill McCarty. 1998. *Object-Oriented Design in Java*. Berkeley, CA: The Waite Group Press.

- Tyma, Paul, Gabriel Torok, and Troy Downing. 1996. *Java Primer Plus*. Berkeley, CA: The Waite Group.

- Jaworski, Jamie. 1997. *Java 1.1 Developers Guide*. Indianapolis, IN: Sams Publishing.

Example Code Used in This Chapter

The following code is presented in C# .NET. Code for other languages, such as VB .NET and Objective-C, are available electronically on the publisher's website. These examples correspond to the Java code that is listed inside the chapter itself.

The `TestMath` Example: C# .NET

```
using System;
using System.Collections.Generic;
using System.Linq;
using System.Text;

namespace TestMath
{
    public class Math
    {
```

```
        public int swap(int a, int b)
        {

            int temp = 0;

            temp = a;
            a = b;
            b = temp;

            return temp;

        }

    }
    class TestMath
    {
        public static void Main()
        {
            Math myMath = new Math();
            myMath.swap(2, 3);
        }
    }
}
```

6

Designing with Objects

When you use a software product, you expect it to behave as advertised. Unfortunately, not all products live up to expectations. The problem is that when many products are produced, the majority of time and effort go into the engineering phase and not into the design phase.

Object-oriented (OO) design has been touted as a robust and flexible software development approach. The truth is that you can create both good and bad OO designs just as easily as you can create both good and bad non-OO designs. Don't be lulled into a false sense of security just because you are using a state-of-the-art design methodology. You must pay attention to the overall design and invest the proper amount of time and effort to create the best possible product.

In Chapter 5, "Class Design Guidelines," we concentrated on designing good classes. This chapter focuses on designing good *systems*. A *system* can be defined as classes that interact with each other. Proper design practices have evolved throughout the history of software development, and there is no reason you should not take advantage of the blood, sweat, and tears of your software predecessors, whether they used OO technologies or not.

Taking advantage of previous efforts is not limited to design practices; you can even incorporate existing legacy code in your object-oriented designs. In many cases, you can take code, which may have been working well for years, and literally wrap it in your objects. The *wrapping* is discussed later in the chapter.

Design Guidelines

One fallacy is that there can ever be one true design methodology. This is certainly not the case. There is no right or wrong way to create a design. Many design methodologies are available today, and they all have their proponents. However, the primary issue is not which design method to use, but whether to use a method at all. This can be expanded beyond design to encompass the entire software development process. Many organizations do not follow a standard software development process, or they have one and don't adhere to it. The most important factor in creating a good design is to find a process that you and your organization feel comfortable with and stick to it. It makes no sense to implement a design process that no one will follow.

Most books that deal with object-oriented technologies offer very similar strategies for designing systems. In fact, except for some of the object-oriented specific issues involved, much of the strategy is applicable to non–OO systems as well.

Generally, a solid OO design process includes the following steps:

1. Doing the proper analysis.

2. Developing a statement of work that describes the system.

3. Gathering the requirements from this statement of work.

4. Developing a prototype for the user interface.

5. Identifying the classes.

6. Determining the responsibilities of each class.

7. Determining how the various classes interact with each other.

8. Creating a high-level model that describes the system to be built.

For object-oriented development, the high-level system model is of special interest. The system, or object model, is made up of class diagrams and class interactions. This model should represent the system faithfully and be easy to understand and modify. We also need a notation for the model. This is where the Unified Modeling Language (UML) comes in. As you know, UML is not a design process, but a modeling tool. In this book, I focus only on the class diagrams within UML. I like to use class diagrams as a visual tool that helps with design as well as documentation.

The Ongoing Design Process

Despite the best intentions and planning, in all but the most trivial cases, the design is an ongoing process. Even after a product is in testing, design changes will pop up. It is up to the project manager to draw the line that says when to stop changing a product and adding features.

It is important to understand that many design methodologies are available. One early methodology, called the waterfall model, advocates strict boundaries between the various phases. In this case, the design phase is completed before the implementation phase, which is completed before the testing phase, and so on. In practice, the waterfall model has been found to be unrealistic. Currently, other design models, such as rapid prototyping, Extreme Programming, Agile, Scrum, and so on, promote a true iterative process. In these models, some implementation is attempted prior to completing the design phase as a type of proof-of-concept. Despite the recent aversion to the waterfall model, the goal behind the model is understandable. Coming up with a complete and thorough design before starting to code is a sound practice. You do not want to be in the release phase of the product and then decide to iterate through the design phase again. Iterating across phase boundaries is unavoidable; however, you should keep these iterations to a minimum (see Figure 6.1).

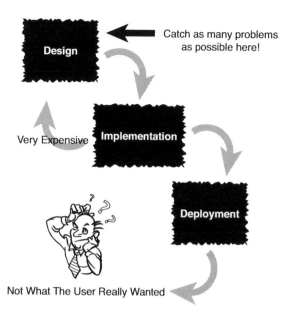

Figure 6.1   The waterfall method.

Simply put, the reasons to identify requirements early and keep design changes to a minimum are as follows:

- The cost of a requirement/design change in the design phase is relatively small.

- The cost of a design change in the implementation phase is significantly higher.

- The cost of a design change after the deployment phase is astronomical when compared to the first item.

Similarly, you would not want to start the construction of your dream house before the architectural design was complete. If I said that the Golden Gate Bridge or the Empire State Building was constructed without any consideration of design issues, you would consider the statement absolutely crazy. Yet, you would most likely not find it crazy if I told you that the software you were using might contain some design flaws, and in fact, might not have been thoroughly tested.

In reality, it might be impossible to thoroughly test software, in the sense that absolutely *no* bugs exist. However, in theory, that should always be the goal. We should always attempt to weed out as many bugs as possible. Bridges and software might not be directly comparable; however, software must strive for the same level of engineering excellence as the "harder" engineering disciplines such as bridge building. Poor-quality software can be lethal—it's not just wrong numbers on payroll checks. For example, inferior software in medical equipment can kill and maim people. Yet, you may be willing to live with having to reboot your computer every now and then. But the same cannot be said for a bridge failing.

Safety Versus Economics

Would you want to cross a bridge that has not been inspected and tested? Unfortunately, with many software packages, users are left with the responsibility of doing much of the testing. This is very costly for both the users and the software providers. Unfortunately, short-term economics often seem to be the primary factor in making project decisions.

Because customers seem to be willing to pay a limited price and put up with software of poor quality, some software providers find that it is cheaper in the long run to let the customers test the product rather than do it themselves. In the short term this might be true, but in the long run it costs far more than the software provider realizes. Ultimately, the software provider's reputation will be damaged.

Some computer software companies are willing to use the beta test phase to let the customers do testing—testing that should, theoretically, have been done before the beta version ever reached the customer. Many customers are willing to take the risk of using prerelease software because they are anxious to get the functionality the product promises.

After the software is released, problems that have not been caught and fixed prior to release become much more expensive. To illustrate, consider the dilemma automobile companies face when they are confronted with a recall. If a defect in the automobile is identified and fixed before it is shipped (ideally before it is manufactured), it is much cheaper than if all delivered automobiles have to be recalled and fixed one at a time. Not only is this scenario very expensive, but it damages the reputation of the company. In an increasingly competitive market, high-quality software, support services, and reputation are *the* competitive advantage (see Figure 6.2).

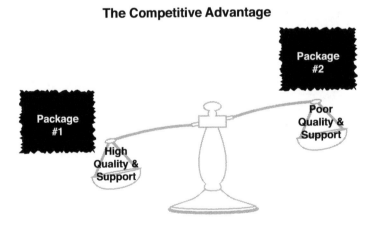

Figure 6.2   The competitive advantage.

The following sections provide brief summaries of the items listed previously as being part of the design process. Later in the chapter, we work through an example that explains in greater detail each of these items.

Performing the Proper Analysis

There are a lot of variables involved in building a design and producing a software product. The users must work hand-in-hand with the developers at all stages. In the analysis phase, the users and the developers must do the proper research and analysis to determine the statement of work, the requirements of the project, and whether to actually do the project. The last point might seem a bit surprising, but it is important. During the analysis phase, there must not be any hesitation to terminate the project if a valid reason exists to do so. Too many times, pet project status or some political inertia keeps a project going, regardless of the obvious warning signs that cry out for project cancellation. Assuming that the project is viable, the primary focus of the analysis phase is for everyone to learn the systems (both the old and the proposed new one) and determine the system requirements.

> Generic Software Principles
> Most of these practices are not specific to OO. They apply to software development in general.

Developing a Statement of Work

The *statement of work* (SOW) is a document that describes the system. Although determining the requirements is the ultimate goal of the analysis phase, at this point the requirements are not yet in a final format. The SOW should give anyone who reads it a complete understanding of the system. Regardless of how it is written, the SOW must represent the complete system and be clear about how the system will look and feel.

The SOW contains everything that must be known about the system. Many customers create a *request for proposal* (RFP) for distribution, which is similar to the statement of work. A customer creates an RFP that completely describes the system the customer wants built and releases it to multiple vendors. The vendors then use this document, along with whatever analysis they need to do, to determine whether they should bid on the project, and if so, what price to charge.

Gathering the Requirements

The *requirements document* describes what the users want the system to do. Even though the level of detail of the requirements document does not need to be of a highly technical nature, the requirements must be specific enough to represent the true nature of the user's needs for the end product. The requirements document must be of sufficient detail for the user to make educated judgments about the completeness of the system. It must also be of specific detail for a design group to use the document to proceed with the design phase.

Whereas the SOW is a document written in paragraph (even narrative) form, the requirements are usually represented as a summary statement or presented as bulleted items. Each individual bulleted item represents one specific requirement of the system. The requirements are distilled from the statement of work. This process is shown later in the chapter.

In many ways, these requirements are the most important part of the system. The SOW might contain irrelevant material; however, the requirements are the final representation of the system that must be implemented. All future documents in the software development process will be based on the requirements.

Developing a Prototype of the User Interface

One of the best ways to make sure users and developers understand the system is to create a *prototype*. A prototype can be just about anything; however, most people consider the prototype to be a simulated user interface. By creating actual screens and screen flows, it is easier for people to get an idea of what they will be working with and what the system will feel like. In any event, a prototype will almost certainly not contain all the functionality of the final system.

Most prototypes are created with an integrated development environment (IDE). However, drawing the screens on a whiteboard or even on paper might be all that is needed. Traditionally, Visual Basic .NET is a good environment for prototyping, although other languages are now in play. Remember that you are not necessarily creating business logic (the logic/code behind the interface that actually does the work) when you build the prototype, although it is possible to do so. The look and feel of the user interface are the major concerns at this point. Having a good prototype can help immensely when identifying classes.

Identifying the Classes

After the requirements are documented, the process of identifying classes can begin. From the requirements, one straightforward way of identifying classes is to highlight all the nouns. These tend to represent objects, such as people, places, and things. Don't be too fussy about getting all the classes right the first time. You might end up eliminating classes, adding classes, and changing classes at various stages throughout the design. It is important to get something down first. Take advantage of the fact that the design is an iterative process. As in other forms of brainstorming, get something down initially, with the understanding that the final result might look nothing like the initial pass.

Determining the Responsibilities of Each Class

You need to determine the responsibilities of each class you have identified. This includes the data that the class must store and what operations the class must perform. For example, an `Employee` object would be responsible for calculating payroll and transferring the money to the appropriate account. It might also be responsible for storing the various payroll rates and the account numbers of various banks.

Determining How the Classes Collaborate with Each Other

Most classes do not exist in isolation. Although a class must fulfill certain responsibilities, many times it will have to interact with another class to get something it wants. This is where the messages between classes apply. One class can send a message to another class when it needs information from that class, or if it wants the other class to do something for it.

Creating a Class Model to Describe the System

When all the classes are determined and the class responsibilities and collaborations are listed, a class model that represents the complete system can be constructed. The class model shows how the various classes interact within the system.

In this book, we are using UML to model the system. Several tools on the market use UML and provide a good environment for creating and maintaining UML class models. As we develop the example in the next section, we will see how the class diagrams fit into the big picture and how modeling large systems would be virtually impossible without some sort of good modeling notation and modeling tool.

Prototyping the User Interface

During the design process, we must create a prototype of our user interface. This prototype will provide invaluable information to help navigate through the iterations of the design process. As Gilbert and McCarty in *Object-Oriented Design in Java* aptly point out, "to a system user, the user interface is the system." There are several ways to create a user interface prototype. You can sketch the user interface by drawing it on paper or a whiteboard. You can use a special prototyping tool, or even a language environment like Visual Basic, which is often used for rapid prototyping. Or you can use the IDE from your favorite development tool to create the prototype.

However you develop the user interface prototype, make sure that the users have the final say on the look and feel.

Object Wrappers

Several times in the previous chapters I have indicated that one of my primary goals in this book is to dispel the fallacy that object-oriented programming is a separate paradigm from structured programming, and is even at odds with it. In fact, as I have already mentioned, I am often asked the following question: "*Are you an object-oriented programmer or a structured programmer?*" The answer is always the same—I am both!

In my mind, there is no way to write a program without using structured code. Thus, when you write a program that uses an object-oriented programming language and are using sound object-oriented design techniques, you are also using structured programming techniques. There is no way around this.

For example, when you create a new object that contains attributes and methods, those methods will include structured code. In fact, I might even say that these methods will contain *mostly* structured code. This approach fits in well with the container concept that we have encountered in earlier chapters. In fact, when I get to the point where I am coding at the method level, my coding thought process hasn't changed much since when I was programming in structured languages, such as Cobol, C, and the like. This is not to say that it is exactly the same, because

I obviously have had to adjust to some object-oriented constructs; however, the fundamental approach to coding at the method level is virtually the same as programming has always been.

Now I'll return to the question *"Are you an object-oriented programmer or a structured programmer?"* I often like to say that *programming is programming.* By this I contend that being a good programmer means understanding the basics of programming logic and having a passion for coding. Often you will see ads for a programmer with a specific skill set—let's say a specific language like Java.

Although I totally understand that an organization may well need an experienced Java programmer in a pinch, over the long run I would prefer to focus on hiring a programmer who has a wide range of programming experience and who can learn and adjust quickly when new technologies emerge. Some of my colleagues do not always agree with this; however, I believe that when hiring, I look more at what a potential employee can learn than what they already know. The passion part is critical because it ensures that an employee will always be exploring new technologies and development methodologies.

Structured Code

Although the basics of programming logic may be debated, as I have stressed, the fundamental object-oriented constructs are *encapsulation, inheritance, polymorphism,* and *composition.* In most textbooks that I have seen, the basic constructs of structured programming are *sequence, conditions,* and *iterations.*

The sequence part is a given, because it seems logical to start at the top and proceed in a logical manner to the bottom. For me, the meat of structured programming resides in the conditions and iterations, which I call if-statements and loops, respectively.

Take a look at the following Java code that starts at 0 and loops 10 times, printing out the value if it equals 5:

```java
class MainApplication {

    public static void main(String args[]) {

        int x = 0;

        while (x <= 10) {

            if (x==5) System.out.println("x = " + x);

            x++;
        }

    }

}
```

Now while this code is written in an object-oriented language, the code that resides inside of the main method is structured code. All three basics of structured programming are present: *sequence, conditions,* and *iterations.*

The sequence part is easy to identify because the first line executed is the following:

```
int x = 0;
```

When that line completes, the next line is executed:

```
while (x <= 10) {
```

And so on. In short, this is tried and true top-down-programming: start at the first line, execute it, and then go on to the next.

There is also a condition present in this code as part of the if-statement:

```
if (x==5)
```

Finally, there is a loop to complete the structured trio:

```
while (x <= 10) {
    }
```

Actually, the while loop also contains a condition:

```
(x <= 10)
```

You can pretty much code anything with just these three constructs. In fact, the concept of the wrapper is basically the same for structured programming as it is for object-oriented programming. In structured design, you wrap the code in functions (such as the main method in this example), and in object-oriented design, you wrap the code in objects and methods.

Wrapping Structured Code

Although defining attributes is considered coding (for example, creating an integer), the behavior of an object resides in the methods. And these methods are where the bulk of the code logic is found.

Consider Figure 6.3. As you can see, an object contains methods, and these methods contain code, which can be anything from variable declarations to conditions to loops.

For example, let's consider a simple example in which we are wrapping the functionality for addition. Here we create a method named add, which accepts two integer parameters and returns their sum:

```
class SomeMath {

    public int add(int a, int b) {

        return a + b;

    }

}
```

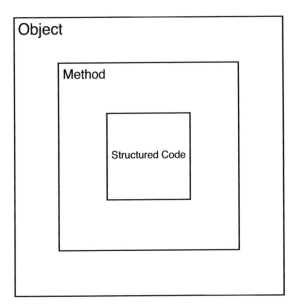

Figure 6.3   Wrapping structured code.

As you can see, the structured code used to perform the addition (*a* + *b*) is *wrapped* inside the add method. Although this is a trivial example, that is all there is to wrapping structured code. Thus, when the user wants to use this method, all that is needed is the signature of the method, as seen next:

```
public class TestMath {

        public static void main(String[] args) {

                int x = 0;

                SomeMath math = new SomeMath();

                x = math.add(1,2);

                System.out.println("x = " + x);

        }
}
```

Finally, let's take a look at some more functionality that is a bit more interesting and complicated. Suppose that we wanted to include a method to calculate the Fibonacci value of a number. We can then add a method like this:

```
public static int fib(int n) {
    if (n < 2) {
```

```
        return n;
    } else {
        return fib(n-1)+fib(n-2);
    }
}
```

The whole point here is to show that we have an object-oriented method that contains (wraps) structured code, because the `fib` method contains conditions, recursion, and so on. And as mentioned in the introduction, it is possible to incorporate existing legacy code in wrappers as well.

Wrapping Nonportable Code

One other use of object wrappers is for the hiding of nonportable (or native) code. The concept is essentially the same; however, in this case, the point is to take code that can be executed on only one platform, (or a few platforms) and encapsulate it in a method providing a simple interface for the programmers using the code.

Consider the task of making the computer make a noise—in this case, a *beep*. On a Windows platform we can execute a *beep* with the following code:

```
System.out.println("\007");
```

Rather than making the programmer memorize the code (or look it up), you can provide a class called Sound that contains a method called `beep`, as shown next:

```
class Sound {

    public void beep() {

            System.out.println("\007");

    }

}
```

Now, rather than having to know the code for making the sound, the programmer can use the class and call the `beep` method:

```
public class TestBeep {

    public static void main(String[] args) {

            Sound mySound = new Sound();

            mySound.beep();

    }
}
```

Not only is this simpler for the programmer to use, but you can extend the functionality of the class to include other sounds. Perhaps, more importantly, when the code is used on a non-Windows platform, the interface for the user remains the same. In short, the team that builds the code for the Sound class will have to deal with the change in platform. For the programmers who utilize the class in their applications, the change will be seamless because they will still call the beep method.

Wrapping Existing Classes

Although the need to wrap legacy structured code, or even nonportable code, into a new (object-oriented) class may seem reasonable, the need to wrap existing classes may not seem so obvious. However, there are also many reasons to create wrappers for existing (object-oriented) classes.

Software developers often utilize code written by someone else. Perhaps the code was purchased from a vendor or even written internally within the same organization. In many of these cases, the code cannot be changed. Perhaps the individual who wrote the code is no longer with the organization, or the vendor cannot perform maintenance updates, and so on. This is where the true power of wrappers emerges.

The idea is to take an existing class and alter its implementation or interface by wrapping it inside a new class—just like we did for the structured code and nonportable code. The difference in this case is that, rather than putting an object-oriented face to the code, we are altering its implementation or interface.

Why would we want to do this? Well, the answer lies with both the implementation and the interface.

Consider the database example that we used in Chapter 2, "How to Think in Terms of Objects." Our goal was to provide the same interface for the developers regardless of which database they were using. In fact, if we need to support another database, our goal would remain the same—to make the transition to the new database transparent to the user (see Figure 2.3, as shown in Chapter 2).

Also, remember our earlier discussion about creating middleware to provide an interface between objects and relational databases. As developers, we want to use objects. Thus, we want functionality that will allow us to persist objects to a database. What we don't want to have to do is write SQL code for every single object transaction performed to a relational database. This is where we can consider middleware to be a wrapper, and many object-relational mapping products are available. This topic is discussed in much more detail in Chapter 12, "Persistent Objects: Serialization, Marshalling, and Relational Databases."

Conceptually, for me, the ultimate example of the interface and implementation paradigm is the discussion that we had regarding the power plant example in Chapter 2, "How to Think in Terms of Objects," and shown in Figure 2.1. In this case, we can swap out (wrap) both: We can alter the interface by changing the outlet, and we can alter the implementation by changing the power generation facility.

The use of wrappers in software development is fairly extensive, not only from a developer's perspective, but also from a vendor's. Wrappers are an important tool when developing software systems.

In this chapter, we have focused on various design considerations. These considerations include writing new code as well as utilizing previously written code, whether in-house or from vendors. In some cases, wrappers are even design paradigms unto themselves. Design patterns, for example, utilize wrappers in various cases. As we will see later, the Decorator pattern focuses on wrapping the implementation, whereas the Adaptor pattern focuses on altering the interface. The discussion concerning design patterns is explored in more detail in Chapter 15, "Design Patterns."

Conclusion

This chapter covers the design process for complete systems. It is important to note that object-oriented and structured code are not mutually exclusive. In fact, you can't create objects without using structured code. Thus, while building object-oriented systems, you are also using structured techniques in the design.

Object wrappers are used to encapsulate many types of functionality, which can range from traditional structured (legacy) and object-oriented (classes) code to nonportable (native) code. The primary purpose of object wrappers is to provide consistent interfaces for the programmers who are using the code.

In the next several chapters, we explore in more detail the relationships between classes. Chapter 7, "Mastering Inheritance and Composition," covers the concepts of inheritance and composition and how they relate to each other.

References

- Ambler, Scott. 2004. *The Object Primer,* 3rd edition. Cambridge, United Kingdom: Cambridge University Press.

- McConnell, Steve. 2004. *Code Complete: A Practical Handbook of Software Construction,* 2nd edition. Redmond WA: Microsoft Press.

- Gilbert, Stephen, and Bill McCarty. 1998. *Object-Oriented Design in Java.* Berkeley, CA: The Waite Group Press.

- Jaworski, Jamie. 1999. *Java 2 Platform Unleashed.* Indianapolis, IN: Sams Publishing.

- Jaworski, Jamie. 1997. *Java 1.1 Developers Guide.* Indianapolis, IN: Sams Publishing.

- Wirfs-Brock, R., B. Wilkerson, and L. Weiner. 1990. *Designing Object-Oriented Software.* Upper Saddle River, NJ: Prentice-Hall.

- Weisfeld, Matt and John Ciccozzi. September, 1999. "Software by Committee," *Project Management Journal* v5, number 1: 30–36.

7

Mastering Inheritance and Composition

Inheritance and composition play major roles in the design of object-oriented (OO) systems. In fact, many of the most difficult and interesting design decisions come down to deciding between inheritance and composition.

These decisions have become much more interesting over the years as object-oriented design practices have evolved. Perhaps one of the most interesting debates revolves around inheritance. Although inheritance is one of the fundamental constructs of object-oriented development (a language has to support inheritance to be considered object-oriented), many developers are increasingly turning away from inheritance in lieu of other design strategies.

Regardless, both inheritance and composition are mechanisms for reuse. *Inheritance*, as its name implies, involves inheriting attributes and behaviors from other classes. In this case, there is a true parent/child relationship. The child (or subclass) inherits directly from the parent (or superclass).

Composition, also as its name implies, involves building objects by using other objects. In this chapter, we explore the obvious and subtle differences between inheritance and composition. Primarily, we will consider the appropriate times to use one or the other.

Reusing Objects

Perhaps the primary reason that inheritance and composition exist is object reuse. In short, you can build classes (which ultimately become objects) by utilizing other classes via inheritance and composition, which in effect, are the only ways to reuse previously built classes.

Inheritance represents the is-a relationship that was introduced in Chapter 1, "Introduction to Object-Oriented Concepts." For example, a dog *is a* mammal.

Composition involves using other classes to build more complex classes—a sort of assembly. No parent/child relationship exists in this case. Basically, complex objects are composed of other objects. Composition represents a has-a relationship. For example, a car *has an* engine. Both the engine and the car are separate, potentially standalone objects. However, the car is a complex object that contains (has an) engine object. In fact, a child object might itself be composed of other objects; for example, the engine might include cylinders. In this case, an engine *has a* cylinder, actually several.

When OO technologies first entered the mainstream, inheritance was often the first example used in how to design an OO system. That you could design a class once and then inherit functionality from it was considered one of the foremost advantages to using OO technologies. Reuse was the name of the game, and inheritance was the ultimate expression of reuse.

However, over time the luster of inheritance has dulled a bit. In fact, even in some early discussions, the use of inheritance itself is questioned. In their book *Java Design*, Peter Coad and Mark Mayfield have a complete chapter titled "Design with Composition Rather Than Inheritance." Many early object-based platforms did not even support true inheritance. As Visual Basic evolved into Visual Basic .NET, early object-based implementations did not include strict inheritance capabilities. Platforms such as the MS COM model were based on interface inheritance. Interface inheritance is covered in great detail in Chapter 8, "Frameworks and Reuse: Designing with Interfaces and Abstract Classes."

Today, the use of inheritance is still a major topic of debate. Abstract classes, which are a form of inheritance, are not directly supported in some languages, such as Objective-C. Interfaces are used even though they don't provide all the functionality that abstract classes do.

The good news is that the discussions about whether to use inheritance or composition are a natural progression toward some seasoned middle ground. As in all philosophical debates, there are passionate arguments on both sides. Fortunately, as is normally the case, these heated discussions have led to a more sensible understanding of how to utilize the technologies.

We will see later in this chapter why some people believe that inheritance should be avoided, and composition should be the design method of choice. The argument is fairly complex and subtle. In actuality, both inheritance and composition are valid class design techniques, and they each have a proper place in the OO developer's toolkit. And, at least, you need to understand both to make the proper design choice.

The fact that inheritance is often misused and overused is more a result of a lack of understanding of what inheritance is all about than a fundamental flaw in using inheritance as a design strategy.

The bottom line is that inheritance and composition are both important techniques in building OO systems. Designers and developers need to take the time to understand the strengths and weaknesses of both and to use each in the proper contexts.

Inheritance

Inheritance was defined in Chapter 1 as a system in which child classes inherit attributes and behaviors from a parent class. However, there is more to inheritance, and in this chapter we explore inheritance in greater detail.

Chapter 1 states that you can determine an inheritance relationship by following a simple rule: If you can say that Class B *is a* Class A, then this relationship is a good candidate for inheritance.

Is-a

One of the primary rules of OO design is that public inheritance is represented by an is-a relationship.

Let's revisit the mammal example used in Chapter 1. Let's consider a `Dog` class. A dog has several behaviors that make it distinctly a dog, as opposed to a cat. For this example, let's specify two: A dog barks, and a dog pants. So, we can create a `Dog` class that has these two behaviors, along with two attributes (see Figure 7.1).

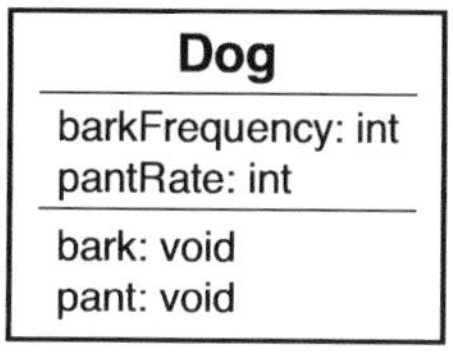

Dog
barkFrequency: int
pantRate: int
bark: void
pant: void

Figure 7.1 A class diagram for the `Dog` class.

Now let's say that you want to create a `GoldenRetriever` class. You could create a brand-new class that contains the same behaviors that the `Dog` class has. However, we could make the following, and quite reasonable, conclusion: A Golden Retriever is-a dog. Because of this relationship, we can inherit the attributes and behaviors from `Dog` and use it in our new `GoldenRetriever` class (see Figure 7.2).

Dog
barkFrequency: int
pantRate: int
bark: void
pant: void
GoldenRetriever
retrievalSpeed: int
retrieves: void

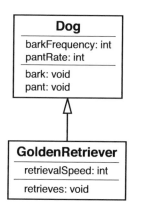

Figure 7.2 The `GoldenRetriever` class inherits from the `Dog` class.

The GoldenRetriever class now contains its own behaviors as well as all the more general behaviors of a dog. This provides us with some significant benefits. First, when we wrote the GoldenRetriever class, we did not have to reinvent part of the wheel by rewriting the bark and pant methods. Not only does this save some design and coding time, but it saves testing and maintenance time as well. The bark and pant methods are written only once and, assuming that they were properly tested when the Dog class was written, they do not need to be heavily tested again; but it does need to be retested because there are new interfaces, and so on.

Now let's take full advantage of our inheritance structure and create a second class under the Dog class: a class called LhasaApso. Whereas retrievers were bred for retrieving, Lhasa Apsos were bred for use as guard dogs. These dogs are not attack dogs; they have acute senses, and when they sense something unusual, they start barking. So, we can create our LhasaApso class and inherit from the Dog class just as we did with the GoldenRetriever class (see Figure 7.3).

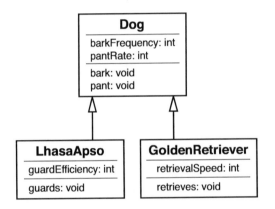

Figure 7.3   The LhasaApso class inherits from the Dog class.

Testing New Code

In our example with the GoldenRetriever class, the bark and pant methods should be written, tested, and debugged when the Dog class is written. Theoretically, this code is now robust and ready to reuse in other situations. However, the fact that you do not need to rewrite the code does not mean it should not be tested. However unlikely, there might be some specific characteristic of a retriever that somehow breaks the code. The bottom line is that you should always test new code. Each new inheritance relationship creates a new context for using inherited methods. A complete testing strategy should take into account each of these contexts.

Another primary advantage of inheritance is that the code for bark() and pant() is in a single place. Let's say there is a need to change the code in the bark() method. When you change it in the Dog class, you do not need to change it in the LhasaApso class and the GoldenRetriever class.

Do you see a problem here? At this level, the inheritance model appears to work very well. However, can you be certain that all dogs have the behavior contained in the Dog class?

In his book *Effective C++*, Scott Meyers gives a great example of a dilemma with design using inheritance. Consider a class for a bird. One of the most recognizable characteristics of a bird is, of course, that it can fly. So, we create a class called Bird with a fly method. You should immediately understand the problem. What do we do with a penguin, or an ostrich? They are birds, yet they can't fly. You could override the behavior locally, but the method would still be called fly. And it would not make sense to have a method called fly for a bird that does not fly but only waddles, runs, or swims.

This leads to some potentially significant problems. For example, if a penguin has a fly method, the penguin might understandably decide to test it out. However, if the fly method was in fact overridden and the behavior to fly did not exist, the penguin would be in for a major surprise when the fly method is invoked after jumping over a cliff. Imagine the penguin's chagrin when the call to the fly method results in waddling instead of flight. In this situation, waddling doesn't cut it. Just imagine if code such as this ever found its way into a spacecraft's guidance system.

In our dog example, we have designed the class so that all dogs have the ability to bark. However, some dogs do not bark. The Basenji breed is a barkless dog. Although these dogs do not bark, they do yodel. So should we reevaluate our design? What would this design look like? Figure 7.4 is an example that shows a more correct way to model the hierarchy of the Dog class.

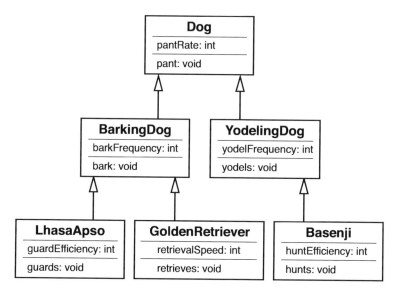

Figure 7.4   The Dog class hierarchy.

Generalization and Specialization

Consider the object model of the Dog class hierarchy. We started with a single class, called Dog, and we factored out some of the commonality between various breeds of dogs. This concept, sometimes called *generalization-specialization*, is yet another important consideration when using inheritance. The idea is that as you make your way down the inheritance tree, things get more specific. The most general case is at the top of the tree. In our Dog inheritance tree, the class Dog is at the top and is the most general category. The various breeds—the GoldenRetriever, LhasaApso, and Basenji classes—are the most specific. The idea of inheritance is to go from the general to the specific by factoring out commonality.

In the Dog inheritance model, we started factoring out common behavior by understanding that although a retriever has some different behavior from that of a LhasaApso, the breeds do share some common behaviors—for example, they both pant and bark. Then we realized that all dogs do not bark—some yodel. Thus, we had to factor out the barking behavior into a separate BarkingDog class. The yodeling behavior went into a YodelingDog class. However, we realized that both barking dogs and barkless dogs still shared some common behavior—all dogs pant. Thus, we kept the Dog class and had the BarkingDog and the YodelingDog classes inherit from Dog. Now Basenji can inherit from YodelingDog, and LhasaApso and GoldenRetriever can inherit from BarkingDog.

We could have decided not to create two distinct classes for BarkingDog and YodelingDog. In this case, we could implement all barking and yodeling as part of each individual breed's class—since each dog would sound differently. This is just one example of some of the design decisions that have to be made. Perhaps the best solution is to implement the barking and yodeling as interfaces, which we discuss in Chapter 8, "Frameworks and Reuse: Designing with Interfaces and Abstract Classes."

Design Decisions

In theory, factoring out as much commonality as possible is great. However, as in all design issues, sometimes it really is too much of a good thing. Although factoring out as much commonality as possible might represent real life as closely as possible, it might not represent your model as closely as possible. The more you factor out, the more complex your system gets. So you have a conundrum: Do you want to live with a more accurate model or a system with less complexity? You have to make this choice based on your situation, for there are no hard guidelines to make the decision.

> ### What Computers Are Not Good At
> Obviously, a computer model can only approximate real-world situations. Computers are good at number crunching but are not as good at more abstract operations.

For example, breaking up the Dog class into BarkingDog and the YodelingDog models real life better than assuming that all dogs bark, but it does add a bit of complexity.

> **Model Complexity**
>
> At this level of our example, adding two more classes does not make things so complex that it makes the model untenable. However, in larger systems, when these kinds of decisions are made over and over, the complexity quickly adds up. In larger systems, keeping things as simple as possible is usually the best practice.

There will be instances in your design when the advantage of a more accurate model does not warrant the additional complexity. Let's assume that you are a dog breeder and that you contract out for a system that tracks all your dogs. The system model that includes barking dogs and yodeling dogs works fine. However, suppose that you do not breed any yodeling dogs—never have and never will. Perhaps you do not need to include the complexity of differentiating between yodeling dogs and barking dogs. This will make your system less complex, and it will provide the functionality that you need.

Deciding whether to design for less complexity or more functionality is a balancing act. The primary goal is always to build a system that is flexible without adding so much complexity that the system collapses under its own weight.

Current and future costs are also a major factor in these decisions. Although it might seem appropriate to make a system more complete and flexible, this added functionality might barely add any benefit—the return on investment might not be there. For example, would you extend the design of your Dog system to include other canines, such as hyenas and foxes (see Figure 7.5)?

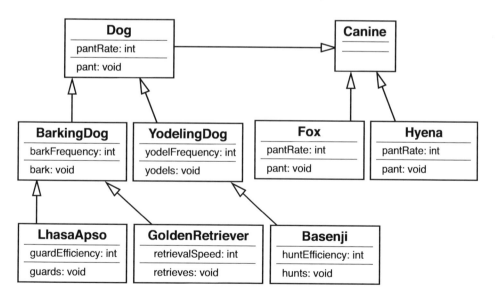

Figure 7.5   An expanded canine model.

Although this design might be prudent if you were a zookeeper, the extension of the `Canine` class is probably not necessary if you are breeding and selling domesticated dogs.

So as you can see, there are always trade-offs when creating a design.

Making Design Decisions with the Future in Mind

You might at this point say, "Never say never." Although you might not breed yodeling dogs now, sometime in the future you might want to do so. If you do not design for the possibility of yodeling dogs now, it will be much more expensive to change the system later to include them. This is yet another of the many design decisions that you have to make. You could possibly override the `bark()` method to make it yodel; however, this is not intuitive, and some people will expect a method called `bark()` to actually bark.

Composition

It is natural to think of objects as containing other objects. A television set contains a tuner and video display. A computer contains video cards, keyboards, and drives. The computer can be considered an object unto itself, and a flash drive is also considered a valid object. You could open up the computer and remove the hard drive and hold it in your hand. In fact, you could take the hard drive to another computer and install it. The fact that it is a standalone object is reinforced because it works in multiple computers.

The classic example of object composition is the automobile. Many books, training classes, and articles seem to use the automobile as the epitome of object composition. Besides the original interchangeable manufacture of the rifle, most people think of the automobile assembly line created by Henry Ford as the quintessential example of interchangeable parts. Thus, it seems natural that the automobile has become a primary reference point for designing OO software systems.

Most people would think it natural for a car to contain an engine. However, a car contains many objects besides an engine, including wheels, a steering wheel, and a stereo. Whenever a particular object is composed of other objects, and those objects are included as object fields, the new object is known as a *compound*, an *aggregate*, or a *composite object* (see Figure 7.6).

Aggregation, Association, and Composition

From my perspective, there are only two ways to reuse classes—with inheritance or composition. In Chapter 9, "Building Objects and Object-Oriented Design," we discuss composition in more detail—specifically, aggregation and association. In this book, I consider aggregation and association to be types of composition, although there are varied opinions on this.

A Car has a Steering Wheel

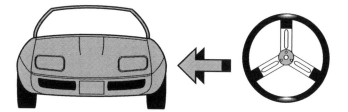

Figure 7.6   An example of composition.

Representing Composition with UML

To model the fact that the car object contains a steering wheel object, UML uses the notation shown in Figure 7.7.

Aggregation, Association, and UML

In this book, aggregations are represented in UML by lines with a diamond, such as an engine as part of a car. Associations are represented by just the line (no diamond), such as a stand-alone keyboard servicing a separate computer box.

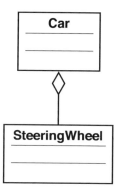

Figure 7.7   Representing composition in UML.

Note that the line connecting the `Car` class to the `SteeringWheel` class has a diamond shape on the `Car` side of the line. This signifies that a `Car` *contains* (has-a) `SteeringWheel`.

Let's expand this example. Suppose that none of the objects in this design use inheritance in any way. All the object relationships are strictly composition, and there are multiple levels of composition. Of course, this is a simplistic example, and there are many, many more object and object relationships in designing a car. However, this design is meant to be a simple illustration of what composition is all about.

Let's say that a car is composed of an engine, a stereo system, and a door.

How Many Doors and Stereos?

Note that a car normally has more than one door. Some have two, and some have four. You might even consider a hatchback a fifth door. In the same vein, it is not necessarily true that all cars have a stereo system. A car could have no stereo system, or it could have one. I have even seen a car with two separate stereo systems. These situations are discussed in detail in Chapter 9. For the sake of this example, just pretend that a car has only a single door (perhaps it's a special racing car) and a single stereo system.

That a car is made up of an engine, a stereo system, and a door is easy to understand because most people think of cars in this way. However, it is important to keep in mind when designing software systems, just like automobiles, that objects are made up of other objects. In fact, the number of nodes and branches that can be included in this tree structure of classes is virtually unlimited.

Figure 7.8 shows the object model for the car, with the engine, stereo system, and door included.

Note that all three objects that make up a car are themselves composed of other objects. The engine contains pistons and spark plugs. The stereo contains a radio and a CD player. The door contains a handle. Also note that there is yet another level. The radio contains a tuner. We could have also added the fact that a handle contains a lock; the CD player contains a fast forward button, and so on. Additionally, we could have gone one level beyond the tuner and created an object for a dial. The level and complexity of the object model is up to the designer.

Model Complexity

As with the inheritance problem of the barking and yodeling dogs, using too much composition can also lead to more complexity. A fine line exists between creating an object model that contains enough granularity to be sufficiently expressive and a model that is so granular that it is difficult to understand and maintain.

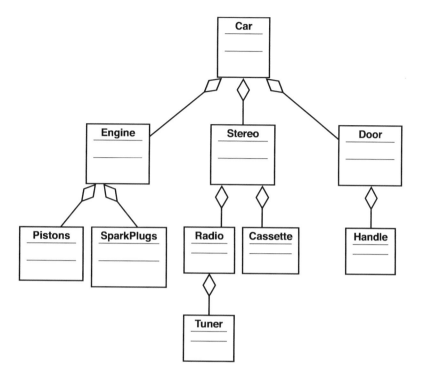

Figure 7.8   The Car class hierarchy.

Why Encapsulation Is Fundamental to OO

Encapsulation is the fundamental concept of OO. Whenever the interface/implementation paradigm is covered, we are talking about encapsulation. The basic question is what in a class should be exposed and what should not be exposed. This encapsulation pertains equally to data and behavior. When talking about a class, the primary design decision revolves around encapsulating both the data and the behavior into a well-written class.

Stephen Gilbert and Bill McCarty define encapsulation as "the process of packaging your program, dividing each of its classes into two distinct parts: the interface and the implementation." This is the message that has been presented over and over in this book.

But what does encapsulation have to do with inheritance, and how does it apply with regard to this chapter? This has to do with an OO paradox. Encapsulation is so fundamental to OO that it is one of OO design's cardinal rules. Inheritance is also considered one of the three primary OO concepts. However, in one way, inheritance actually breaks encapsulation! How can this be? Is it possible that two of the three primary concepts of OO are incompatible with each other? Let's explore this possibility.

How Inheritance Weakens Encapsulation

As already stated, encapsulation is the process of packaging classes into the public interface and the private implementation. In essence, a class hides everything that is not necessary for other classes to know about.

Peter Coad and Mark Mayfield make a case that when using inheritance, encapsulation is inherently weakened within a class hierarchy. They talk about a specific risk: Inheritance connotes strong encapsulation with other classes but weak encapsulation between a superclass and its subclasses.

The problem is that if you inherit an implementation from a superclass and then change that implementation, the change from the superclass *ripples through* the class hierarchy. This rippling effect potentially affects all the subclasses. At first, this might not seem like a major problem; however, as we have seen, a rippling effect such as this can cause unanticipated problems. For example, testing can become a nightmare. In Chapter 6, "Designing with Objects," we talked about how encapsulation makes testing systems easier. In theory, if you create a class called Cabbie (see Figure 7.9) with the appropriate public interfaces, any change to the implementation of Cabbie should be transparent to all other classes. However, in any design, a change to a superclass is certainly not transparent to a subclass. Do you see the conundrum?

If the other classes were directly dependent on the implementation of the Cabbie class, testing would become more difficult, if not untenable.

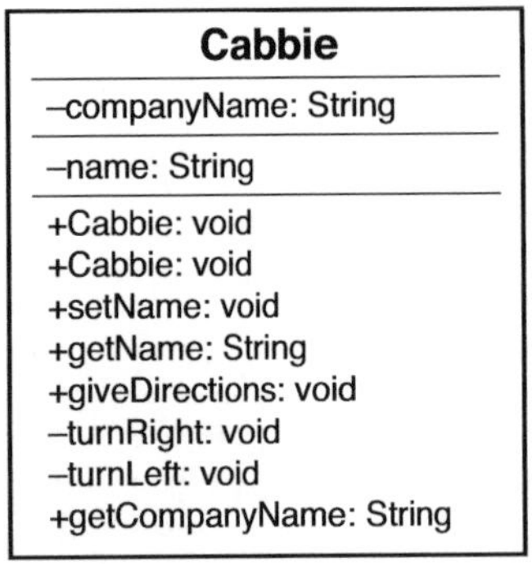

Cabbie
–companyName: String
–name: String
+Cabbie: void
+Cabbie: void
+setName: void
+getName: String
+giveDirections: void
–turnRight: void
–turnLeft: void
+getCompanyName: String

Figure 7.9   A UML diagram of the Cabbie class.

Keep Testing

Even with encapsulation, you would still want to retest the classes that use Cabbie to verify that no problem has been introduced by the change.

If you then create a subclass of Cabbie called PartTimeCabbie, and PartTimeCabbie inherits the implementation from Cabbie, changing the implementation of Cabbie directly affects the PartTimeCabbie class.

For example, consider the UML diagram in Figure 7.10. PartTimeCabbie is a subclass of Cabbie. Thus, PartTimeCabbie inherits the public implementation of Cabbie, including the method giveDirections(). If the method giveDirections()is changed in Cabbie, it will have a direct impact on PartTimeCabbie and any other classes that might later be subclasses of Cabbie. In this subtle way, changes to the implementation of Cabbie are not necessarily encapsulated within the Cabbie class.

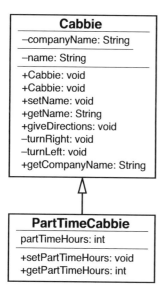

Figure 7.10   A UML diagram of the Cabbie/PartTimeCabbie classes.

To reduce the risk posed by this dilemma, it is important that you stick to the strict is-a condition when using inheritance. If the subclass were truly a specialization of the superclass, changes to the parent would likely affect the child in ways that are natural and expected. To illustrate, if a Circle class inherits implementation from a Shape class, and a change to the implementation of Shape breaks Circle, then Circle was not truly a Shape to begin with.

How can inheritance be used improperly? Consider a situation in which you want to create a window for the purposes of a graphical user interface (GUI). One impulse might be to create a window by making it a subclass of a rectangle class:

```
public class Rectangle {

}

public class Window extends Rectangle {

}
```

In reality, a GUI window is much, much more than a rectangle. It is not a specialized version of a rectangle, as is a square. A true window might contain a rectangle (in fact, many rectangles); however, it is not a true rectangle. In this approach, a `Window` class should not inherit from `Rectangle`, but it should contain `Rectangle` classes:

```
public class Window {

    Rectangle menubar;
    Rectangle statusbar;
    Rectangle mainview;

}
```

A Detailed Example of Polymorphism

Many people consider polymorphism a cornerstone of OO design. Designing a class for the purpose of creating totally independent objects is what OO is all about. In a well-designed system, an object should be able to answer all the important questions about it. As a rule, an object should be responsible for itself. This independence is one of the primary mechanisms of code reuse.

As stated in Chapter 1, polymorphism literally means *many shapes*. When a message is sent to an object, the object must have a method defined to respond to that message. In an inheritance hierarchy, all subclasses inherit the interfaces from their superclass. However, because each subclass is a separate entity, each might require a separate response to the same message.

To review the example in Chapter 1, consider a class called `Shape`. This class has a behavior called `Draw`. However, when you tell somebody to draw a shape, the first question is likely to be, "What shape?" Simply telling a person to draw a shape is too abstract (in fact, the `Draw` method in `Shape` contains no implementation). You must specify which shape you mean. To do this, you provide the actual implementation in `Circle` and other subclasses. Even though `Shape` has a `Draw` method, `Circle` overrides this method and provides its own `Draw` method. Overriding basically means replacing an implementation of a parent with your own.

Object Responsibility

Let's revisit the `Shape` example from Chapter 1 (see Figure 7.11).

Polymorphism is one of the most elegant uses of inheritance. Remember that a `Shape` cannot be instantiated. It is an abstract class because it has an abstract method, `getArea()`. Chapter 8 explains abstract classes in great detail.

However, `Rectangle` and `Circle` can be instantiated because they are concrete classes. Although `Rectangle` and `Circle` are both shapes, they have some differences. As shapes, their area can be calculated. Yet the formula to calculate the area is different for each. Thus, the area formulas cannot be placed in the `Shape` class.

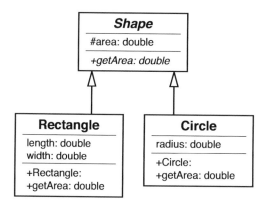

Figure 7.11   The Shape class hierarchy.

This is where polymorphism comes in. The premise of polymorphism is that you can send messages to various objects, and they will respond according to their object's type. For example, if you send the message getArea() to a Circle class, you will invoke a different calculation than if you send the same getArea() message to a Rectangle class. This is because both Circle and Rectangle are responsible for themselves. If you ask Circle to return its area, it knows how to do this. If you want a circle to draw itself, it can do this as well. A Shape object could not do this even if it could be instantiated because it does not have enough information about itself. Notice that in the UML diagram (Figure 7.11), the getArea() method in the Shape class is italicized. This designates that the method is abstract.

As a very simple example, imagine that there are four classes: the abstract class Shape, and concrete classes Circle, Rectangle, and Star. Here is the code:

```
public abstract class Shape{

    public abstract void draw();

}

public class Circle extends Shape{

    public void draw() {

        System.out.println("I am drawing a Circle");

    }
}

public class Rectangle extends Shape{

    public void draw() {
```

```
        System.out.println("I am drawing a Rectangle");

    }

}

public class Star extends Shape{

    public void draw() {

        System.out.println("I am drawing a Star");

    }

}
```

Notice that only one method exists for each class: draw(). Here is the important point regarding polymorphism and an object being responsible for itself: The concrete classes themselves have responsibility for the drawing function. The Shape class does not provide the code for drawing; the Circle, Rectangle, and Star classes do this for themselves. Here is some code to prove it:

```
public class TestShape {

    public static void main(String args[]) {

        Circle circle = new Circle();
        Rectangle rectangle = new Rectangle();
        Star star = new Star();

        circle.draw();
        rectangle.draw();
        star.draw();

    }

}
```

The test application TestShape creates three classes: Circle, Rectangle, and Star. To draw these classes, TestShape asks the individual classes to draw themselves:

```
circle.draw();
rectangle.draw();
star.draw();
```

When you execute TestShape, you get the following results:

```
C:\>java TestShape
I am drawing a Circle
I am drawing a Rectangle
I am drawing a Star
```

This is polymorphism at work. What would happen if you wanted to create a new shape, such as `Triangle`? Simply write the class, compile it, test it, and use it. The base class `Shape` does not have to change—nor does any other code:

```java
public class Triangle extends Shape{

    public void draw() {

        System.out.println("I am drawing a Triangle");

    }
}
```

A message can now be sent to `Triangle`. And even though `Shape` does not know how to draw a triangle, the `Triangle` class does:

```java
public class TestShape {

    public static void main(String args[]) {

        Circle circle = new Circle();
        Rectangle rectangle = new Rectangle();
        Star star = new Star();
        Triangle triangle = new Triangle ();

        circle.draw();
        rectangle.draw();
        star.draw();
        triangle.draw();

    }

}
```

```
C:\>java TestShape
I am drawing a Circle
I am drawing a Rectangle
I am drawing a Star
I am drawing a Triangle
```

To see the real power of polymorphism, you can pass the shape to a method that has absolutely no idea what shape is coming. Take a look at the following code, which includes the specific shapes as parameters:

```java
public class TestShape {

    public static void main(String args[]) {

        Circle circle = new Circle();
```

```
        Rectangle rectangle = new Rectangle();
        Star star = new Star();

        drawMe(circle);
        drawMe(rectangle);
        drawMe(star);

    }

    static void drawMe(Shape s) {
      s.draw();
    }

}
```

In this case, the Shape object can be passed to the method drawMe(), and the drawMe() method can handle any valid Shape—even one you add later. You can run this version of TestShape just like the previous one.

Abstract Classes, Virtual Methods, and Protocols

Abstract classes, as they are defined in Java, can be directly implemented in .NET and C++ as well. Not surprisingly, the C# .NET code looks similar to the Java code, as shown in the following:

```
public abstract class Shape
{

    is a construct similar to a Java-type interface, called a protocol (discussed
further public abstract void draw();

}
```

The Visual Basic .NET code is written like this:

```
Public MustInherit Class Shape

    Public MustOverride Function draw()

End Class
```

The same functionality can be provided in C++ using virtual methods with the following code:

```
class Shape
{
    public:
        virtual void draw() = 0;
}
```

As mentioned in previous chapters, Objective-C does not fully implement the functionality of abstract classes.

For example, consider the following Java interface code for the Shape class we have seen many times:

```
public abstract class Shape{

    public abstract void draw();

}
```

The corresponding Objective-C protocol is shown in the following code. Note that in both the Java code and the Objective-C code, there is no implementation for the draw () method:

```
@protocol Shape

@required
- (void) draw;

@end // Shape
```

At this point, the functionality for the abstract class and the protocol are pretty much equivalent; however, here is where the Java-type interface and the Objective-C protocol diverge. Consider the following Java code:

```
public abstract class Shape{

    public abstract void draw();
    public void print() {
        System.out.println("I am printing");
    };

}
```

In the preceding Java code, the print () method provides code that can be inherited by a subclass. Although this is also the case with C# .NET, VB .NET, and C++, the same cannot be said for an Objective-C protocol, which would look like this:

```
@protocol Shape

@required
- (void) draw;
- (void) print;

@end // Shape
```

In this protocol, the print () method signature is provided, and thus must be implemented by a subclass; however, no code can be included. In short, subclasses cannot directly inherit any code from a protocol. Thus, the protocol cannot be used in the same way as an abstract class, and this has implications when designing an object model.

Conclusion

This chapter gives a basic overview of what inheritance and composition are and how they are different. Many well-respected OO designers have stated that composition should be used whenever possible, and inheritance should be used only when necessary.

However, this is a bit simplistic. I believe that the idea that composition should be used whenever possible hides the real issue, which might be that composition is more appropriate in more cases than inheritance—not that it should be used whenever possible. The fact that composition might be more appropriate in most cases does not mean that inheritance is evil. Use both composition and inheritance, but only in their proper contexts.

In earlier chapters, the concepts of abstract classes and Java interfaces arose several times. In Chapter 8, we explore the concept of development contracts and how abstract classes and Java interfaces are used to satisfy these contracts.

References

- Holzner, Steven. 2010. *Visual Quickstart Guide, Objective-C*. Berkeley, CA: Peachpit Press.

- Booch, Grady, Robert A. Maksimchuk, Michael W. Engel, Bobbi J. Young, Jim Conallen, and Kelli A. Houston. 2007. *Object-Oriented Analysis and Design with Applications*, 3rd edition. Boston, MA: Addison-Wesley.

- Meyers, Scott. 2005. *Effective C++*, 3rd edition. Boston, MA: Addison-Wesley Professional.

- Coad, Peter, and Mark Mayfield. 1997. *Java Design*. Upper Saddle River, NJ: Prentice-Hall.

- Gilbert, Stephen, and Bill McCarty. 1998. *Object-Oriented Design in Java*. Berkeley CA: The Waite Group Press.

Example Code Used in This Chapter

The following code is presented in C# .NET. Code for other languages, such as VB .NET and Objective-C, are available electronically on the publisher's website. These examples correspond to the Java code that is listed inside the chapter itself:

```
using System;

namespace TestShape
{
    public class TestShape
    {

        public static void Main()
        {

            Circle circle = new Circle();
```

```csharp
            Rectangle rectangle = new Rectangle();

            circle.draw();
            rectangle.draw();

        }

    }

public abstract class Shape
{

    public abstract void draw();

}

public class Circle : Shape
{

    public override void draw()
    {

        Console.WriteLine("I am drawing a Circle");

    }
}

public class Rectangle : Shape
{

    public override void draw()
    {

        Console.WriteLine("I am drawing a Rectangle");

    }
}

public class Star : Shape
{

    public override void draw()
    {

        Console.WriteLine("I am drawing a Star");

    }
```

```
    }

    public class Triangle : Shape
    {

        public override void draw()
        {

            Console.WriteLine("I am drawing a Triangle");

        }
    }
}
```

8

Frameworks and Reuse: Designing with Interfaces and Abstract Classes

Chapter 7, "Mastering Inheritance and Composition," explains how inheritance and composition play major roles in the design of object-oriented (OO) systems. This chapter expands upon the concepts of Java-style interfaces, Objective-C protocols, and abstract classes.

Interfaces, protocols, and abstract classes are powerful mechanisms for code reuse, providing the foundation for a concept I call *contracts*. This chapter covers the topics of code reuse, frameworks, contracts, interfaces, protocols, and abstract classes (for the remainder of the chapter, unless otherwise indicated, when I use the term interface to include Objective-C protocols). At the end of the chapter, we'll work through an example of how all these concepts can be applied to a real-world situation.

Code: To Reuse or Not to Reuse?

Programmers have been dealing with the issue of code reuse ever since writing their first line of code. Many software development paradigms stress code reuse as a major part of the process. Since the dawn of computer software, the concept of reusing code has been reinvented several times. The OO paradigm is no different. One of the major advantages touted by OO proponents is that if you write code properly the first time, you can reuse it to your heart's content.

This is true only to a certain degree. As with all design approaches, the utility and the reusability of code depends on how well it was designed and implemented. OO design does not hold the patent on code reuse. There is nothing stopping anyone from writing very robust and reusable code in a non–OO language. Certainly, countless numbers of routines and functions, written in structured languages such as COBOL, C, and traditional VB, are of high quality and are quite reusable.

Thus, it is clear that following the OO paradigm is not the only way to develop reusable code. However, the OO approach does provide several mechanisms for facilitating the development of reusable code. One way to create reusable code is to create frameworks. In this chapter, we focus on using interfaces and abstract classes to create frameworks and encourage reusable code.

What Is a Framework?

Hand in hand with the concept of code reuse is the concept of *standardization*, which is sometimes called *plug and play*. The idea of a framework revolves around these plug-and-play and reuse principles. One of the classic examples of a framework is a desktop application. Let's take an office suite application as an example. The document editor that I am currently using (Microsoft Word, as of this edition part of Office 2010) has a ribbon that includes multiple tab options. These options are similar to those in the presentation package (Microsoft PowerPoint 2010) and the spreadsheet software (Microsoft Excel 2010) that I also have open. In fact, the first two menu items (Home, Insert) are the same in all three programs. Not only are the menu options similar, but many of the options look remarkably alike as well (New, Open, Save, and so on). Below the ribbon is the document area—whether it be for a document, a presentation, or a spreadsheet. The common framework makes it easier to learn various applications within the office suite. It also makes a developer's life easier by allowing maximum code reuse, not to mention that we can reuse portions of the design as well.

The fact that all these menu bars have a similar look and feel is obviously not an accident. In fact, when you develop in most integrated development environments, on a certain platform like Microsoft Windows, for example, you get certain things without having to create them yourself. When you create a window in a Windows environment, you get elements like the main title bar and the file Close button in the top-right corner. Actions are standardized as well—when you double-click the main title bar, the screen always minimizes/maximizes. When you click the Close button in the top-right corner, the application always terminates. This is all part of the framework. Figure 8.1 is a screenshot of a word processor. Note the menu bars, toolbars, and other elements that are part of the framework.

A word processing framework generally includes operations such as creating documents, opening documents, saving documents, cutting text, copying text, pasting text, searching through documents, and so on. To use this framework, a developer must use a predetermined interface to create an application. This predetermined interface conforms to the standard framework, which has two obvious advantages. First, as we have already seen, the look and feel are consistent, and the end users do not have to learn a new framework. Second, a developer can take advantage of code that has already been written and tested (and this testing issue is a huge advantage). Why write code to create a brand-new Open dialog when one already exists and has been thoroughly tested? In a business setting, when time is critical, people do not want to have to learn new things unless it is absolutely necessary.

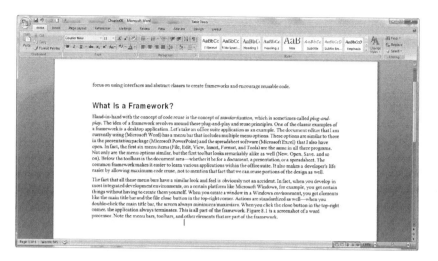

Figure 8.1   A word processing framework.

Code Reuse Revisited

In Chapter 7, we talked about code reuse as it pertains to inheritance—basically one class inheriting from another class. This chapter is about frameworks and reusing whole or partial systems.

The obvious question is this: If you need a dialog box, how do you use the dialog box provided by the framework? The answer is simple: You follow the rules that the framework provides you. And where might you find these rules? The rules for the framework are found in the documentation. The person or persons who wrote the class, classes, or class libraries should have provided documentation on how to use the public interfaces of the class, classes, or class libraries (at least we hope). In many cases, this takes the form of the application-programming interface (API).

For example, to create a menu bar in Java, you would bring up the API documentation for the JMenuBar class and take a look at the public interfaces it presents. Figure 8.2 shows a part of the Java API. By using these APIs, you can create a valid Java applet and conform to required standards. If you follow these standards, your applet will be set to run in Java-enabled browsers.

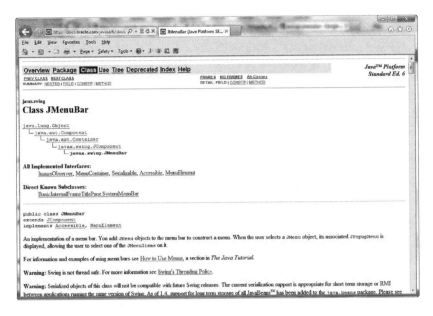

Figure 8.2   API documentation.

What Is a Contract?

In the context of this chapter, we will consider a *contract* to be any mechanism that requires a developer to comply with the specifications of an API. Often, an API is referred to as a framework. The online dictionary, Dictionary.com (http://www.dictionary.com), defines a contract as "an agreement between two or more parties for the doing or not doing of something specified" and "an agreement enforceable by law."

This is exactly what happens when a developer uses an API—with the project manager, business owner, or industry standard providing the enforcement. When using contracts, the developer is required to comply with the rules defined in the framework. This includes issues such as method names, number of parameters, and so on (signatures, and the like). In short, standards are created to facilitate good development practices.

> ### The Term *Contract*
>
> The term *contract* is widely used in many aspects of business, including software development. Do not confuse the concept presented here with other possible software design concepts called contracts.

Enforcement is vital because it is always possible for a developer to break a contract. Without enforcement, a rogue developer could decide to reinvent the wheel and write her own code rather than use the specification provided by the framework. There is little benefit to a standard if people routinely disregard or circumvent it. In Java and the .NET languages, the two ways to implement contracts are to use abstract classes and interfaces.

Abstract Classes

One way a contract is implemented is via an abstract class. An *abstract class* is a class that contains one or more methods that do not have any implementation provided. Suppose that you have an abstract class called Shape. It is abstract because you cannot instantiate it. If you ask someone to draw a shape, the first thing the person will most likely ask you is, "What kind of shape?" Thus, the concept of a shape is abstract. However, if someone asks you to draw a circle, this does not pose quite the same problem, because a circle is a concrete concept. You know what a circle looks like. You also know how to draw other shapes, such as rectangles.

How does this apply to a contract? Let's assume that we want to create an application to draw shapes. Our goal is to draw every kind of shape represented in our current design, as well as ones that might be added later. There are two conditions we must adhere to.

First, we want all shapes to use the same syntax to draw themselves. For example, we want every shape implemented in our system to contain a method called draw(). Thus, seasoned developers implicitly know that to draw a shape, you invoke the draw() method, regardless of what the shape happens to be. Theoretically, this reduces the amount of time spent fumbling through manuals, and it cuts down on syntax errors.

Second, remember that it is important that every class be responsible for its own actions. Thus, even though a class is required to provide a method called draw(), that class must provide its own implementation of the code. For example, the classes Circle and Rectangle both have a draw() method; however, the Circle class obviously has code to draw a circle, and as expected, the Rectangle class has code to draw a rectangle. When we ultimately create classes called Circle and Rectangle, which are subclasses of Shape, these classes must implement their own version of Draw (see Figure 8.3).

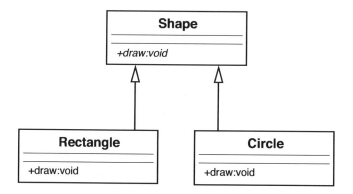

Figure 8.3 An abstract class hierarchy.

In this way, we have a Shape framework that is truly polymorphic. The Draw method can be invoked for every single shape in the system, and invoking each shape produces a different result. Invoking the Draw method on a Circle object draws a circle, and invoking the Draw method on a Rectangle object draws a rectangle. In essence, sending a message to an object evokes a different response, depending on the object. This is the essence of polymorphism:

```
circle.draw();        // draws a circle
rectangle.draw();     // draws a rectangle
```

Let's look at some code to illustrate how Rectangle and Circle conform to the Shape contract. Here is the code for the Shape class:

```
public abstract class Shape {

    public abstract void draw(); // no implementation

}
```

Note that the class does not provide any implementation for draw(); basically there is no code, and this is what makes the method abstract (providing any code would make the method concrete). There are two reasons why there is no implementation. First, Shape does not know what to draw, so we could not implement the draw() method even if we wanted to.

Structured Analogy

This is an interesting issue. If we did want the Shape class to contain the code for all possible shapes present and future, some conditional statement (like a Case statement) would be required. This would be very messy and difficult to maintain. This is one example of where the strength of an object-oriented design comes into play.

Second, we want the subclasses to provide the implementation. Let's look at the Circle and Rectangle classes:

```
public class Circle extends Shape {

    public void Draw() {System.out.println ("Draw a Circle")};

}

public class Rectangle extends Shape {

    public void Draw() {System.out.println ("Draw a Rectangle")};

}
```

Note that both Circle and Rectangle extend (that is, inherit from) Shape. Also notice that they provide the actual implementation (in this case, the implementation is trivial). Here is where the contract comes in. If Circle inherits from Shape and fails to provide a draw()

method, `Circle` won't even compile. Thus, `Circle` would fail to satisfy the contract with `Shape`. A project manager can require that programmers creating shapes for the application must inherit from `Shape`. By doing this, all shapes in the application will have a `draw()` method that performs in an expected manner.

> **Circle**
>
> If `Circle` does indeed fail to implement a `draw()` method, `Circle` will be considered abstract itself. Thus, yet another subclass must inherit from `Circle` and implement a `draw()` method. This subclass would then become the concrete implementation of both `Shape` and `Circle`.

Although the concept of abstract classes revolves around abstract methods, nothing is stopping `Shape` from providing some implementation. (Remember that the definition for an abstract class is that it contains *one or more* abstract methods—this implies that an abstract class can also provide concrete methods.) For example, although `Circle` and `Rectangle` implement the `draw()` method differently, they share the same mechanism for setting the color of the shape. So, the `Shape` class can have a color attribute and a method to set the color. This `setColor()` method is a concrete implementation and would be inherited by both `Circle` and `Rectangle`. The only methods that a subclass must implement are the ones that the superclass declares as abstract. These abstract methods are the contract.

> **Caution**
>
> Be aware that in the cases of `Shape`, `Circle`, and `Rectangle`, we are dealing with a strict inheritance relationship, as opposed to an interface, which we discuss in the next section. `Circle` *is-a* `Shape`, and `Rectangle` *is-a* `Shape`. This is an important point because contracts are not used in cases of composition, or has-a relationships.

Some languages, such as C++, use only abstract classes to implement contracts; however, Java and .NET have another mechanism that implements a contract called an interface. In other cases, such as Objective-C, abstract classes are not provided by the language. Thus, to implement a contract in Objective-C, you need to use a protocol, which is Objective-C's version of an interface.

Interfaces

Before defining an interface, it is interesting to note that C++ does not have a construct called an interface. When using C++, you can essentially create an interface by using a syntax subset of an abstract class. For example, the following C++ code is an abstract class. However, because the only method in the class is a virtual method, there is no implementation. As a result, this abstract class provides the same functionality as an interface:

```
class Shape
{
    public:
        virtual void draw() = 0;
}
```

Interface Terminology

This is another one of those times when software terminology gets confusing—very confusing. Be aware that you can use the term interface in several ways, so be sure to use each in the proper context.

First, the graphical user interface (GUI) is widely used when referring to the visual interface that a user interacts with—often on a monitor.

Second, the interface to a class is basically the signatures of its methods.

Third, in Objective-C you break the code up into physically separate modules called the interface and implementation.

Fourth, a Java-style interface and an Objective-C protocol are basically a contract between a parent class and a child class.

Can you think of any others?

The obvious question is this: If an abstract class can provide the same functionality as an interface, why do Java and .NET bother to provide this construct called an interface? And why does Objective-C provide the protocol?

For one thing, C++ supports multiple inheritance, whereas Java, Objective-C, and .NET do not. Although Java, Objective-C, and .NET classes can inherit from only one parent class, they can implement many interfaces. Using more than one abstract class constitutes multiple inheritance; thus, Java and .NET cannot go this route. In short, when using an interface, you do not have to concern yourself with a formal inheritance structure—you can theoretically add an interface to any class if the design makes sense. However, an abstract class requires you to inherit from that abstract class and, by extension, all of its potential parents.

Circle

Because of these considerations, interfaces are often thought to be a workaround for the lack of multiple inheritance. This is not technically true. Interfaces are a separate design technique, and although they can be used to design applications that could be done with multiple inheritance, they do not replace or circumvent multiple inheritance.

As with abstract classes, interfaces are a powerful way to enforce contracts for a framework. Before we get into any conceptual definitions, it's helpful to see an actual interface UML diagram and the corresponding code. Consider an interface called Nameable, as shown in Figure 8.4.

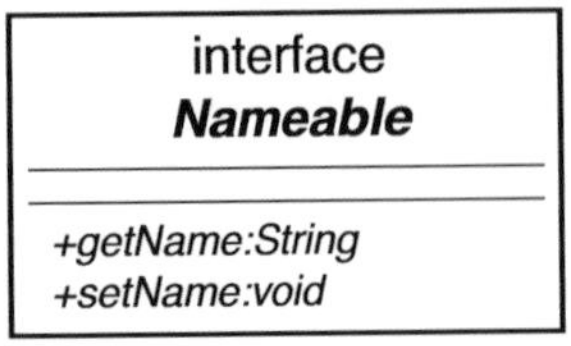

```
┌─────────────────────────┐
│       interface         │
│       Nameable          │
├─────────────────────────┤
│                         │
├─────────────────────────┤
│ +getName:String         │
│ +setName:void           │
└─────────────────────────┘
```

Figure 8.4   A UML diagram of a Java interface.

Note that Nameable is identified in the UML diagram as an interface, which distinguishes it from a regular class (abstract or not). Also note that the interface contains two methods, getName() and setName(). Here is the corresponding code:

```
public interface Nameable {

    String getName();
    void setName (String aName);

}
```

For comparison purposes, here is the code for the corresponding Objective-C protocol:

```
@protocol Nameable

@required
        - (char *) getName;
        - (void) setName: (char *) n;
@end // Nameable
```

In the code, notice that Nameable is not declared as a class, but as an interface. Because of this, both methods, getName() and setName(), are considered abstract and there is no implementation provided. An interface, unlike an abstract class, can provide *no* implementation at all. As a result, any class that implements an interface must provide the implementation for all methods. For example, in Java, a class inherits from an abstract class, whereas a class implements an interface.

Implementation Versus Definition Inheritance

Sometimes inheritance is referred to as *implementation inheritance*, and interfaces are called *definition inheritance*.

Tying It All Together

If both abstract classes and interfaces provide abstract methods, what is the real difference between the two? As we saw before, an abstract class provides both abstract and concrete methods, whereas an interface provides only abstract methods. Why is there such a difference?

Assume that we want to design a class that represents a dog, with the intent of adding more mammals later. The logical move would be to create an abstract class called Mammal:

```
public abstract class Mammal {

    public void generateHeat() {System.out.println("Generate heat");}

    public abstract void makeNoise();

}
```

This class has a concrete method called `generateHeat()` and an abstract method called `make-Noise()`. The method `generateHeat()` is concrete because all mammals generate heat. The method `makeNoise()` is abstract because each mammal will make noise differently.

Let's also create a class called `Head` that we will use in a composition relationship:

```
public class Head {

    String size;

    public String getSize() {

        return size;

    }

    public void setSize(String aSize) { size = aSize;}

}
```

`Head` has two methods: `getSize()` and `setSize()`. Although composition might not shed much light on the difference between abstract classes and interfaces, using composition in this example does illustrate how composition relates to abstract classes and interfaces in the overall design of an object-oriented system. I feel that this is important because the example is more complete. Remember that there are two ways to build object relationships: the *is-a* relationship, represented by inheritance, and the *has-a* relationship, represented by composition. The question is: Where does the interface fit in?

To answer this question and tie everything together, let's create a class called `Dog` that is a subclass of `Mammal`, implements `Nameable`, and has a `Head` object (see Figure 8.5).

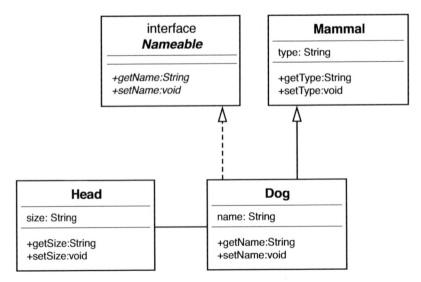

Figure 8.5   A UML diagram of the sample code.

In a nutshell, Java and .NET build objects in three ways: inheritance, interfaces, and composition. Note the dashed line in Figure 8.5 that represents the interface. This example illustrates when you should use each of these constructs. When do you choose an abstract class? When do you choose an interface? When do you choose composition? Let's explore further.

You should be familiar with the following concepts:

- `Dog` is a `Mammal`, so the relationship is inheritance.
- `Dog` implements `Nameable`, so the relationship is an interface.
- `Dog` has a `Head`, so the relationship is composition.

The following code shows how you would incorporate an abstract class and an interface in the same class:

```
public class Dog extends Mammal implements Nameable {

    String name;

    Head head;

    public void makeNoise(){System.out.println("Bark");}

    public void setName (String aName) {name = aName;}
    public String getName () {return (name);}

}
```

After looking at the UML diagram, you might come up with an obvious question: Even though the dashed line from `Dog` to `Nameable` represents an interface, isn't it still inheritance? At first glance, the answer is not simple. Although interfaces are a special type of inheritance, it is important to know what *special* means. Understanding these *special* differences are key to a strong object-oriented design.

Although inheritance is a strict is-a relationship, an interface is not quite. For example:

- A dog is a mammal.
- A reptile is not a mammal.

Thus, a `Reptile` class could not inherit from the `Mammal` class. However, an interface transcends the various classes. For example:

- A dog is nameable.
- A lizard is nameable.

The key here is that classes in a strict inheritance relationship must be related. For example, in this design, the `Dog` class is directly related to the `Mammal` class. A dog is a mammal. Dogs and lizards are not related at the mammal level because you can't say that a lizard is a mammal.

However, interfaces can be used for classes that are not related. You can name a dog just as well as you can name a lizard. This is the key difference between using an abstract class and using an interface.

The abstract class represents some sort of implementation. In fact, we saw that `Mammal` provided a concrete method called `generateHeat()`. Even though we do not know what kind of mammal we have, we know that all mammals generate heat. However, an interface models only behavior. An interface *never* provides any type of implementation, only behavior. The interface specifies behavior that is the same across classes that conceivably have no connection. Not only are dogs nameable, but so are cars, planets, and so on.

The Compiler Proof

Can we prove or disprove that interfaces have a true is-a relationship? In the case of Java (and this can also be done in C# or VB), we can let the compiler tell us. Consider the following code:

```
Dog D = new Dog();
Head H = D;
```

When this code is run through the compiler, the following error is produced:

```
Test.java:6: Incompatible type for Identifier. Can't convert Dog to Head. Head H = D;
```

Obviously, a dog is not a head. Not only do we know this, but the compiler agrees. However, as expected, the following code works just fine:

```
Dog D = new Dog();
Mammal M = D;
```

This is a true inheritance relationship, and it is not surprising that the compiler parses this code cleanly because a dog is a mammal.

Now we can perform the true test of the interface. Is an interface an actual is-a relationship? The compiler thinks so:

```
Dog D = new Dog();
Nameable N = D;
```

This code works fine. So, we can safely say that a dog is a nameable entity. This is a simple but effective proof that both inheritance and interfaces constitute an is-a relationship.

> ### Nameable Interface
>
> An interface specifies certain behavior, but not the implementation. By implementing the `Nameable` interface, you are saying that you will provide nameable behavior by implementing methods called `getName()` and `setName()`. How you implement these methods is up to you. All you have to do is to provide the methods.

Making a Contract

The simple rule for defining a contract is to provide an unimplemented method, via either an abstract class or an interface. Thus, when a subclass is designed with the intent of implementing the contract, it must provide the implementation for the unimplemented methods in the parent class or interface.

As stated earlier, one of the advantages of a contract is to standardize coding conventions. Let's explore this concept in greater detail by providing an example of what happens when coding standards are not used. In this case, there are three classes: Planet, Car, and Dog. Each class implements code to name the entity. However, because they are all implemented separately, each class has different syntax to retrieve the name. Consider the following code for the Planet class:

```
public class Planet {

    String planetName;

    public void getplanetName() {return planetName;};

}
```

Likewise, the Car class might have code like this:

```
public class Car {

    String carName;

    public String getCarName() { return carName;};

}
```

And the Dog class might have code like this:

```
public class Dog {

    String dogName;

    public String getDogName() { return dogName;};

}
```

The obvious issue here is that anyone using these classes would have to look at the documentation (what a horrible thought!) to figure out how to retrieve the name in each of these cases. Even though looking at the documentation is not the worst fate in the world, it would be nice if all the classes used in a project (or company) would use the same naming convention—it would make life a bit easier. This is where the Nameable interface comes in.

The idea would be to make a contract for any type of class that needs to use a name. As users of various classes move from one class to the other, they would not have to figure out the current syntax for naming an object. The Planet class, the Car class, and the Dog class would all have the same naming syntax.

To implement this lofty goal, we can create an interface (we can use the Nameable interface that we used previously). The convention is that all classes must implement Nameable. In this way, the users have to remember only a single interface for all classes when it comes to naming conventions:

```
public interface Nameable {

    public String getName();
    public void setName(String aName);

}
```

The new classes, Planet, Car, and Dog, should look like this:

```
public class Planet implements Nameable {

    String planetName;

    public String getName() {return planetName;}
    public void setName(String myName) { planetName = myName;}

}

public class Car implements Nameable {

    String carName;

    public String getName() {return carName;}
    public void setName(String myName) { carName = myName;}

}

public class Dog implements Nameable {

    String dogName;

    public String getName() {return dogName;}
    public void setName(String myName) { dogName = myName;}

}
```

In this way, we have a standard interface, and we've used a contract to ensure that it is the case. In fact, one of the major benefits of using a modern IDE is that, when implementing an interface, the IDE will automatically stub out the required methods. This feature saves lots of time and effort when using interfaces.

There is one little issue that you might have thought about. The idea of a contract is great as long as everyone plays by the rules, but what if some shady individual doesn't want to play by the rules (the rogue programmer)? The bottom line is that there is nothing to stop people from breaking the standard contract; however, in some cases, doing so will get them in deep trouble.

On one level, a project manager can insist that everyone use the contract, just like team members must use the same variable naming conventions and configuration management system. If a team member fails to abide by the rules, he could be reprimanded, or even fired.

Enforcing rules is one way to ensure that contracts are followed, but there are instances in which breaking a contract will result in unusable code. Consider the Java interface `Runnable`. Java applets implement the `Runnable` interface because it requires that any class implementing `Runnable` must implement a `run()` method. This is important because the browser that calls the applet will call the `run()` method within `Runnable`. If the `run()` method does not exist, things will break.

System Plug-in Points

Basically, contracts are "plug-in points" into your code. Anyplace where you want to make parts of a system abstract, you can use a contract. Instead of coupling to objects of specific classes, you can connect to any object that implements the contract. You need to be aware of where contracts are useful; however, you can overuse them. You want to identify common features such as the `Nameable` interface, as discussed in this chapter. However, be aware that there is a trade-off when using contracts. They might make code reuse more of a reality, but they make things somewhat more complex.

An E-Business Example

It's sometimes hard to convince a decision maker, who may have no development back-ground, of the monetary savings of code reuse. However, when reusing code, it is pretty easy to understand the advantage to the bottom line. In this section, we'll walk through a simple but practical example of how to create a workable framework using inheritance, abstract classes, interfaces, and composition.

An E-Business Problem

Perhaps the best way to understand the power of reuse is to present an example of how you would reuse code. In this example, we'll use inheritance (via interfaces and abstract classes) and composition. Our goal is to create a framework that will make code reuse a reality, reduce coding time, and reduce maintenance—all the typical software development wish-list items.

Let's start our own Internet business. Let's assume that we have a client, a small pizza shop called Papa's Pizza. Despite the fact that it is a small, family owned business, Papa realizes that a Web presence can help the business in many ways. Papa wants his customers to access his website, find out what Papa's Pizza is all about, and order pizzas right from the comfort of their browsers.

At the site we develop, customers will be able to access the website, select the products they want to order, and select a delivery option and time for delivery. They can eat their food at the restaurant, pick up the order, or have the order delivered. For example, a customer decides at 3:00 that he wants to order a pizza dinner (with salads, breadsticks, and drinks), to be delivered to his home at 6:00. Let's say the customer is at work (on a break, of course). He gets on the Web and selects the pizzas, including size, toppings, and crust; the salads, including dressings; breadsticks; and drinks. He chooses the delivery option and requests that the food be delivered to his home at 6:00. Then he pays for the order by credit card, gets a confirmation number, and exits. Within a few minutes, he gets an email confirmation as well. We will set up accounts so that when people bring up the site, they will get a greeting reminding them of who they are, what their favorite pizza is, and what new pizzas have been created this week.

When the software system is finally delivered, it is deemed a total success. For the next several weeks, Papa's customers happily order pizzas and other food and drinks over the Internet. During this rollout period, Papa's brother-in-law, who owns a donut shop called Dad's Donuts, pays Papa a visit. Papa shows Dad the system, and Dad falls in love with it. The next day, Dad calls our company and asks us to develop a Web-based system for his donut shop. This is great, and exactly what we had hoped for. Now, how can we leverage the code that we used for the pizza shop in the system for the donut shop?

How many more small businesses, besides Papa's Pizza and Dad's Donuts, could take advantage of our framework to get on the Web? If we can develop a good, solid framework, we will be able to efficiently deliver Web-based systems at lower costs than we were able to do before. There will also be an added advantage that the code will have been tested and implemented previously, so debugging and maintenance should be greatly reduced.

The Non-Reuse Approach

For many reasons, the concept of code reuse has not been as successful as some software developers would like. First, many times reuse is not even considered when developing a system. Second, even when reuse is entered into the equation, the issues of schedule constraints, limited resources, and budgetary concerns often short-circuit the best intentions.

In many instances, code ends up highly coupled to the specific application for which it was written. This means that the code within the application is highly dependent on other code within the same application.

A lot of code reuse is the result of using cut, copy, and paste operations. While one application is open in a text editor, you copy code and then paste it into another application. Sometimes certain functions or routines can be used without any change. As is unfortunately often the case, even though most of the code may remain identical, a small bit of code must change to work in a specific application.

For example, consider two separate applications, as represented by the UML diagram in Figure 8.6.

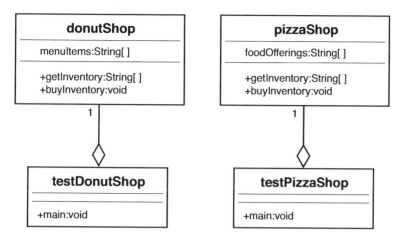

Figure 8.6   Applications on divergent paths.

In this example, the applications testDonutShop and testPizzaShop are totally independent code modules. The code is kept separate, and there is no interaction between the modules. However, these applications might use some common code. In fact, some code might have been copied verbatim from one application to another. At some point, someone involved with the project might decide to create a library of these shared pieces of code to use in these and other applications. In many well-run and disciplined projects, this approach works well. Coding standards, configuration management, change management, and so on are all very well run. However, in many instances, this discipline breaks down.

Anyone who is familiar with the software development process knows that when bugs crop up and time is of the essence, there is the temptation to put some fixes or additions into a system that are specific to the application currently in distress. This might fix the problem for the distressed application, but could have unintended, possibly harmful, implications for other applications. Thus, in situations like these, the initially shared code can diverge, and separate code bases must be maintained.

For example, one day Papa's website crashes. He calls us in a panic, and one of our developers is able to track down the problem. The developer fixes the problem, knowing that the fix works but is not quite sure why. The developer also does not know what other areas of the system the fix might inadvertently affect. So the developer makes a copy of the code, strictly for use in the Papa's Pizza system. This is affectionately named Version 2.01papa. Because the developer does not yet totally understand the problem and because Dad's system is working fine, the code is not migrated to the donut shop's system.

Tracking Down a Bug

The fact that the bug turned up in the pizza system does not mean that it will also turn up in the donut system. Even though the bug caused a crash in the pizza shop, the donut shop might never encounter it. It may be that the fix to the pizza shop's code is more dangerous to the donut shop than the original bug.

The next week Dad calls in a panic, with a totally unrelated problem. A developer fixes it, again not knowing how the fix will affect the rest of the system, makes a separate copy of the code, and calls it Version 2.03dad. This scenario gets played out for all the sites we now have in operation. There are now a dozen or more copies of the code, with various versions for the various sites. This becomes a mess. We have multiple code paths and have crossed the point of no return. We can never merge them again. (Perhaps we could, but from a business perspective, this would be costly.)

Our goal is to avoid the mess of the previous example. Although many systems must deal with legacy issues, fortunately for us, the pizza and donut applications are brand-new systems. Thus, we can use a bit of foresight and design this system in a reusable manner. In this way, we will not run into the maintenance nightmare just described. What we want to do is factor out as much commonality as possible. In our design, we will focus on all the common business functions that exist in a Web-based application. Instead of having multiple application classes like testPizzaShop and testDonutShop, we can create a design that has a class called Shop that all the applications will use.

Notice that testPizzaShop and testDonutShop have similar interfaces, getInventory() and buyInventory(). We will factor out this commonality and require that all applications that conform to our Shop framework implement getInventory() and buyInventory() methods. This requirement to conform to a standard is sometimes called a contract. By explicitly setting forth a contract of services, you isolate the code from a single implementation. In Java, you can implement a contract by using an interface or an abstract class. Let's explore how this is accomplished.

An E-Business Solution

Now let's show how to use a contract to factor out some of the commonality of these systems. In this case, we will create an abstract class to factor out some of the implementation, and an interface (our familiar Nameable) to factor out some behavior.

Our goal is to provide customized versions of our Web application with the following features:

- An interface, called Nameable, which is part of the contract.
- An abstract class, called Shop, which is also part of the contract.
- A class called CustList, which we use in composition.
- A new implementation of Shop for each customer we service.

The UML Object Model

The newly created Shop class is where the functionality is factored out. Notice in Figure 8.7 that the methods getInventory() and buyInventory() have been moved up the hierarchy tree from DonutShop and PizzaShop to the abstract class Shop. Now, whenever we want to provide a new, customized version of Shop, we plug in a new implementation of Shop (such as a grocery shop). Shop is the contract that the implementations must abide by:

```
public abstract class Shop  {

    CustList customerList;

    public void CalculateSaleTax() {

        System.out.println("Calculate Sales Tax");

    }

    public abstract String[] getInventory();

    public abstract void buyInventory(String item);

}
```

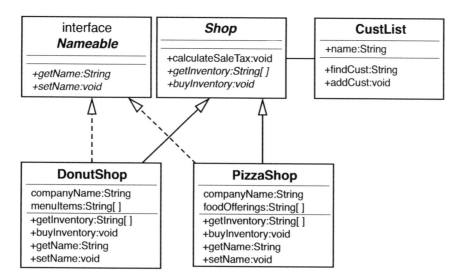

Figure 8.7   A UML diagram of the Shop model.

To show how composition fits into this picture, the Shop class has a customer list. Thus, the class CustList is contained within Shop:

```
public class CustList {

    String name;

    public  String findCust() {return name;}
    public  void addCust(String Name){}

}
```

To illustrate the use of an interface in this example, an interface called `Nameable` is defined:

```
public interface Nameable {

    public abstract String getName();
    public abstract void setName(String name);

}
```

We could potentially have a large number of different implementations, but all the rest of the code (the application) is the same. In this small example, the code savings might not look like a lot. But in a large, real-world application, the code savings is significant. Let's take a look at the donut shop implementation:

```
public class DonutShop extends Shop implements Nameable {

    String companyName;

    String[] menuItems = {
        "Donuts",
        "Muffins",
        "Danish",
        "Coffee",
        "Tea"
};

    public String[] getInventory() {

        return menuItems;

    }

    public void buyInventory(String item) {

        System.out.println("\nYou have just purchased " + item);

    }

    public String getName(){

        return companyName;
    }

    public void setName(String name){

        companyName = name;
    }
}
```

The pizza shop implementation looks very similar:

```java
public class PizzaShop extends Shop implements Nameable {

    String companyName;


    String[] foodOfferings = {
        "Pizza",
        "Spaghetti",
        "Garden Salad",
        "Antipasto",
        "Calzone"
    }

    public String[] getInventory() {

        return foodOfferings;

    }

    public void buyInventory(String item) {

        System.out.println("\nYou have just purchased " + item);

    }

    public String getName(){

        return companyName;
    }

    public void setName(String name){

        companyName = name;
    }

}
```

Unlike the initial case, where a large number of customized applications exist, we now have only a single primary class (Shop) and various customized classes (PizzaShop, DonutShop). There is no coupling between the application and any of the customized classes. The only thing the application is coupled to is the contract (Shop). The contract specifies that any implementation of Shop must provide an implementation for two methods, getInventory() and buyInventory(). It also must provide an implementation for getName() and setName() that relates to the interface Nameable that is implemented.

Although this solution solves the problem of highly coupled implementations, we still have the problem of deciding which implementation to use. With the current strategy, we would still have to have separate applications. In essence, you have to provide one application for each Shop implementation. Even though we are using the Shop contract, we still have the same situation as before we used the contract:

```
DonutShop myShop= new DonutShop();

PizzaShop myShop = new PizzaShop ();
```

How do we get around this problem? We can create objects dynamically. In Java, we can use code like this:

```
String className = args[0];

Shop  myShop;

myShop = (Shop)Class.forName(className).newInstance();
```

In this case, you set className by passing a parameter to the code. (There are other ways to set className, such as by using a system property.)

Let's look at Shop using this approach. (Note that there is no exception handling and nothing else besides object instantiation.)

```
class TestShop {

   public static void main (String args[]) {

      Shop shop = null;

      String className = args[0];

      System.out.println("Instantiate the class:" + className + "\n");


      try {

       // new pizzaShop();
         shop = (Shop)Class.forName(className).newInstance();

      } catch (Exception e) {

         e.printStackTrace();
      }

      String[] inventory = shop.getInventory();
```

```
    // list the inventory

    for (int i=0; i<inventory.length; i++) {
        System.out.println("Argument" + i + " = " + inventory[i]);
    }


    // buy an item

    shop.buyInventory(Inventory[1]);

    }

}
```

In this way, we can use the same application code for both PizzaShop and DonutShop. If we add a GroceryShop application, we only have to provide the implementation and the appropriate string to the main application. No application code needs to change.

Conclusion

When designing classes and object models, it is vitally important to understand how the objects are related to each other. This chapter discusses the primary topics of building objects: inheritance, interfaces, and composition. In this chapter, you have learned how to build reusable code by designing with contracts.

In Chapter 9, "Building Objects and Object-Oriented Design," we complete our OO journey and explore how objects that might be totally unrelated can interact with each other.

References

- Holzner, Steven. 2010. *Visual Quickstart Guide, Objective-C*. Berkeley, CA: Peachpit Press.

- Booch, Grady, Robert A. Maksimchuk, Michael W. Engel, Bobbi J. Young, Jim Conallen, and Kelli A. Houston. 2007. *Object-Oriented Analysis and Design with Applications*, 3rd edition. Boston, MA: Addison-Wesley.

- Meyers, Scott. 2005. *Effective C++*, 3rd edition. Boston, MA: Addison-Wesley Professional.

- Coad, Peter, and Mark Mayfield. 1997. *Java Design*. Upper Saddle River, NJ: Prentice-Hall.

Example Code Used in This Chapter

The following code is presented in C# .NET. Code for other languages, such as VB .NET and Objective-C, are available electronically on the publisher's website. These examples correspond to the Java code that is listed inside the chapter itself.

The `TestShop` Example: C# .NET

```csharp
using System;


namespace TestShop
{
    class TestShop
    {

        public static void Main()
        {

            Shop shop = null;

            Console.WriteLine("Instantiate the PizzaShop class:" + "\n");

            shop = new PizzaShop();

            string[] inventory = shop.getInventory();


            // list the inventory

            for (int i = 0; i < 5; i++)
            {
                Console.WriteLine("Argument" + i + " = " + inventory[i]);
            }


            // buy an item

            shop.buyInventory(inventory[1]);

        }

    }


    public abstract class Shop  {

        public void CalculateSaleTax() {

            Console.WriteLine("Calculate Sales Tax");

        }
```

```csharp
    public abstract string[] getInventory();

    public abstract void buyInventory(string item);

}

public interface Nameable {

    string getName();
    void setName(string name);

}

public class PizzaShop : Shop , Nameable
{

    string _CompanyName;

    string[] foodOfferings = {
        "Pizza",
        "Spaghetti",
        "Garden Salad",
        "Antipasto",
        "Calzone"
    };

    public override string[] getInventory() {

        return foodOfferings;

    }

    public override void buyInventory(string item) {

        Console.WriteLine("\nYou have just purchased " + item);

    }

    public string getName(){

        return _CompanyName;
    }

    public void setName(string name){

        _CompanyName = name;
```

```csharp
        }

    }

    public class DonutShop : Shop , Nameable {

        string _CompanyName;

        string[] menuItems = {
            "Donuts",
            "Muffins",
            "Danish",
            "Coffee",
            "Tea"
        };

        public override string[]  getInventory() {

            return menuItems;

        }

        public override void  buyInventory(string item) {

            Console.WriteLine(string.format("\nYou have just purchased {0}.", item);

        }

        public string getName(){

            return _CompanyName;
        }

        public void setName(string name){

            _CompanyName = name;
        }
    }
}
```

9

Building Objects and Object-Oriented Design

The previous two chapters cover the topics of inheritance and composition. In Chapter 7, "Mastering Inheritance and Composition," we learned that inheritance and composition represent the primary ways to build objects. In Chapter 8, "Frameworks and Reuse: Designing with Interfaces and Abstract Classes," we learned that there are varying degrees of inheritance and how inheritance, interfaces, abstract classes, and composition all fit together.

This chapter covers the issue of how objects are related to each other in an overall design. You might say that this topic was already introduced, and you would be correct. Both inheritance and composition represent ways that objects interact. However, inheritance and composition have one significant difference in the way objects are built. When inheritance is used, the end result is, at least conceptually, a single class that incorporates all the behaviors and attributes of the inheritance hierarchy. When composition is used, one or more classes are used to build another class.

Although it is true that inheritance is a relationship between two classes, what is really happening is that a parent is created that incorporates the attributes and methods of a child class. Let's revisit the example of the `Person` and `Employee` classes (see Figure 9.1).

Although there are indeed two separately designed classes here, the relationship is not simply interaction—it is inheritance. Basically, an employee is a person. An `Employee` object does not send a message to a `Person` object. An `Employee` object does need the services of a `Person` object. This is because an `Employee` object is a `Person` object.

However, composition is a different situation. Composition represents interactions between distinct objects. So, whereas Chapter 8 primarily covers the different flavors of inheritance, this chapter delves into the various flavors of composition and how objects interact with each other.

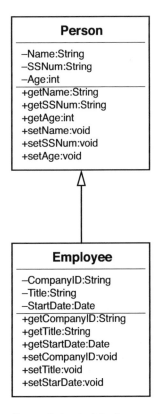

Figure 9.1   An inheritance relationship.

Composition Relationships

We have already seen that composition represents a part of a whole. Although the inheritance relationship is stated in terms of is-a, composition is stated in terms of has-a. We know intuitively that a car "has-a" steering wheel (see Figure 9.2).

Is-a and Has-a

Please forgive my grammar: For consistency, I will stick with "has a engine," even though "has an engine" is grammatically correct. I do this because I want to simply state the rules as "is-a" and "has-a."

The reason to use composition is that it builds systems by combining less complex parts. This is a common way for people to approach problems. Studies show that even the best of us can keep, at most, seven chunks of data in our short-term memory at one time. Thus, we like to use abstract concepts. Instead of saying that we have a large unit with a steering wheel, four tires, an engine, and so on, we say that we have a car. This makes it easier for us to communicate and keep things clear in our heads.

A Car has a Steering Wheel

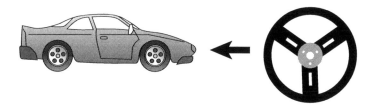

Figure 9.2   A composition relationship.

Composition also helps in other ways, such as making parts interchangeable. If all steering wheels are the same, it does not matter which specific steering wheel is installed in a specific car. In software development, interchangeable parts mean reuse.

In Chapters 7 and 8 of their book *Object-Oriented Design in Java*, Stephen Gilbert and Bill McCarty present many examples of associations and composition in much more detail. I highly recommend referencing this material for a more in-depth look into these subjects. Here we address some of the more fundamental points of these concepts and explore some variations of their examples.

Building in Phases

Another major advantage in using composition is that systems and subsystems can be built independently, and perhaps more importantly, tested and maintained independently.

There is no question that software systems are quite complex. To build quality software, you must follow one overriding rule to be successful: keep things as simple as possible. For large software systems to work properly and be easily maintained, they must be broken into smaller, more manageable parts. How do you accomplish this? In a 1962 article titled "The Architecture of Complexity," Nobel Prize winner Herbert Simon noted the following thoughts regarding stable systems:

- **"Stable complex systems usually take the form of a hierarchy, where each system is built from simpler subsystems, and each subsystem is built from simpler subsystems still."**—You might already be familiar with this principle because it forms the basis for functional decomposition, the method behind procedural software development. In object-oriented design, you apply the same principles to composition—building complex objects from simpler pieces.

- **"Stable, complex systems are nearly decomposable."**—This means you can identify the parts that make up the system and can tell the difference between interactions between the parts and inside the parts. Stable systems have fewer links between their parts than they have inside their parts. Thus, a modular stereo system, with simple links between the speakers, turntable, and amplifier, is inherently more stable than an integrated system, which isn't easily decomposable.

- **"Stable complex systems are almost always composed of only a few different kinds of subsystems, arranged in different combinations."**—Those subsystems, in turn, are generally composed of only a few different kinds of parts.

- **"Stable systems that work have almost always evolved from simple systems that worked."**—Rather than build a new system from scratch—reinventing the wheel—the new system builds on the proven designs that went before it.

In our stereo example (see Figure 9.3), suppose the stereo system was totally integrated and was not built from components (that is, the stereo system was one big black-box system). In this case, what would happen if the CD player broke and became unusable? You would have to take in the entire system for repair. Not only would this be more complicated and expensive, but you would not have the use of any of the other components.

This concept becomes very important to languages such as Java and those included in the .NET framework. Because objects are dynamically loaded, decoupling the design is quite important. For example, if you distribute a Java application and one of the class files needs to be re-created (for bug fixes or maintenance), you would be required to redistribute only that particular class file. If all code was in a single file, the entire application would need to be redistributed.

Suppose the system is broken into components rather than a single unit. In this case, if the CD player broke, you could disconnect the CD player and take it in for repair. (Note that all the components are connected by patch cords.) This would be less complicated and less expensive, and it would take less time than having to deal with a single, integrated unit. As an added benefit, you could still use the rest of the system. You could even buy another CD player because it is a component. The repairperson could then plug your broken CD player into his repair systems to test and fix it. All in all, the component approach works quite well. Composition is one of the primary strategies that you, as a software designer, have in your arsenal to fight software complexity.

One major advantage of using components is that you can use components that were built by other developers, or even third-party vendors. However, using a software component from another source requires a certain amount of trust. Third-party components must come from a reliable source, and you must feel comfortable that the software is properly tested, not to mention that it must perform the advertised functions properly. There are still many who would rather build their own than trust components built by others.

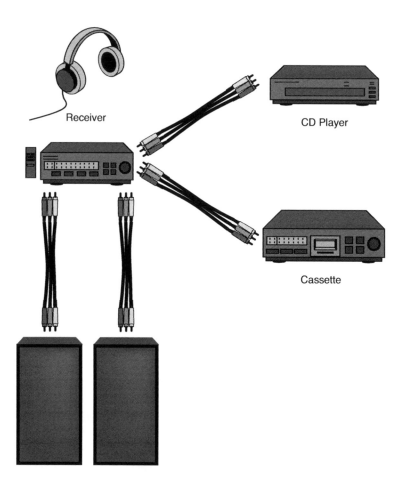

Figure 9.3   Building, testing, and verifying a complete system one step at a time.

Types of Composition

Generally, there are two types of composition: association and aggregation. In both cases, these relationships represent collaborations between the objects. The stereo example we just used to explain one of the primary advantages of composition represents an association.

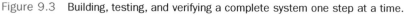

Is Composition a Form of Association?

Composition is another area in OO technologies where there is a question of which came first, the chicken or the egg. Some texts say that composition is a form of association, and some say that an association is a form of composition. In any event, in this book, we consider inheritance and composition the two primary ways to build classes. Thus, in this book, association is considered a form of composition.

All forms of composition include a has-a relationship. However, subtle differences exist between associations and aggregations based on how you visualize the parts of the whole. In an aggregation, you normally see only the whole, and in associations, you normally see the parts that make up the whole.

Aggregations

Perhaps the most intuitive form of composition is aggregation. Aggregation means that a complex object is composed of other objects. A TV set is a clean, neat package that you use for entertainment. When you look at your TV, you see a single TV. Most of the time, you do not stop to think about the fact that the TV contains some microchips, a screen, a tuner, and so on. Sure, you see a switch to turn the set on and off, and you certainly see the picture screen. However, this is not the way people normally think of TVs. When you go into an appliance store, the salesperson does not say, "Let me show you this aggregation of microchips, a picture screen, a tuner, and so on." The salesperson says, "Let me show you this TV."

Similarly, when you go to buy a car, you do not pick and choose all the individual components of the car. You do not decide which spark plugs to buy or which door handles to buy. You go to buy a car. Of course, you do choose some options, but for the most part, you choose the car as a whole, a complex object made up of many other complex and simple objects (see Figure 9.4).

Associations

Whereas aggregations represent relationships where you normally see only the whole, associations present both the whole and the parts. As stated in the stereo example, the various components are presented separately and connect to the whole by use of patch cords (the cords that connect the various components).

Consider a computer system as an example (see Figure 9.5); the whole is the computer system. The components are the monitor, keyboard, mouse, and main box. Each is a separate object, but together they represent the whole of the computer system. The main computer is using the keyboard, the mouse, and the monitor to delegate some of the work. In other words, the computer box needs the service of a mouse, but does not have the capability to provide this service by itself. Thus, the computer box requests the service from a separate mouse via the specific port and cable connecting the mouse to the box.

> **Aggregation Versus Association**
>
> An aggregation is a complex object composed of other objects. An association is used when one object wants another object to perform a service for it.

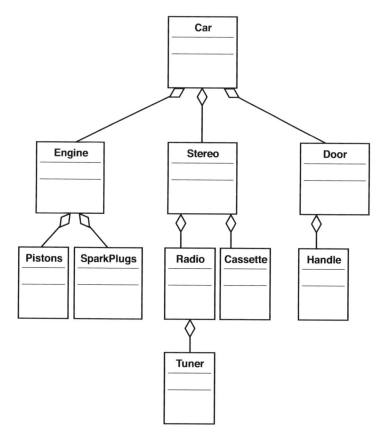

Figure 9.4   An aggregation hierarchy for a car.

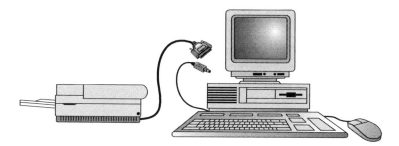

Figure 9.5   Associations as a separate service.

Using Associations and Aggregations Together

One thing you might have noticed in all the examples is that the dividing lines between what is an association and what is an aggregation are often blurred. Suffice it to say that many of your most interesting design decisions will come down to whether to use associations or aggregations.

For example, the computer system example used to describe associations also contains some aggregation. Although the interaction between the computer box, the monitor, the keyboard, and the mouse is association, the computer box itself represents aggregation. You see only the computer box, but it is actually a complex system made up of other objects, including chips, motherboards, video cards, and so on.

Consider that an `Employee` object might be composed of an `Address` object and a `Spouse` object. You might consider the `Address` object as an aggregation (basically a part of the `Employee` object), and the `Spouse` object as an association. To illustrate, suppose both the employee and the spouse are employees. If the employee is fired, the spouse is still in the system, but the association is broken.

Similarly, in the stereo example, the receiver has an association with the speakers as well as the CD. Yet, the speakers and the CD are themselves aggregations of other objects, such as power chords.

In the car example, although the engine, spark plugs, and doors represent composition, the stereo also represents an association relationship.

No One Right Answer

As usual, there isn't a single, absolutely correct answer when it comes to making a design decision. Design is not an exact science. Although we can make general rules to live by, these rules are not hard and fast.

Avoiding Dependencies

When using composition, it is desirable to avoid making objects highly dependent on one another. One way to make objects very dependent on each other is to mix domains. In the best of all worlds, an object in one domain should not be mixed with an object in another domain, except under certain circumstances. We can return again to the stereo example to explain this concept.

By keeping the receiver and the CD player in separate domains, the stereo system is easier to maintain. For example, if the CD component breaks, you can send the CD player off to be repaired individually. In this case, the CD player and the MP3 player have separate domains. This provides flexibility, such as buying the CD player and the MP3 player from separate manufacturers. So, if you decide you want to swap out the CD player with a brand from another manufacturer, you can.

Sometimes there is a certain convenience in mixing domains. A good example of this pertains to the existence of TV/VCR and TV/DVD combinations. Not only has object-oriented design evolved since the first edition of this book was published, but consumer technology has evolved as well. VCRs are not as prevalent as they once were, and DVDs are following the same path. The movement of consumer preferences from VCRs to DVDs to streaming technologies in such a short period of time is a good example of why avoiding dependencies is a preferred design choice at many levels.

You need to determine what is more important in specific situations: whether you want convenience or stability. There is no right answer. It all depends on the application and the environment. In the case of the TV/VCR combination, we decided that the convenience of the integrated unit far outweighed the risk of lower unit stability (see Figure 9.6).

More Convenient/Less Stable

TV part

Figure 9.6   Convenience versus stability.

Mixing Domains

The convenience of mixing domains is a design decision. If the power of having a TV/VCR combination outweighs the risk and potential downtime of the individual components, the mixing of domains may well be the preferred design choice.

Cardinality

In their book *Object-Oriented Design in Java*, Gilbert and McCarty describe cardinality as the number of objects that participate in an association and whether the participation is optional or mandatory. To determine cardinality, Gilbert and McCarty ask the following questions:

- Which objects collaborate with which other objects?
- How many objects participate in each collaboration?
- Is the collaboration optional or mandatory?

For example, let's consider the following example. We are creating an `Employee` class that inherits from `Person` and has relationships with the following classes:

- `Division`
- `JobDescription`
- `Spouse`
- `Child`

What do these classes do? Are they optional? How many does an `Employee` need?

- `Division`
    - This object contains the information relating to the division that the employee works for.
    - Each employee must work for a division, so the relationship is mandatory.
    - The employee works for one, and only one, division.
- `JobDescription`
    - This object contains a job description, most likely containing information such as salary grade and salary range.
    - Each employee must have a job description, so the relationship is mandatory.
    - The employee can hold various jobs during the tenure at a company. Thus, an employee can have many job descriptions. These descriptions can be kept as a history if an employee changes jobs, or it is possible that an employee might hold two different jobs at one time. For example, a supervisor might take on an employee's responsibilities if the employee quits and a replacement has not yet been hired.
- `Spouse`
    - In this simplistic example, the `Spouse` class contains only the anniversary date.
    - An employee can be married or not married. Thus, a spouse is optional.
    - An employee can have only one spouse.
- `Child`
    - In this simple example, the `Child` class contains only the string `FavoriteToy`.
    - An employee can have children or not have children.
    - An employee can have no children or an infinite number of children (wow!). You could make a design decision as to the upper limit of the number of children that the system can handle.

To sum up, Table 9.1 represents the cardinality of the associations of the classes we just considered.

Table 9.1   **Cardinality of Class Associations**

Optional/Association	Cardinality	Mandatory
Employee/Division	1	Mandatory
Employee/JobDescription	1 ... n	Mandatory
Employee/Spouse	0 ... 1	Optional
Employee/Child	0 ... n	Optional

Cardinality Notation

The notation of 0 . . . 1 means that an employee can have either zero or one spouse. The notation of 0 . . . n means that an employee can have any number of children from zero to an unlimited number. The *n* basically represents infinity.

Figure 9.7 shows the class diagram for this system. Note that in this class diagram, the cardinality is indicated along the association lines. Refer to Table 9.1 to see whether the association is mandatory.

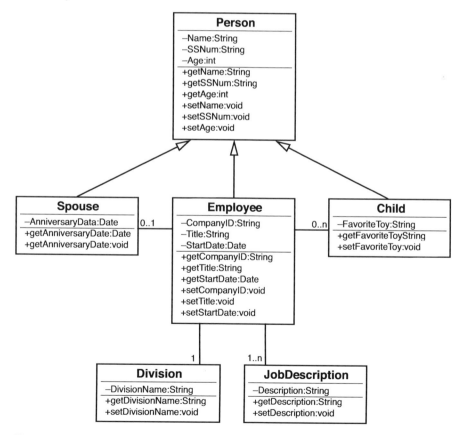

Figure 9.7   Cardinality in a UML diagram.

Multiple Object Associations

How do we represent an association that might contain multiple objects (such as 0 to many children) in code? Here is the code for the `Employee` class:

```
import java.util.Date;

public class Employee extends Person{

        private String CompanyID;
        private String Title;
        private Date StartDate;

        private Spouse spouse;
        private Child[] child;
        private Division division;
        private JobDescription[] jobDescriptions;

        public String getCompanyID() {return CompanyID;}
        public String getTitle() {return Title;}
        public Date getStartDate() {return StartDate;}

        public void setCompanyID(String CompanyID) {}
        public void setTitle(String Title) {}
        public void setStartDate(int StartDate) {}

}
```

Note that the classes that have a one-to-many relationship are represented by arrays in the code:

```
private Child[] child;
private JobDescription[] jobDescriptions;
```

Optional Associations

One of the most important issues when dealing with associations is to make sure that your application is designed to check for optional associations. This means that your code must check to see whether the association is `null`.

Suppose in the previous example that your code assumes that every employee has a spouse. However, if one employee is not married, the code will have a problem (see Figure 9.8). If your code does indeed expect a spouse to exist, it may well fail and leave the system in an unstable state. The bottom line is that the code must check for a `null` condition, and must handle this as a valid condition.

For example, if no spouse exists, the code must not attempt to invoke a spouse method. This could lead to an application failure. Thus, the code must be able to process an `Employee` object that has no spouse.

Object Mary

```
public String getSpouse(Employee e) {
    return Spouse;

}
```

OOPS!! Mary has no spouse

Must check all optional associations for null!!!

Figure 9.8   Checking all optional associations.

Tying It All Together: An Example

Let's work on a simple example that will tie the concepts of inheritance, interfaces, composition, associations, and aggregations together into a single, short system diagram.

Consider the example used in Chapter 8, with one addition: We will add an `Owner` class that will take the dog out for walks.

Recall that the `Dog` class inherits directly from the `Mammal` class. The solid arrow represents this relationship between the `Dog` class and the `Mammal` class in Figure 9.9. The `Nameable` class is an interface that `Dog` implements, which is represented by the dashed arrow from the `Dog` class to the `Nameable` interface.

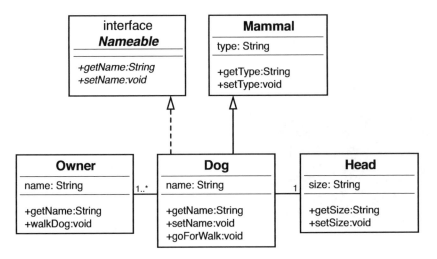

Figure 9.9   A UML diagram for the Dog example.

In this chapter, we are mostly concerned with associations and aggregations. The relationship between the Dog class and the Head class is considered aggregation because the head is actually part of the dog. The cardinality on the line connecting the two class diagrams specifies that a dog can have only a single head.

The relationship between the Dog class and the Owner class is association. The owner is clearly not part of the dog, or vice versa, so we can safely eliminate aggregation. However, the dog does require a service from the owner—the act of taking him on a walk. The cardinality on the line connecting the Dog and Owner classes specifies that a dog can have one or more owners (for example, a wife and husband can both be considered owners, with shared responsibility for walking the dog).

These relationships—inheritance, interfaces, composition, associations, and aggregations—represent the bulk of the design work you will encounter when designing OO systems.

Where Is the Head?

You might decide that it makes sense to attach the Head class to the Mammal class instead of the Dog class, because all mammals supposedly have a head. For this model, I was using the Dog class as the focal point of the example, so that is why I attached the Head to the Dog itself.

Conclusion

In this chapter, we have explored some of the finer points of composition and its two primary types: aggregation and association. Whereas inheritance represents a new kind of already existing object, composition represents the interactions between various objects.

The past three chapters have covered the basics of inheritance and composition. Using these concepts and your skills in the software development process, you are on your way to designing solid classes and object models. The next chapter explores how to use UML class diagrams to assist in the modeling of object models.

References

- Booch, Grady, Robert A. Maksimchu, Michael W. Engel, Bobbi J. Young, Jim Conallen, and Kelli A. Houston. 2007. *Object-Oriented Analysis and Design with Applications*, 3rd edition. Boston, MA: Addison-Wesley.

- Meyers, Scott. 2005. *Effective C++*, 3rd edition. Boston, MA: Addison-Wesley Professional.

- Coad, Peter, and Mark Mayfield. 1997. *Java Design*. Upper Saddle River, NJ: Prentice-Hall.

- Gilbert, Stephen, and Bill McCarty. 1998. *Object-Oriented Design in Java*. Berkeley, CA: The Waite Group Press.

10

Creating Object Models

I believe very strongly that learning the fundamental OO concepts should come before learning any specific modeling tools. Thus, the placement of this chapter was somewhat problematic. In many ways, this chapter could go first, because the Unified Modeling Language (UML)
diagrams are present throughout this book, including in Chapter 1, "Introduction to Object-
Oriented Concepts." Finally, it was decided to place this chapter at the end of the "conceptual"
chapters, which I consider to be Chapters 1–9. The remaining chapters cover some specific
application technology issues as well as concepts.

This chapter is a brief overview of the UML class diagram notation used in this book. It is
not a comprehensive tutorial on UML because that would require an entire book unto itself,
and there are many such books. For several good sources, see the references at the end of this
chapter. Because this book deals with fundamentals, it only scratches the surface of what UML
offers.

In this book, the UML class diagrams that we use concern modeling object-oriented systems
or, as I like to call it, *object-modeling*. This notation utilizes class diagrams for system modeling purposes. Many components of UML are not covered in this book, such as State Chart
Diagrams and Activity Diagrams. Each of those topics could warrant a complete chapter or
more. Again, the purpose of this chapter is to provide a quick overview of object models and,
specifically, class diagrams so that if you are unfamiliar with class diagrams, you can pick up
the basics quickly. With this introduction, the examples in the book will be more meaningful.

What Is UML?

UML, as its name implies, is a modeling language. The UML User Guide defines UML as "a
graphical language for visualizing, specifying, constructing, and documenting the artifacts of a
software-intensive system." UML gives you a standard way to write the system's blueprints. In
a nutshell, UML offers a way to graphically represent and manipulate an object-oriented (OO)
software system. It is not only the representation of the design of a system, but a tool to assist
in this design.

UML is a synthesis of different modeling languages developed independently by Grady Booch, James Rumbaugh, and Ivar Jacobson, affectionately called the Three Amigos. The software company Rational brought the three modeling languages together under one roof—thus the name Unified Modeling Language. As stated previously, object modeling is one part of UML.

However, it is important not to link UML and OO development too closely. In his article "What the UML Is—and Isn't," Craig Larman states:

> Yet unfortunately, in the context of software engineering and the UML diagramming language, acquiring the skills to read and write UML notation seems to sometimes be equated with skill in object-oriented analysis and design. Of course, this is not so, and the latter is much more important than the former. Therefore, I recommend seeking education and educational materials in which intellectual skill in object-oriented analysis and design is paramount rather than UML notation or the use of a case tool.

Although UML is very important, it is much more important to learn the OO skills first. Learning UML before learning OO concepts is similar to learning how to read an electrical diagram without first knowing anything about electricity.

The Structure of a Class Diagram

A class diagram is constructed of three parts: the class name, the attributes, and the methods (constructors are considered methods). The class diagram is essentially a rectangle that separates these three parts with horizontal lines. This book often uses a cabbie metaphor as an illustration. Figure 10.1 shows the UML class diagram representing this class.

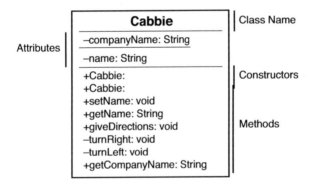

Figure 10.1   A UML diagram of the Cabbie class.

This UML diagram corresponds exactly to the following Java code:

```
/*

    This class defines a cabbie and assigns a cab
```

```java
*/
public class Cabbie {

    // Place the name of the company here
    private static String companyName = "Blue Cab Company";

    // Name of the cabbie
    private String name;

    // Car assigned to cabbie

    // Default constructor for the cabbie
    public Cabbie() {

        name = null;
        myCab = null;

    }

    // Initializing the constructor for the cabbie
    public Cabbie(String iName, String serialNumber) {

        Name = iName;
        myCab = new Cab(serialNumber);

    }

    // Set the name of the cabbie
    public void setName(String iName) {
        name = iName;
    }

    // Get the name of the cabbie
    public String getName() {
        return name;
    }

    // Give the cabbie directions
    public void giveDirections(){
    }

    // Cabbie turns right
    private void turnRight(){
    }

    // Cabbie turns left
    private void turnLeft() {
```

```
    }

    // Get the name of the company
    public static String getCompanyName() {
        return companyName;
    }

}
```

Take a moment to look at the code and compare it to the UML class diagram. Notice how the class name, attributes, and methods in the code relate to the designation in the class diagram. Really, that is all there is to the class diagram as far as the structure goes. However, a lot more information can be gleaned from the diagram. This information is discussed in the following sections.

Attributes and Methods

Besides presenting the structure of the class, the class diagram also presents information about the attributes and methods.

Attributes

Normally, attributes are not thought of as having signatures, as do methods. However, an attribute has a type, and this type is represented in the class diagram. Consider the two attributes that are in the Cabbie example:

```
-companyName:String
-name:String
```

Both of these attributes are defined as strings. This is represented by the name of the attribute followed by the type (in these cases, String). There could have been attributes that were defined as int and float as well, as in this example:

```
-companyNumber:float
-companyAge:int
```

By looking at the class diagram, you can tell the data type of the parameter. You can also tell that the attributes are declared as private because of the minus sign (-) that precedes them. A plus sign (+) would denote that they were public, which should evoke a gag reflex. Based on all discussion in the previous chapters, we know that all attributes should be declared as private. Every now and then someone makes a case for the use of public attributes, but the approach taken in this book is to always make attributes private.

Methods

The same logic used with attributes works for methods. Rather than express the type, the diagram shows the return type of the method.

If you look at the following snippet from the `Cabbie` example, you can see that the name of the method is presented, along with the return type and the access modifier (for example, `public`, `private`):

```
+Cabbie:
+giveDirections:void
+getCompanyName:String
```

In all three cases, the access modifier is public (designated by the plus sign). If a method were private, there would be a minus sign. Each method name is followed by a colon that separates the method name from the return type.

It is possible to include a parameter list, in the following manner:

```
+getCompanyName(parameter-list):String
```

Commas separate the parameters in the parameter list:

```
+getCompanyName(parameter1, parameter2, parameter3):String
```

I like keeping the object models as simple as possible. Thus, I normally include only the class name, attributes, and methods in the class diagrams. This allows us to concentrate on the big picture of the design and does not place focus on details. Including too much information (such as parameters) in the class diagrams makes the object-model difficult to read. This is one of those issues that depends on your specific tastes.

Access Designations

As mentioned previously, the plus signs (+) and minus signs (-) to the left of the attributes and methods signify whether the attributes and methods are public or private. The attribute or method is considered private if there is a minus sign. This means that no other class can access the attribute or method; only methods in the class can inspect or change it.

If the attribute or method has a plus sign to the left, the attribute or method is public, and any class can inspect or modify it. For example, consider the following:

```
-companyNumber:float
+companyAge:int
```

In this example, `companyNumber` is private, and only methods of its class can do anything with it. However, `companyAge` is public, and thus it is fair game for any class to access and modify it.

If no access designation is present in the code, the system considers the access to be the default, and no plus or minus is used:

```
companyNumber:float
companyAge:int
```

In Java, the default type of access is protected. Protected access means that only classes in the package can access the attribute or method. A Java package is a collection of related classes that are intentionally grouped together by the developer.

In .NET the access modifiers, per Microsoft's MSDN, are as follows:

- **public**—The type or member can be accessed by any other code in the same assembly or another assembly that references it.

- **private**—The type or member can be accessed only by code in the same class or struct.

- **protected**—The type or member can be accessed only by code in the same class or struct, or in a derived class.

- **internal**—The type or member can be accessed by any code in the same assembly, but not from another assembly. Objective-C provides public (@public) and private (@ private) access modifiers as well. The default access for Objective-C is protected, which allows access to the members of the subclass.

Inheritance

To understand how inheritance is represented, consider the Dog example presented in Chapter 7, "Mastering Inheritance and Composition." In this example, the class GoldenRetriever inherits from the class Dog, as shown in Figure 10.2. This relationship is represented in UML by a line with an arrowhead pointing in the direction of the parent or superclass.

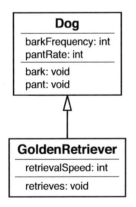

Figure 10.2   UML diagram of the Dog hierarchy.

The notation is straightforward, and when the line with the arrowhead is encountered, an inheritance relationship is indicated.

Because Java is primarily used for the code examples in this book, we do not have to worry about multiple inheritance. The same goes for .NET and Objective-C. C++ does implement multiple inheritance.

However, several subclasses can inherit from the same superclass. Again, we can use the Dog example from Chapter 7 (see Figure 10.3).

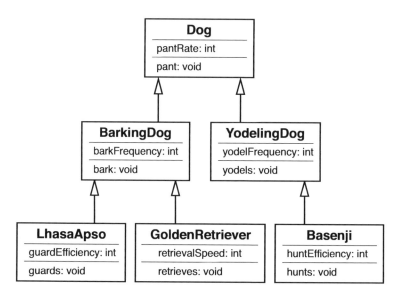

Figure 10.3   UML diagram of the expanded Dog hierarchy.

This example illustrates two concepts when modeling an inheritance tree. First, a superclass can have more than one subclass. Second, the inheritance tree can extend for more than one level. The example in Figure 10.3 shows three levels. We could add further levels by adding specific types of retrievers, or even by adding a higher level by creating a Canine class (see Figure 10.4).

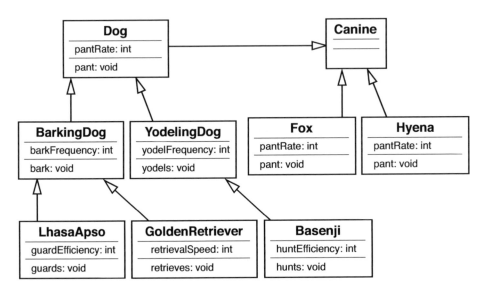

Figure 10.4   UML diagram of the `Canine` hierarchy.

Interfaces

Because interfaces are a special type of inheritance, the notations are similar and can cause some confusion. Earlier we said that a line with an arrowhead represents inheritance. An interface is also represented by a line with an arrowhead—but the arrowhead is connected to a dashed line. This notation indicates the relationship between inheritance and interfaces, but also differentiates them. Take a look at Figure 10.5, which is an abbreviated version of an example in Chapter 8, "Frameworks and Reuse: Designing with Interfaces and Abstract Classes." The `Dog` class inherits from the class `Mammal` and implements the interface `Nameable`.

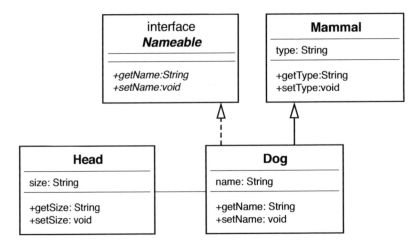

Figure 10.5   UML diagram of an interface relationship.

Composition

Composition indicates that a has-a relationship is being used. When inheritance is not the proper design choice (because the is-a relationship is not appropriate), composition is normally used.

Chapter 9, "Building Objects and Object-Oriented Design," discusses two types of composition: aggregations and associations. Composition is used when classes are built with other classes. This can happen with aggregation when a class is a component of another class (as a tire is to a car). Or it can happen with association when a class needs the services of another class (for example, when a client needs the services of a server).

Aggregations

An aggregation is represented by a line with a diamond at the head. In the car example of Chapter 9, to represent that a steering wheel is part of a car, you use the notation shown in Figure 10.6.

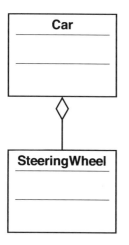

Figure 10.6   UML diagram representing composition.

As with the inheritance tree, there is no limit (theoretically) to the number of levels of aggregation you can represent. In the example shown in Figure 10.7, there are four levels. Notice that the various levels can represent various aggregations. For example, although a stereo is part of the car, the radio is part of the stereo, and the tuner is part of the radio.

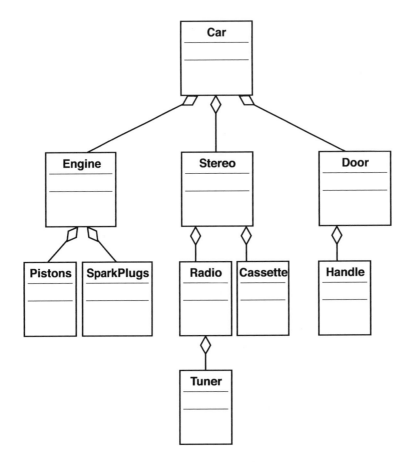

Figure 10.7   An expanded composition UML diagram.

Associations

Although aggregations represent parts of a whole, meaning that one class is logically built with parts of another, associations are services provided between classes.

As mentioned earlier, a client/server relationship fits this model. Although it is obvious that a client is not part of a server, and likewise a server is not part of a client, they both depend on each other. In most cases, you can say that a server provides the client a service. In UML notation, a plain line represents this service, with no shape on either end (see Figure 10.8).

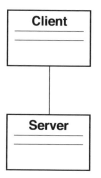
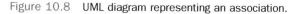

Figure 10.8   UML diagram representing an association.

Note that because there is no shape on either end of the line, there is no indication about which way the service flows. The figure shows only that an association exists between the two classes.

To illustrate, consider the example of the computer system from Chapter 9. In this case, there are multiple components, such as a computer, monitor, scanner, keyboard, and mouse. Each is a totally separate component that interacts, to some degree, with the computer itself (see Figure 10.9).

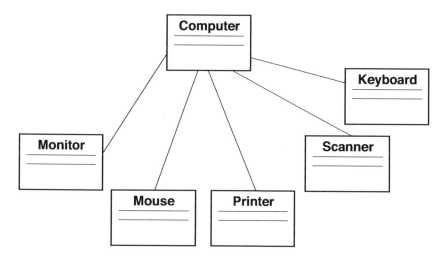

Figure 10.9   An expanded UML diagram representing association.

The important thing to note here is that the monitor is technically part of the computer. If you were to create a class for a computer system, you could model it by using aggregation. However, the computer represents some form of aggregation, because it is made up of a motherboard, RAM, and so on (see Figure 10.10).

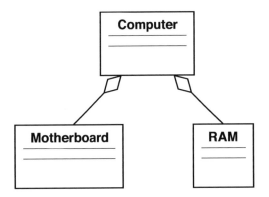

Figure 10.10   UML representation of aggregation.

Cardinality

The last issue to visit in this chapter is cardinality. Basically, cardinality pertains to the range of objects that correspond to the class. Using the earlier computer example, we can say that a computer is made up of one, and only one, motherboard. This cardinality is represented as 1. There is no way that a computer can be without a motherboard and, in PCs today, no computer has more than one. On the other hand, a computer must have at least one RAM chip, but it may have as many chips as the machine can hold. Thus, we can represent the cardinality as 1 . . . n, where *n* represents an unlimited value—at least in the general sense.

> **Limited Cardinality Values**
>
> If we know that there are slots for six RAM chips, the upper limit number is not unlimited. Thus, the *n* would be replaced by a 6, and the cardinality would be 1 . . . 6.

Consider the example shown in Figure 9.7 from Chapter 9.

In this example, we have several representations of cardinality. First, the Employee class has an association with the Spouse class. Based on conventional rules, an employee can have either no spouses or one spouse (at least in our culture, an employee cannot have more than one spouse). Thus, the cardinality of this association is represented as 0 . . . 1.

The association between the Employee class and the Child class is somewhat different in that an employee has no theoretical limits to the number of children that the employee can have. Although it is true that an employee might have no children, if the employee does have children, no upper limit exists. Thus, the cardinality of this association is represented as 0 . . . n, and *n* means that there is no upper limit to the number of children that the system can handle.

The relationship between the Employee class and the Division class states that each employee can be associated with one, and only one, division. A simple 1 represents this association. The placement of the cardinality indicator is tricky, but it's a very important part of the object model.

More Design Issues

In certain situations, it is possible for an employee to be associated with more than one division. For example, a college might allow an individual to hold concurrent positions in the mathematics department and the computer science department. This is another design issue you must consider.

The last cardinality association we will discuss is the association between the Employee class and the JobDescription class. In this system, it is possible for an employee to have an unlimited number of job descriptions. However, unlike the Child class, where there can be zero children, in this system there must be at least one job description per employee. Thus, the cardinality of this association is represented as 1 . . . n. The association involves at least one job description per employee, but possibly more (in this case, an unlimited number).

Keeping History

You must also consider that an employee can have job descriptions for past jobs, as well as for current jobs. In this case, there needs to be a way to differentiate current job descriptions from past ones. This could be implemented using inheritance by creating a collection of job objects with an attribute indicating which job is currently active.

Conclusion

This chapter gives a very brief overview of the UML class diagram notation used in this book. As stated in the introduction, UML is a very complex and important topic, and the complete coverage of UML requires a book (or several) unto itself.

Class diagrams are used to illustrate OO examples throughout this book. You do not need UML to design OO systems, but UML is a tool that can be used to assist in the development of OO systems. However, I really like to use class diagrams as a visual tool in creating object models.

Learning UML in detail is one of the steps that you should take after you are comfortable with the underlying OO concepts. However, as happens so many times, the chicken-and-the-egg conundrum presents itself. In an effort to illustrate some of the examples in the book, it is very useful to use UML.

It's good to introduce a little of a modeling language (such as UML) and a little of a programming language (such as Java) while explaining OO concepts. Of course, we could have used

C++ instead of Java, and another modeling system rather than UML. It is important to keep in mind that whatever examples you use, you should stay focused on the OO concepts themselves.

Thus far, this book has covered a lot of material relating to the basic object-oriented concepts. The intent is to provide a high-level overview to the concepts involved in the OO thought process. The fundamental OO concepts, encapsulation, inheritance, polymorphism, and composition, have all been covered in detail. The remainder of the book will focus on several of OO technologies.

References

- Schmuller, Joseph. 2006. *Teach Yourself UML in 24 Hours,* 3rd ed., Indianapolis, IN: Sams Publishing.

- Booch, G., I. Jacobson, and J. Rumbagh. 2005. *The UML Users Guide,* 2nd ed., Boston, MA: Addison-Wesley.

- Lee, Richard, and William Tepfenhart. 2003. *Practical Object-Oriented Development with UML and Java.* Upper Saddle River, NJ: Prentice Hall.

- Ambler, Scott. 2003. *The Elements of UML Style.* Cambridge, United Kingdom: Cambridge University Press.

- Fowler, Martin. 2003. *UML Distilled*, 3rd ed. Boston, MA: Addison-Wesley Longman.

- Larman, Craig. May 1999. "What the UML Is—and Isn't." *Java Report*, 4(5): 20–24.

11

Objects and Portable Data: XML and JSON

Object-oriented technologies have made significant inroads in the past decade. Objects have become one of the primary technologies in the application development industry. Objects have also made major headway in the definition and movement of data. Much excitement has been generated over the past several years regarding the portability of code. For example, much of Java's success is due to the fact that it is highly portable across multiple platforms.

The bytecodes produced by Java can be executed on various platforms, as long as the system has a Java virtual machine loaded. The .NET framework provides another, very important, type of portability—portability across various languages. The assemblies produced by C# .NET can be used within Visual Basic .NET applications, or any other .NET language for that matter. Certainly, although many technology standards are in place, the major programming languages (Java, .NET, Objective-C, etc.) are still proprietary. Perhaps the future will bring a programming language that will be fully and economically portable across both languages and platforms.

Although portable languages are powerful tools, they are really only half of the application development equation. The programs that are written using these languages must process data, and this data must be turned into information. It is this information that drives businesses. Information is the other half of the portability equation.

XML is a standard mechanism for defining and transporting data between potentially disparate systems (JSON is another available option). By using object-oriented languages such as Java, VB, and C# in conjunction with an object-oriented data definition language such as XML and JSON, moving data between various destinations is much more efficient and secure. XML and JSON provide a mechanism for independent applications to share data.

Portable Data

Historically, a major business problem has been the diversity of data storage formats. For example, assume that Alpha Company uses an Oracle database system to operate its sales system. Assume further that Beta Company uses a SQL Server database system to operate its purchasing system. Now consider the problem that occurs when Alpha Company and Beta Company want to do business over the Internet. Although several issues must be addressed when building a system, the one problem we address here is that the two proprietary databases are not directly compatible. Our goal is to create an electronic purchase order for Beta Company using SQL Server, which will interact directly with Alpha Company's sales system, which uses Oracle.

Furthermore, many companies must move the information within their organization, as well as to other companies. Much electronic commerce is transacted over both the Internet and local intranets, and the types of business systems that require electronic commerce are quite varied.

XML provides standards to move data in a variety of ways. Often we can think of data as moving vertically and horizontally. The term *vertical* means that data is meant to move through multiple industry groups. Industry groups such as those in accounting and finance (FpML, or Financial products Markup Language) have developed their own markup languages that provide standard data definitions. These vertical applications provide the specific business models and terminology to move information across multiple industries. These standards are often called a *vocabulary*. Thus, industry groups are using XML to form a vocabulary.

The other approach to XML standards is that of horizontal applications. *Horizontal* applications are specific to a particular industry, such as retail or transportation. In all electronic commerce applications, the sharing of data is paramount. Figure 11.1 represents how data can move vertically and horizontally through various industries.

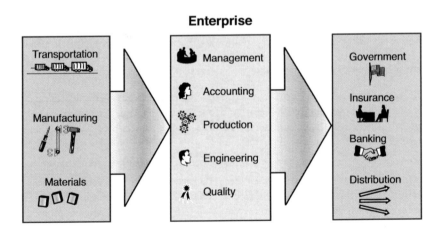

Figure 11.1   XML across industries.

One interesting example of an industry XML application is that of the Recipe Markup Language (RecipeML). RecipeML is an XML vocabulary that defines standards for industries involved with food, such as hotels, restaurants, publishers, and so on. Using RecipeML allows these industries to move data back and forth in a standard and portable manner. Some of the industries with XML-based standards include legal, hospitality, accounting, retail, travel, finance, and education.

Here is where we consider the concept of portable data. Although the low-level data (at the machine level) is certainly not portable, we want to create a higher-level portability at the information level. Whereas Java, .NET, and Objective-C provide various levels of portability at the programming language level, XML provides this information portability that we are looking for.

The Extensible Markup Language (XML)

XML stands for Extensible Markup Language. You probably are already familiar with another markup language called Hypertext Markup Language (HTML). Both XML and HTML are descendants of SGML, the Standard Generalized Markup Language. Surprisingly, SGML appeared as early as the 1970s and was standardized in the 1980s.

The primary function of HTML is to present data in a browser. It was developed to organize data using hyperlinks, and the browser is a perfect vehicle for this purpose. However, HTML is meant to format and present data, not to define and verify it. HTML is a subset of SGML but did not include the data verification constructs provided by the SGML specification. The reason for this is that SGML is very complex and sophisticated, and implementing SGML completely can be quite expensive. At least early on, HTML did not concern itself with the data verification issues, among other things.

XML, on the other hand, *does* concern itself with data verification issues. XML was defined in 1997 as a subset of SGML. XML is much more strict with its format than HTML and was designed to represent data. XML is not proprietary and the World Wide Web Consortium (W3C) is the organization that proposes recommendations and that promotes the distribution of its standards. For many web technologies, I like to reference the w3schools website (http://www.w3schools.com/).

In subsequent chapters, we will see how XML is used within various object-oriented technologies such as web services, distributed computing, object persistence, and so on. In this chapter, we cover the concepts and syntax behind XML (and JSON).

One of the philosophical problems with Java is that it is proprietary (owned by Oracle). The .NET framework is also proprietary (owned by Microsoft), as is Objective-C (Apple). The beauty of XML is that it is an open technology. In fact, it is one of the few technologies that have been embraced by most of the IT industry leaders. Thus, XML is not about to go away anytime soon.

XML Versus HTML

Soon after XML emerged, there was speculation that XML would replace HTML. Many believed that because they were both descendants of SGML, XML was an upgrade. In reality, HTML and

XML are designed for different purposes. HTML, along with Cascading Style Sheets (CSS), determines the structure and presentation of a document, whereas XML describes data. Both HTML and XML are important tools in the development of web-based systems.

XML looks a lot like HTML. This is not surprising, because they come from the same source. However, XML provides two primary advantages that HTML does not—validity and well-formed documents.

HTML tags are all predefined. Tags such as <HTML>, <HEAD>, <BODY>, and so on are all defined in the HTML specification. You cannot add your own tags. Because HTML is intended for formatting purposes, this is not a problem. XML, however, is meant to define data. To define data, you need to create your own tag names. This is where a document called the *Document Type Definition (DTD)* comes into play. The DTD is where you define the tags that describe your data. When you create an XML document, you can use only tags that are predefined. All XML documents are checked for validity. The XML processor reads the DTD and determines whether the document is valid. If the document is not valid, a syntax error is produced.

Valid Documents

You are not required to use a DTD. However, using a DTD provides a great benefit to validating XML documents. XML only checks to see whether there is a well-formed document. You need to explicitly include a DTD to check for document validity. You define the parameters in the DTD.

For example, if you are creating a purchase order system, you might want to create a tag called <PurchaseOrder> in the DTD. If you then misspell the tag like this: <PurchasOrder>, this problem will be detected, and the document will be flagged as invalid.

A validated document makes XML documents much more robust—a necessity when dealing with data. For example, HTML has many tags that are part of a pair, such as <FONT> and </FONT>. If you were to forget to close the pair with the </FONT> tag, the browser will still load the document, but the results could be unpredictable. HTML will make a best guess and continue. XML, when used with a DTD, will not attempt a best guess. If the document is not constructed properly, an error will be generated and the document will not be valid.

Enforcing the validity of a document and ensuring that a document is well-formed provides industries with an important mechanism to share information.

XML and Object-Oriented Languages

XML works hand-in-hand with object-oriented languages to provide what I have termed "portable information." Often, an application written in an object-oriented language is developed to interact with XML. To illustrate, let's revisit the example earlier in the chapter. Alpha Company, a department store, uses an Oracle database, and Beta Company, a vacuum machine manufacturer, uses a SQL Server database. Alpha Company wants to purchase some vacuum cleaners from Beta Company for its inventory. All transactions will be handled electronically over the Internet.

To make a long story short, the problem is that the data is stored in two totally different data-bases. Even if the databases were the same, the formats of the records in the database would most likely be designed differently. Thus, the goal is to share data between Alpha Company and Beta Company, which means sharing the data between their databases. This does not mean a direct physical connection between the databases; the issue here is how to transact business—for example, one company sending a purchase order and the receiving company processing it.

Proprietary Solutions

We could create a proprietary application for connectivity between the Alpha and Beta Companies. Although this would work for this one application, it is preferable to have a more general solution (as is the object-oriented way). For example, Alpha Company might be in the market position to require that all suppliers conform to its purchase order specification. This is where XML shines. Alpha Company can create an XML specification to which all its suppliers can connect.

To accomplish the goal of connecting the systems of the two companies, Alpha Company can come up with an XML specification describing what information is required to complete a transaction and store the information in its database. Here is where the object-oriented languages come in. A language such as Java, VB, or C# can be used to extract the data from Alpha Company's SQL Server database and create an XML document based on the agreed-upon standards.

This XML document can then be sent over the Internet to Beta Company, which uses the agreed-upon XML standard to extract the information in the XML document and enters it into its Oracle database. Figure 11.2 represents the flow of data from one database to another. In this figure, data is extracted from a SQL database by an application\parser and then sent over a network to another application\parser. This parser then converts the data into an Oracle format.

Figure 11.2   Application-to-application data transfer.

Parsers

A *parser* is an application that reads a document and extracts specific information. For exam-ple, a compiler contains a parser. The parser reads each line of a program and uses specific grammar rules to determine how to produce code. A parser would verify that a print statement was written with the appropriate syntax.

Sharing Data Between Two Companies

At this point, it is helpful to implement, to a certain extent, our example of the collaboration between the Alpha and Beta Companies. The scope of this discussion is to create the XML document that will contain a simple transaction between the two companies. For this example, we create a simple document that contains the information contained in Table 11.1. This table defines the data that will be transferred from one company to the other.

Table 11.1   **Specification for Data to Be Transferred**

Object	Category	Field
supplier		
	name	
		`<companyname>`
	address	
		`<street>`
		`<city>`
		`<state>`
		`<zip>`
	product	
		type
		price
		count

Validating the Document with the Document Type Definition (DTD)

In this example, we will be sending an XML document from Beta Company to Alpha Company. The XML document will represent a transaction that contains the name of the company, the address of the company, and certain product information. Note that the information is nested. This is to say that the overall document, which can be described as an object, is that of a supplier, and nested within the supplier identification are the company name, the company address, and the product information. Note that there is also information nested within the address and the product identifications. Before going any further, let's define a DTD that will drive all the transactions for this example. The DTD is presented in Listing 11.1.

Listing 11.1   **The Data Definition Document for Validation**

```
<!-- DTD for supplier document -->
<!ELEMENT supplier ( name, address)>
<!ELEMENT name ( companyname)>
<!ELEMENT companyname ( #PCDATA)>
<!ELEMENT address ( street+, city, state, zip)>
<!ELEMENT street ( #PCDATA)>
<!ELEMENT city ( #PCDATA)>
<!ELEMENT state ( #PCDATA)>
<!ELEMENT zip ( #PCDATA)>
```

The DTD defines how the XML document is constructed. It is composed of tags that look very similar to HTML tags. The first line is an XML comment:

```
<!-- DTD for supplier document -->
```

XML comments provide the same function as any other programming language's comments—to document the code. As with any code, XML uses comments to make the document easier to read and understand. Do not put too many comments in it, or the document will be more difficult to read. This document contains only one comment.

The remaining lines define the structure of the XML document. Let's look at the first line:

```
<!ELEMENT supplier ( name, address, product)>
```

This tag defines an element called `supplier`. As specified in the preceding DTD, a `supplier` contains a `name`, an `address`, and a `product`. Thus, when an XML parser actually parses an XML document, the document must be a `supplier`, which contains a `name`, an `address`, and a `product`.

Taking things to the next level, we see that the element name is made up of yet another element called `<companyname>`:

```
<!ELEMENT name ( companyname)>
```

The `<companyname>` element is then defined to be a data element designated by #PCDATA:

```
<!ELEMENT companyname ( #PCDATA)>
```

This tag terminates the hierarchy of the element tree. This DTD is named `supplier.dtd`. You can use any text editor to create the DTD. Many integrated tools and environments can be used to create this document as well. Figure 11.3 uses Notepad to show how a DTD for this application might look.

Document Validity

An XML document that specifies a DTD is either valid or invalid based on the DTD. If a document does not specify a DTD, the XML document is not judged either valid or invalid. An XML document can specify a DTD internally or externally. Because external DTDs provide a very powerful mechanism, we will use an external DTD here.

Figure 11.3   Creating the DTD in Notepad.

> PCDATA
>
> PCDATA stands for *Parsed Character Data* and is standard character information parsed from
> the text file. Any numbers, such as integers, will need to be converted by the parser.

Integrating the DTD into the XML Document

Now that we have created the DTD, it is time to create an actual XML document. Remember
that the XML document must conform to the supplier DTD we have just written.

In Table 11.2, we have identified some of the actual information that will be contained in the
XML document. Again, note that the data is contained only in the end elements, not the aggregate elements, such as address and name.

Table 11.2   **Adding the Values to the Table**

Object	Category	Field	Value
supplier			
	name		
		<companyname>	The Beta Company
	address		
		<street>	12000 Ontario St
		<city>	Cleveland
		<state>	OH
		<zip>	24388

Object	Category	Field	Value
	product		
		type	Vacuum Cleaner
		price	50.00
		count	20

To enter this information into an XML document, we can use a text editor, as we used for the DTD. However, as we will see later, tools have been created specifically for this purpose. Figure 11.4 shows the XML document written using Notepad. This document is called `beta.xml`.

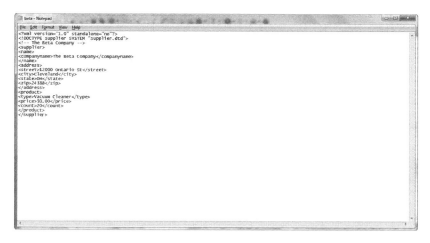

```
<?xml version="1.0" standalone="no"?>
<!DOCTYPE supplier SYSTEM "supplier.dtd">
<!-- The Beta Company -->
<supplier>
<name>
<companyname>The Beta Company</companyname>
</name>
<address>
<street>12000 Ontario St</street>
<city>Cleveland</city>
<state>OH</state>
<zip>24388</zip>
</address>
<product>
<type>Vacuum Cleaner</type>
<price>50.00</price>
<count>20</count>
</product>
</supplier>
```

Figure 11.4   The Beta Company XML document with the DTD.

Note that the second line ties this document to the supplier DTD that we defined earlier:

```
<!DOCTYPE supplier SYSTEM "supplier.dtd">
```

Looking at Figure 11.4, we can see that the tag structure mimics the specification. It is important to realize that the tags are nested and that only the end tags contain any data. Some of the tags are basically high-level tags. In some ways, it is similar to the concept of abstract classes. You can think of the `<address>` tag as being "abstract" because we don't really define it. However, the `<street>` tag can be considered "concrete" given that we actually assign a value to it. In other words, the `<street>` tag does contain information, whereas the address tag does not:

```
<address>
<street>12000 Ontario St</street>
```

There is a better way to inspect the XML document. As stated previously, many tools have been written to assist in the development of XML documents. One of these early tools is called XML Notepad, and it has a similar look and feel to Notepad provided in the Microsoft operating systems.

XML Notepad

Currently, you can find XML Notepad by doing a simple Internet search for "XML Notepad." It is available on various sites.

XML Notepad can help us understand the structure of an XML document. After you install XML Notepad, you can open the `beta.xml` file. Figure 11.5 shows what happens when you open the `beta.xml` file with XML Notepad. When the document opens, expand all the plus signs to look at all the elements.

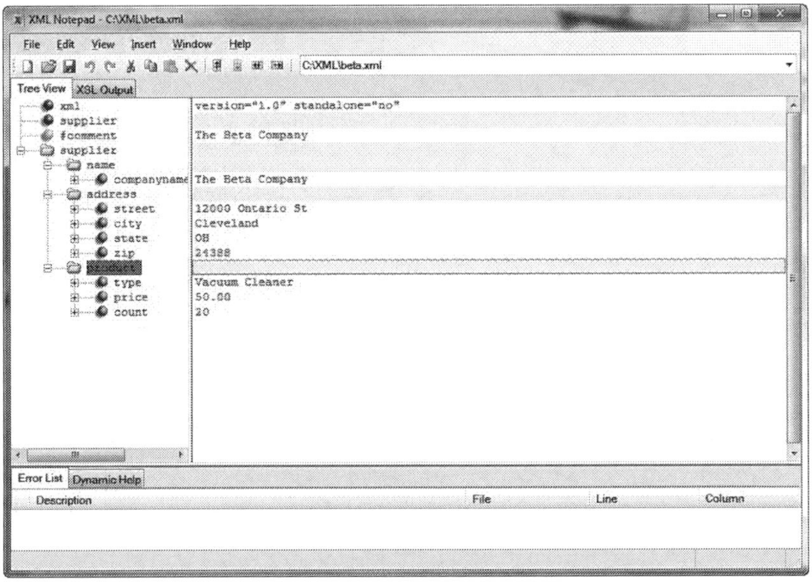

Figure 11.5   Opening the `beta.xml` file with XML Notepad.

XML Notepad lists each level of the document, starting with the supplier tag. Note that as we have said before, only the end elements contain any information.

The obvious advantage to developing the DTD is that it can be used for more than one document—in this case, for more than one supplier. Suppose we have a company that makes skates, called Gamma Company, which wants to supply Alpha Company. What Gamma Company needs to do is create an XML document that conforms to the supplier DTD. Opening up this document with XML Notepad presents the picture seen in Figure 11.6.

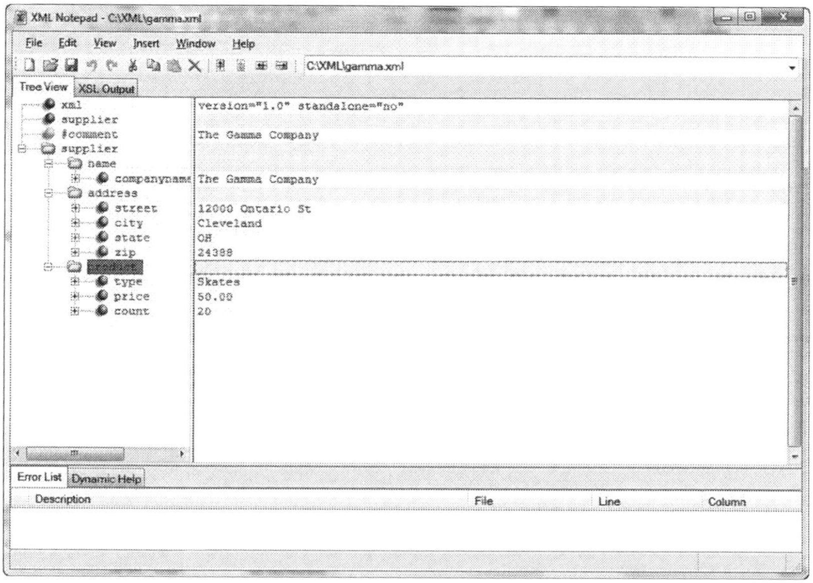

Figure 11.6   Opening the `gamma.xml` file with XML Notepad.

Note that `beta.xml` and `gamma.xml` conform to the supplier DTD. The question is, what happens when the XML document does not conform to the DTD? At this point we see the power of the DTD. Let's purposely create an error in the `gamma.xml` file by taking out all the information pertaining to the name:

```
<name>
<companyname>The Gamma Company</companyname>
</name>
```

Basically, we are creating an invalid document—invalid per the supplier DTD. The invalid document is found in Figure 11.7. Be aware that Notepad will not indicate that the document is invalid because Notepad does not check for validity. You need to use an XML validator to check for validity.

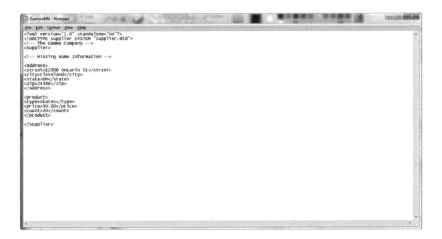

Figure 11.7   An invalid document (no name information).

We now have an invalid document based on the supplier DTD. How do we verify that it is invalid? We can open the invalid gamma.xml document with an XML validator, such as the one on the w3schools site (www.w3schools.com/xml/xml_validator.asp). Notice the result, as indicated in Figure 11.8. Here the XML validator provides a dialog box indicating that an invalid document was detected.

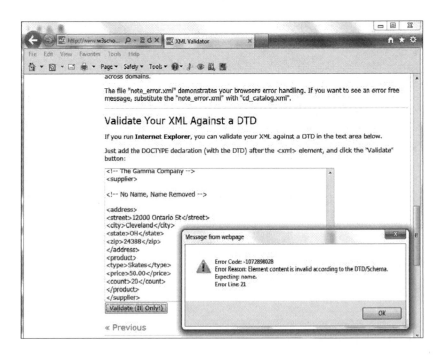

Figure 11.8   The invalid gamma.xml document verified at the w3schools site.

XML Validation

Many applications will validate XML code. The XML validator at the w3schools site is one that is easily accessible.

Because the supplier DTD was expecting a document to conform to its definition, an error was generated. In fact, the error message is quite specific as to what the problem is. The DTD was expecting the name information. Thus, to create a proper XML document for this system, all the appropriate information must be supplied, and supplied in the proper format. The <address> tag must be provided for the document to be valid.

One of the primary points to recognize here is that this error checking would not have happened in HTML. In fact, even with the invalid structure, you can open up the invalid XML file with a browser, as seen in Figure 11.9.

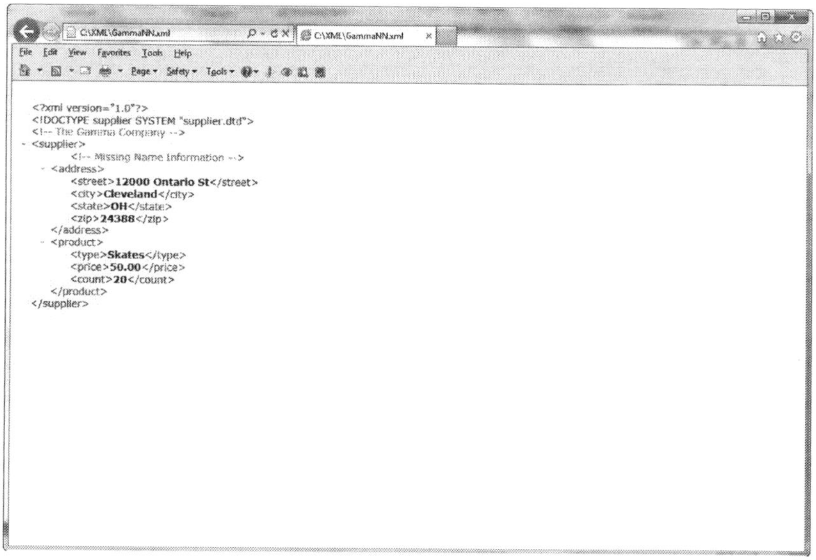

Figure 11.9   The gamma.xml document (with no name info) opened in Internet Explorer.

Note that even though the document is invalid, the browser opens it and even displays it. This is because the browser is not checking to make sure the document conforms to the DTD, whereas XML validators do perform this check. In theory, this is one of the major advantages that XML provides when working with data (when using a validator). Although HTML is used to *display* the data, XML is used to *format* the data and this means it has to be a bit more vigilant. This is a very important distinction.

You might ask, what benefit does a tool like XML Notepad provide in the overall supplier example, and what is it used for? To answer the first part of the question, XML Notepad, or some editor like it, allows us to verify that the document is valid early on in the process. To answer the second part of the question, XML Notepad or a similar editor can be used to construct the document.

Using Cascading Style Sheets

From a technical perspective, the concept of portable data often focuses on the movement of data between two points. However, getting the data from point A to point B provides no real value unless the data is presented in an appropriate way. Thus, we must consider how the data transported in an XML system is presented to a user.

Remember that although XML is primarily used to define data, HTML is basically a presentation mechanism. However, XML and HTML can be used in tandem to present data via a browser.

Although XML is not generally used for presentation purposes, there are ways to format XML. One of these is to use CSS. CSS are used heavily in the HTML world to format content. To a certain degree, CSS can be used to format XML. Recall that the supplier XML document contains definitions for `<companyname>`, `<street>`, `<city>`, `<state>`, and `<zip>`. Suppose that we want to format each of these definitions, as seen in Table 11.3, to provide a specification that formats the elements of the XML document.

Table 11.3 **Cascading Style Sheet Specification**

Tag	Font Family	Size	Color	Display
`<companyname>`	Arial, sans serif	24	Blue	Block
`<street>`	Times New Roman, serif	12	Red	Block
`<city>`	Courier New, serif	18	Black	Block
`<state>`	Tahoma; serif	16	Gray	Block
`<zip>`	Arial Black, sans serif	6	Green	Block

We can represent this in a CSS with the following style sheet:

```
companyname{font-family:Arial, sans-serif;
    font-size:24;
    color:blue;
    display:block;}
```

```
street {font-family:"Times New Roman", serif;
    font-size:12;
    color:red;
    display:block;}
city {font-family:"Courier New", serif;
    font-size:18;
    color:black;
    display:block;}
state {font-family:"Tahoma"; serif;
    font-size:16;
    color:gray;
    display:block;}
zip {font-family:"Arial Black", sans-serif;
    font-size:6;
    color:green;
    display:block;}
```

This style sheet is implemented by adding a line of code in our XML document:

```
<?xml-stylesheet href="supplier.css" type="text/css" ?>
```

For example, in the case of the ZIP Code, the simple text displayed earlier is now formatted with a font of Arial Black, the color green, and a font size of 6. The attribute `display:block` in this case will bring each attribute to a new line.

This code is inserted in the following manner:

```
<?xml version="1.0" standalone="no"?>
<?xml-stylesheet href="supplier.css" type="text/css" ?>
<!DOCTYPE supplier SYSTEM "supplier.dtd">
<!-- The XML data -->
<supplier>
<name>
<companyname>The Beta Company</companyname>
</name>
<address>
<street>12000 Ontario St</street>
<city>Cleveland</city>
<state>OH</state>
<zip>24388</zip>
</address>
</supplier>
```

With the CSS in the XML document, we can now open the document with a browser. Figure 11.10 illustrates how this looks.

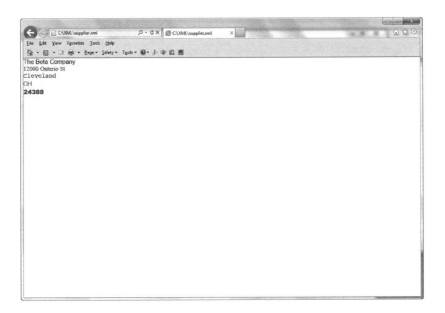

Figure 11.10   The XML document using a cascading style sheet.

Take a look at Figure 11.9 again to see how this document was presented without the CSS.

JavaScript Object Notation (JSON)

Although the concept of portable data is quite powerful, and XML is a widely accepted standard in the exchange of data, there are alternatives. Striving for an industry standard, a noble pursuit, is extremely difficult in an industry that is constantly innovating and changing. For example, many developers see advantages of strongly typed, compiled languages as too hard to ignore, whereas others appreciate the flexibility of languages, such as Perl, which are more loosely typed. The same goes for the discussion on data.

Although XML is much more structured, especially when using a DTD, technologies such as the JavaScript Object Notation, or JSON, fall into the category of "more flexible." The w3schools site (http://www.w3schools.com/json/default.asp) provides the following bullet item description of JSON:

- JSON is lightweight text-data interchange format.
- JSON is language independent.
- JSON is "self-describing" and easy to understand.

* JSON uses JavaScript syntax for describing data objects, but JSON is still language and platform independent. JSON parsers and JSON libraries exist for many different programming languages.

The primary point to understand is that JSON uses the identical syntax for creating objects that JavaScript does. Thus, as the w3schools site explains: *Instead of using a parser, a JavaScript program can use the built-in eval() function and execute JSON data to produce native JavaScript objects.* In fact, you can parse this data in various ways; some developers shy away from using the `eval()` function.

As is always the case with this book, for the purpose of honing in on the concepts, let's convert the XML object that we created earlier in the chapter into an equivalent JSON example. In fact, let's take a look at the simple JSON object created at the w3schools site:

```
{
"employees": [
{ "firstName":"John" , "lastName":"Doe" },
{ "firstName":"Anna" , "lastName":"Smith" },
{ "firstName":"Peter" , "lastName":"Jones" }
]
}
```

Note that the actual JSON is represented by the code within the outer curly braces. Also note that the JSON object is basically a property—a name/value pair. To see how the JSON object fits into the big picture, take a look at a complete code example also from the w3schools site. You can try things out with the editor they provide at the site: (http://www.w3schools.com/json/json_intro.asp):

```
<!DOCTYPE html>
<html>
 <body>
 <h2>JSON Object Creation in JavaScript</h2>
<p>
 Name: <span id="jname"></span><br />
Age: <span id="jage"></span><br />
Address: <span id="jstreet"></span><br />
Phone: <span id="jphone"></span><br />
</p>

<script type="text/javascript">
 var JSONobject= {
 "name":"John Johnson",
 "street":"Oslo West 555",
"age":33,
 "phone":"555 1234567"};
document.getElementById("jname").innerHTML=JSONObject.name
document.getElementById("jage").innerHTML=JSONObject.age
document.getElementById("jstreet").innerHTML=JSONObject.street
document.getElementById("jphone").innerHTML=JSONObject.phone
</script>
</body>
</html>
```

JSON Editor at w3schools Site

Note that the editor used at the w3schools site processes a single, complete file. Thus, if you want to use a separate file (such as a style sheet, and so on), you will have to embed the file in this editor. In short, you can process only a single file in this editor, which is meant for testing out some concepts. When you create your application, you will want to structure the code into logically separate files.

Using this example, let's implement the XML object created earlier as a JSON object:

```
var address= {
 "street":"23456 Main St",
 "city":"Cleveland",
 "state":"OH",
 "zip":"24388"
 };
```

In this case, the JSON object is created as a JavaScript associative array, with the name/value pairing that was mentioned in a previous paragraph. Figure 11.11 shows how the JSON object is embedded inside an actual HTML document for use.

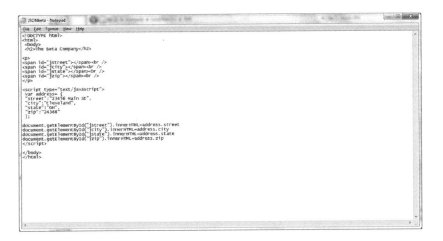

Figure 11.11   The HTML document using a JSON object.

To understand how we can process and display this JSON code in a similar manner to our XML example earlier, we can use a style sheet like this:

```
<!DOCTYPE html>
<html>
 <head>
 <style type="text/css">
```

```
companyname{font-family:Arial, sans-serif;
    font-size:24;
    color:blue;
    display:block;}
street {font-family:"Times New Roman", serif;
    font-size:12;
    color:red;
    display:block;}
city {font-family:"Courier New", serif;
    font-size:18;
    color:black;
    display:block;}
state {font-family:"Tahoma"; serif;
    font-size:16;
    color:gray;
    display:block;}
zip {font-family:"Arial Black", sans-serif;
    font-size:6;
    color:green;
    display:block;}
</style>
</head>

<body>
<companyname>The Beta Company</companyname>

<p>
<street> <span id="jstreet"></span><br /> </street>
<city> <span id="jcity"></span><br /> </city>
<state> <span id="jstate"></span><br /> </state>
<zip> <span id="jzip"></span><br /> </zip>
</p>

<script type="text/javascript">
 var address= {
 "street":"23456 Main St",
 "city":"Cleveland",
 "state":"OH",
 "zip":"24388"
 };

document.getElementById("jstreet").innerHTML=address.street
document.getElementById("jcity").innerHTML=address.city
document.getElementById("jstate").innerHTML=address.state
document.getElementById("jzip").innerHTML=address.zip
</script>
</body>
</html>
```

Executing this code in the w3schools editor results in the output displayed in Figure 11.12.

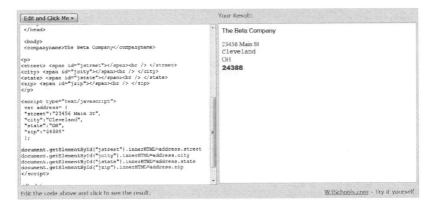

Figure 11.12   The HTML/CSS document using a JSON object in the w3schools editor.

Finally, let's compare the output from the XML example in Internet Explorer, which is provided in Figure 11.10 to the JSON example. To do this, we use the same mechanism; open the JSON (embedded in HTML) file in Internet Explorer. This output is displayed in Figure 11.13.

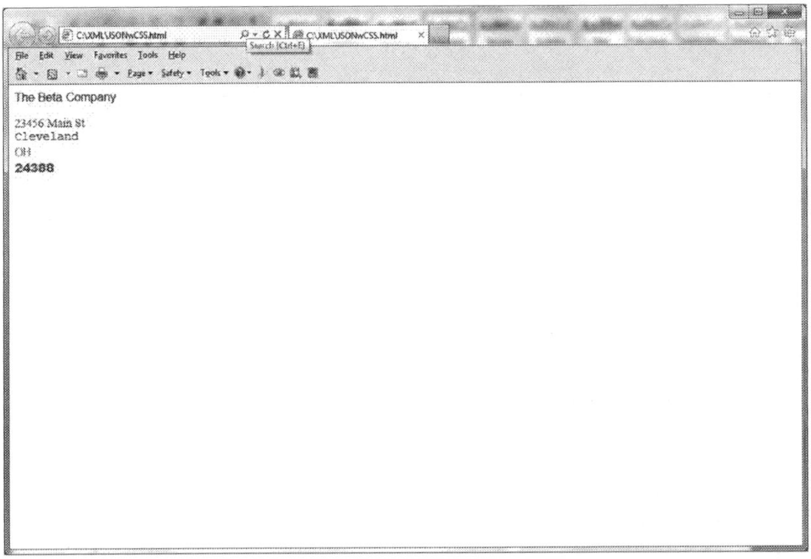

Figure 11.13   JSON implementation of similar XML example.

As you can see, although XML and JSON approach the concept of portable data differently, the objectives are the same. In both cases, the goal is to allow the transmission of data contained in objects that can be easily parsed, shared, and utilized. As mentioned earlier in this section, many people like using JSON because it is less structured than XML, and they claim that it is faster.

Conclusion

In this chapter, we discussed many aspects of XML and why it is a very important technology within the IT community. It is rare when many major players in the IT market buy into the same standard, but this has happened in the case of XML. We also took a quick look at an alternative technology, JSON. Both XML and JSON are used for the transmission of what I like to call "portable data."

From the object-oriented perspective, you should come away from this chapter with the understanding that object-oriented development goes far beyond OO languages and encompasses the data as well. Because data is the fundamental part of information systems, it is important to design object-oriented systems that focus on the data. In today's business environment, moving data from one point to another is of paramount importance.

There are many levels of investigation you can visit when it comes to XML and JSON. This book is about concepts, and by the end of this chapter, you should have a good general idea of what XML and JSON are, as well as some of the tools that are used with them. Another level that was mentioned briefly in this chapter was that of the style sheets. By using CSS and other technologies, you can better format your XML documents.

References

- Marcotte, Ethan. 2011. *Responsive Web Design*. New York, NY: A Book Apart.

- http://www.w3schools.com/json/default.asp

- Deitel, Harvey and Paul Deitel. 2010. *JavaScript for Programmers*, Upper Saddle River, NJ: Pearson Education, Inc.

- Hughes, Cheryl. 2003. *The Web Wizard's Guide to XML*. Boston, MA: Addison-Wesley.

- Watt, Andrew H. 2003. *Teach Yourself XML in 10 Minutes*. Indianapolis, IN: Sams Publishing.

- McKinnon, Al and Linda. 2003. *XML: Web Warrior Series*. Boston, MA: Course Technology.

- Holtzer, Steven. 2003. *Real World XML*. Indianapolis, IN: New Riders.

12

Persistent Objects: Serialization, Marshaling, and Relational Databases

No matter what type of business application you create, a database most likely will be part of the equation. In fact, one of my favorite lines when it comes to software development is, "It's all about the data." In short, no matter what hardware, operating system, application software, and so on is used when developing a software application, the need for the data is usually the reason for creating the system in the first place.

Persistent Objects Basics

Recall that when an object is instantiated by an application, it lives only as long as the application itself. Thus, if you instantiate an `Employee` object that contains attributes such as `name`, `ss#`, and so on, that `Employee` object will cease to exist when the application terminates. Figure 12.1 illustrates the traditional object life cycle that is pretty straightforward. When an application creates an object, an object lives within the confines of that application. When the application ends, the object goes out of scope. For the object to live on, it must be written to some sort of persistent storage.

When the `Employee` object is instantiated and initialized, it has a specific state. Remember that the state of an object is defined by the value of its attributes. If we want to save the state of the `Employee` object, we must take some sort of action to save the state of this object. The concept of saving the state of an object so that it can be used later is called *persistence*. Thus, we used the term *persistent object* to define an object that can be restored and used independently of a single application. Figure 12.2 illustrates the traditional object life cycle with persistence. In this figure, the object is created in application 1, which then writes the object out to a storage device, perhaps a database. Because the object is in persistent storage, other applications can access it. In this figure, application 2 can now instantiate an object and load the contents of the persistent object.

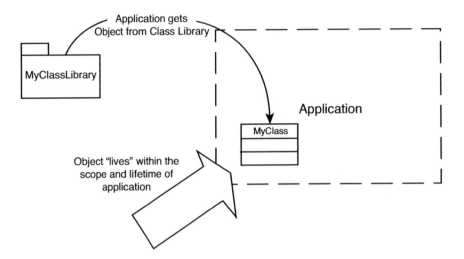

Figure 12.1   Object life cycle.

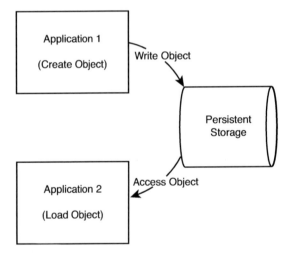

Figure 12.2   Object life cycle with persistence.

There are many ways to save the state of an object. Some of these are as follows:

- Save to a flat file.
- Save to a relational database.
- Save to an object database.

The easiest way to demonstrate how to save an object is to create code that will write the object to a flat file, because many people do not have access to an object database or an industrial strength relational database on their home computers. However, whereas using a flat file to illustrate how to save an object is good for illustration purposes, using a flat file for business applications is certainly not the norm.

Saving the Object to a Flat File

In this section, we use a flat file to illustrate object persistence. I define a flat file as a simple file managed by the operating system. This is a very basic concept, so don't get too caught up in this description.

Flat Files

Many people are not totally comfortable with the term *flat file*. The word *flat* implies that the object is literally *flattened*, and in a way it is. You almost can think of this *flattening* process as necessary to store and transport an object, regardless of its complexity.

One of the issues you might have considered is that an object cannot be saved to a file like a simple variable—and this is true. In fact, this problem of saving the state of an object has spawned a major segment of the software product industry, which we discuss at length later in this chapter. Normally, when you save a number of variables to a file, you know the order and type of each variable (perhaps comma-delimited, and the like), and then you write them out to the file. It could be a comma-delimited file or any other protocol that you may decide to implement.

The problem with an object is that it is not simply a collection of primitive variables. An object can be thought of as an indivisible unit that is composed of a number of parts. Thus, the object must be decomposed into a unit that can be written to a storage medium such as a flat file. After the object is decomposed and written to a flat file, there is one major issue left to consider—reconstituting the object, basically putting it back together.

Another major problem with storing objects relates to the fact that an object can contain other objects. Consider that a `Car` object might contain objects like `Engines` and `Wheels`. When you save the object to a flat file, you must consider saving the entire object, `Car`, `Engines`, and the like.

Modern languages have built-in mechanisms for object persistence. For example, like other C-based languages, Java often uses the concept of a stream to deal with I/O. To save an object to a file, Java writes it to the file via a `Stream`. To write to a `Stream`, objects must implement either the `Serializable` or `Externalizable` interface.

The downside to this approach is that the solution is proprietary—you must be using Java to get this to work. In fact, Java must be on both sides of the "pipe." Another more portable approach to this problem is to create an XML document as the intermediate file and decompose and reconstitute an object using open XML technologies.

We cover both approaches in this chapter. First, Java will be used to demonstrate the Java serialization technology, and then we will use an XML strategy to implement a .NET example using C#.

Serializing a File

As an example, consider the following Java code for a class called `Person`:

```
package Serialization;
import java.util.*;
import java.io.*;

class Person implements Serializable{

    private String name;

    public Person(){
    }

    public Person(String n){
        System.out.println("Inside Person's Constructor");
        name = n;
    }

    String getName() {
        return name;
    }

}
```

This class is a simple one that contains only a single attribute representing the name of the person.

The one line to pay special attention to identifies the class as `Serializable`. If you inspect the Java documentation, you will realize that the `Serializable` interface does not contain much—in fact, it is meant solely to identify that the object will be serialized:

```
class Person implements Serializable
```

This class also contains a method called `getName` that returns the name of the object. Besides the `Serializable` interface, there is really nothing new about this class that we have not seen before. Here is where the interesting stuff starts. We now want to write an application that will write this object to a flat file. The application is called `SavePerson` and is as follows:

```
package Serialization;
import java.util.*;
import java.io.*;
```

```java
public class SavePerson implements Serializable{

    public SavePerson(){

        Person person = new Person("Jack Jones");

        try{
            FileOutputStream fos = new FileOutputStream("Name.txt");
            ObjectOutputStream oos = new ObjectOutputStream(fos);
            System.out.print("Person's Name Written: ");
            System.out.println(person.getName());

            oos.writeObject(person);
            oos.flush();
            oos.close();
        } catch(Exception e){
            e.printStackTrace();
        }

    }
}
```

Although some of this code delves into some more sophisticated Java functionality, we can get a general idea of what is happening when an object gets serialized and written to a file.

Java Code

Although we have not explicitly covered some of the code in this example, such as file I/O, you can study the code in much greater detail with a few of the books referenced at the end of this chapter.

By now you should realize that this is an actual application. How can you tell? The fact that the code has a main method in it is a sure tip. This application basically does three things:

- Instantiates a `Person` object
- Serializes the object
- Writes the object to the file `Name.txt`

The act of serializing and writing the object is accomplished in the following code:

```java
oos.writeObject(person);
```

This is a lot simpler than writing out each individual attribute one at a time. It is very convenient to write the object directly to the file.

Implementation and Interface Revisited

It is interesting to note that the underlying implementation of the serialization of a file is not quite as simple as the interface used. Remember that one of the most important themes of this book is the concept of separating the implementation from the interface. By providing an intuitive and easy-to-use interface that hides the underlying implementation, life for the user is much easier.

Serializing a file is yet another great example of the difference between the interface and the implementation. The programmer's interface is to write the object to the file. You don't care about all the technical issues required to accomplish this feat. All you care about is the following:

- That you can write the object as an indivisible unit
- That you can restore the object exactly as you stored it

It's just like using a car. The interface to turn on the car is your key in the ignition, which starts it. Most people do not know or care about the technical issues regarding how things work—all they care about is that the car starts.

The program SavePerson writes the object to the file Name.txt. The following code restores the object:

```java
package Serialization;
import java.io.*;
import java.util.*;

public class RestorePerson{

    public RestorePerson(){
        try{
            FileInputStream fis = new FileInputStream("Name.txt");
            ObjectInputStream ois = new ObjectInputStream(fis);

            Person person = (Person )ois.readObject();
            System.out.print("Person's Name Restored: ");
            System.out.println(person.getName());
            ois.close();
        } catch(Exception e){
            e.printStackTrace();
        }

    }
}
```

The main line of interest is the code that retrieves the object from the file Name.txt:

```java
Person person = (Person )ois.readObject();
```

It is important to note that the object is reconstructed from the flat file, and a new instance of a `Person` object is instantiated and initialized. This `Person` object is an exact replica of the `Person` object that we stored in the `SavePerson` application. Figure 12.3 shows the output of both the `SavePerson` and the `RestorePerson` applications.

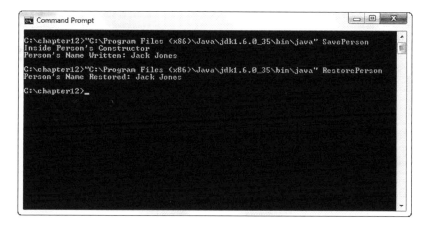

Figure 12.3   Serializing an object.

Note that in Figure 12.3, the name "Jack Jones," part of the `Person` object, is stored in the file `Name.txt` when the file is executed, and then the object is restored when `RestorePerson` is executed. When the object is restored, we can access the `Person` attribute.

What About the Methods?

One question that may cross your mind when we talk about object persistence is this: "When the object is saved, it is easy to visualize how the attributes are saved, but what about the methods?"

One of the definitions of an object is that it contains attributes and behaviors or, in other words, data and methods. What happens to the methods when the object is stored?

In the case of the Java serialization example, the methods are not explicitly stored. Remember that we indicated that Java had to be at both ends of the "pipe." In actuality, the class definitions that you are using have to be on both ends of the "pipe" as well.

Thus, in the `Person` object example, both the `SavePerson` application and the `RestorePerson` application must have access to the `Person` class. Although it is possible to access the `Person` class dynamically, the application that uses the class must have access to it. Thus, the methods themselves are not necessarily kept in the data store.

However, as far as the programmer is concerned, the attributes and behaviors are still encapsulated as part of the object. There is no conceptual distinction—despite the fact that the physical implementation may not match the conceptual model.

Using XML in the Serialization Process

Although using a proprietary serialization technique may be efficient and compact, it is not portable. XML is the standard for defining data, so we can create an XML model of our serialization example that can, at least theoretically, be used across various platforms and languages. In this section, the XML model that we create will be accessible by code written in C# .NET. In fact, there is nothing to stop you from accessing the generated XML file from a Java program, or any other language for that matter.

The primary difference between the XML model and the Java serialization model is that with the XML model, we generate an XML document. This document represents the attributes and properties of the `Person` class. This approach adds a bit of complexity to the `Person` class; however, the syntax provides a more encapsulated construction of the class.

Let's first look at the C# code. The primary difference of the `Person` class is the way that the attributes are defined. Although much of the code is similar to the non-XML model (like the constructors, behaviors, and so on), the data is defined with XML in mind.

For example, you embed the definitions of the XML roots, attributes, and elements directly in the code. The definitions would appear as follows:

```
    [XmlRoot("person")]
    public class Person
...
    [XmlAttribute("name")]
    public String Name
...
    [XmlElement("age")]
    public int Age
```

The interesting addition to this strategy is that the attributes themselves have specific properties. Although this may add more lines of code, and thus some complexity, the benefit is that the encapsulation of the class is much tighter. For example, throughout this book, we often proclaim the benefits of private attributes and how access to these attributes should be through defined *getters* and *setters*. This is obviously a strong and important concept, but the fact remains that the definition (and thus signature) of the *getters* and *setters* are left to the discretion of the programmer. In short, *getters* and *setters* may be defined with whatever method names the programmer conjures up. In this XML model, the *getters* and *setters* are properties of the attribute and are thus bound to that attribute in a standard manner.

For example, when creating an XML attribute called `Name`, the definition looks like this:

```
[XmlAttribute("name")]
public String Name
{
    get
    {
        return this.strName;
    }
```

```
    set
    {
        if (value == null) return;
        this.strName = value;
    }
}
```

Inspecting this code, we can see that there is a lot more code than a simple attribute declaration:

```
public String Name;
```

However, although we have still defined the attribute as a type of String, the major addition is that the Name attribute is now defined as an XML attribute, and the corresponding *getter* and *setter* are properties of the Name attribute itself.

The data validation and verification is still performed in the same way; however, it is much more intuitive (at least after you figure it out).

The syntax to set the Name attribute now becomes a simple assignment statement like this line of code:

```
this.Name = name;
```

When this line is executed, the set property of the attribute is invoked. It is essentially an operator overload (for those of us who programmed a lot in C and C++). When the assignment operator (equal sign) is seen in the context of the Name attribute (on the left side), the getter is called. It is almost like an inline compiler directive.

The concept of using the XML version of the Person class is similar to the Java serialization model. Here is some sample code:

```
public void Serialize()
{
    Person[] myPeople = new Person[3];
    myPeople[0] = new Person("John Q. Public", 32, 95);
    myPeople[1] = new Person("Jacob M. Smith", 35, 67);
    myPeople[2] = new Person("Joe L. Jones", 65, 77);
    XmlSerializer mySerializer = new XmlSerializer(typeof(Person[]));
    TextWriter myWriter = new StreamWriter("person.xml");
    mySerializer.Serialize(myWriter, myPeople);
    myWriter.Close();
}
```

The primary difference is that, instead of being serialized to a proprietary Java format, the file produced is in XML:

```
<?xml version="1.0" encoding="utf-8"?>
<ArrayOfPerson xmlns:xsi="http://www.w3.org/2001/XMLSchema-instance"
xmlns:xsd="http://www.w3.org/2001/XMLSchema">
  <Person name="John Q. Public">
```

```
    <age>32</age>
  </Person>
  <Person name="Jacob M. Smith">
    <age>35</age>
  </Person>
  <Person name="Joe L. Jones">
    <age>65</age>
  </Person>
</ArrayOfPerson>
```

To restore the object, we use the following code:

```
public void DeSerialize()
{
Person[] myRestoredPeople;
XmlSerializer mySerializer = newXmlSerializer(typeof(Person[]));
TextReader myReader = new StreamReader("person.xml");
myRestoredPeople = (Person[])mySerializer.Deserialize(myReader);
Console.WriteLine("My People restored:");
foreach (Person listPerson in myRestoredPeople)
{
Console.WriteLine(listPerson.Name + " is " + listPerson.Age
                                  + " years old.");
}
Console.WriteLine("Press any key to continue...");
Console.ReadKey();
}
```

Note that we iterate through a data structure using a `foreach` loop. The complete code for this C# example is listed at the end of this chapter.

As we have noted, one of the major advantages of this approach is that the XML file is accessible by any and all languages and platforms that implement the XML interface, including Java. Although we implemented the Java example in a proprietary way, this was done for example purposes. There is nothing stopping a programmer from using the XML approach in Java as well.

Writing to a Relational Database

The relational database is perhaps one of the most successful tools ever devised in the information technology field. Although some people might not buy into this statement completely, and there certainly are many other important candidates, the relational database has had a huge impact on the IT industry. In fact, the relational database remains a powerhouse despite the fact that other technologies may well be technologically better.

The reason for this is that relational databases are the database of choice for most businesses today. From Oracle to SQLServer in the large applications, to Microsoft Access in small to medium applications, relational databases are everywhere.

Although relational databases are a wonderful technology, they provide a bit of a problem when it comes to interfacing with objects. Just as with the issue of writing to a flat file, taking an object that may be composed of other objects and writing it to relational databases, which are not designed in an object-oriented manner, can be problematic.

Relational databases are built on the concept of tables. Figure 12.4 shows a typical Microsoft Access table relationship. This relational model is so widespread that many people intuitively think of all data models in this way. However, the object-oriented model is not table driven. Figure 12.4 shows the familiar Northwind relational database model that ships with Microsoft Access.

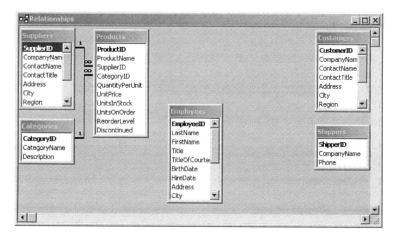

Figure 12.4   A relational model.

Because objects do not map conveniently to tables, object-oriented database systems were developed in the 1990s. An interesting bit of history is that although these databases represented the object-oriented model well, and might even have performed better, there was one major problem: legacy data.

Legacy Data

Legacy data may be decades of data that are stored in various storage devices. In this chapter, we consider legacy data to be the historical data stored in relational databases. Many people don't like the term "legacy" because they think it implies *obsolete*. In fact, important legacy data is not obsolete but an important part of the system.

Because most companies use relational databases, most of today's business data is stored in relational databases. This means that there is a huge investment made in these relational databases. And one more issue is involved when it comes to these systems—they work. Even though object databases might perform better when writing objects to a database, the cost of converting all the relational data to object data is unacceptable. In short, to use an object database, a company would have to convert all its data from a relational database to an object database. This has many drawbacks.

First, anyone who has performed the conversion of data from one database to another knows that this is a very painful process. Second, even if the data converts successfully, there is no way to know how the change of database tools will affect the application code. Third, when problems occur (and they almost always do), it's difficult to determine whether the problem is with the database or the application code. It can be a nightmare. Most company decision makers were not willing to take these chances. Thus, object databases were relegated to totally new systems written with object-oriented code.

However, we still have the following problem: We want to write object-oriented applications, but we need to access the legacy data in the relational databases. This is where object-to-relational mapping comes in.

Accessing a Relational Database

All databases applications have the following structure:

- Database client
- Database server
- Database

The database client is the user application that provides the interface to the system. Often it is a GUI application that allows users to query and update the database.

> ## SQL
>
> SQL stands for Structured Query Language. It is a standard way for database clients to communicate with varied vendor database systems that implement this standard.

The database client communicates with the database server via SQL statements. Figure 12.5 displays a general solution to the database client/server model.

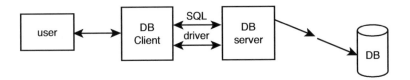

Figure 12.5   Database client server model.

As an example, let's use Java to communicate to a Microsoft Access database, which is a relational database. Java uses JDBC (Java Database Connectivity) to communicate with database servers.

Part of the problem with database drivers is that they tend to be vendor specific. This is a common problem with any type of driver. As you probably know, when you purchase a new printer, the printer comes with a driver that's specific to that printer, and you might even have to download specific updates for that driver. Software products have similar issues. Each vendor has a specific protocol for communicating with its product. This solution might work well if you continue to use a specific vendor. However, if you want to maintain the option of changing vendors, you might be in trouble.

Microsoft has produced a standard called Open Database Connectivity (ODBC). According to Jamie Jaworski in *Java 2 Platform Unleashed*, "ODBC drivers abstract away vendor-specific protocols, providing a common application-programming interface to database clients. By writing your database clients to the ODBC API, you enable your programs to access more database servers." Take a look at Figure 12.6. This figure illustrates how ODBC fits into the picture.

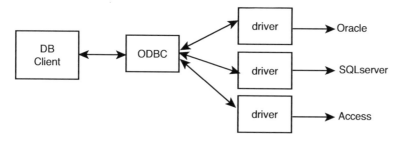

Figure 12.6   Database client/server model using ODBC.

Again we see the words *abstract* and *interface* in a definition of a software API. By using ODBC, we can write applications to a specific standard, and we do not need to know the implementation. Theoretically, we can write code to the ODBC standard and not care whether the database implementation is a Microsoft Access database or an Oracle database—theoretically, at least.

As we see in Figure 12.5, the client uses the driver to send SQL statements to the database servers. Java uses JDBC to communicate with the database servers. JDBC can work in various ways. First, some JDBC drivers can connect directly to the database servers. Others use ODBC as a connection to the database servers, as in Figure 12.7. Depending on how you decide to write your applications, you might need to download various drivers and servers. These specifics are well beyond the scope of this book because here we are concerned mainly with the general concepts. For more detailed information on how to set up a database and how to connect to it with your applications, refer to more advanced books, such as *Java 2 Platform Unleashed*—it is not a trivial endeavor.

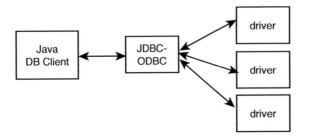

Figure 12.7   Database client/server model using ODBC/JDBC.

Conclusion

In this chapter, we covered the concept of object persistence. Previously, we had focused mainly on the fundamental object-oriented concepts and treated the object as an entity that persists only in the life cycle of the application that creates it. We considered the issue of objects that need to persist beyond the life cycle of one or more applications.

For example, an application might need to restore an object that was created by another application or might create an object for later use by itself or other applications. One way to persist an object is to serialize it to a conventional file. Another is to use a relational database.

References

- Savitch, Walter. 2008. *Absolute Java*, 3rd ed. Boston, MA: Addison-Wesley.

- Walther, Stephen. 2008. *ASP.NET 3.5 Unleashed*. Indianapolis, IN: Sams Publishing.

- Skeet, Jon. 2008. *C# in Depth: What You Need to Master C# 2 and 3*. Greenwich, CT: Manning.

- Bob Leasure and James Leasure. 2004. *The Web Warrior Guide to Web Database Technologies*. Boston, MA: Course Technology (Cengage).

- Deitel, et al. 2003. *C# for Experienced Programmers*. Upper Saddle River, NJ: Prentice Hall.

- Deitel, et al. 2003. *Visual Basic .NET for Experienced Programmers*. Upper Saddle River, NJ: Prentice Hall.

- Jaworski, Jamie. 1999. *Java 2 Platform Unleashed*. Indianapolis, IN: Sams Publishing.

- Flanagan, David, et al. 1999.*Java Enterprise in a Nutshell*. Sebastopol, CA: O'Reilly.

- Farley, Jim. 1998. *Java Distributed Computing*. Sebastopol, CA: O'Reilly.

- Oracle: http://www.oracle.com/technetwork/java/index.html

Example Code Used in This Chapter

The following code is presented in C# .NET. Code for other languages is available electronically on the publisher's website. These examples correspond to the Java code that is listed inside the chapter itself.

The `Person` Class Example: C# .NET

```csharp
// Class Person
using System;
using System.Collections;
using System.IO;
using System.Xml;
using System.Xml.Serialization;

namespace CSSerial
{
    [XmlRoot("person")]
    public class Person
    {
        private String strName;
        private int intAge;
        private int intScore;

        public Person()
        {
            this.Name = "John Doe";
            this.Age=25;
            this.Score=50;
        }

        public Person(String name, int age, int score)
        {
            this.Name = name;
            this.Age = age;
            this.Score = score;
        }
        [XmlAttribute("name")]
        public String Name
        {
            get
            {
                return this.strName;
            }
            set
            {
```

```
                        if (value == null) return;
                        this.strName = value;
                    }
                }

                [XmlElement("age")]
                public int Age
                {
                    get
                    {
                        return this.intAge;
                    }
                    set
                    {
                        this.intAge = value;
                    }
                }

                [XmlIgnore()]
                public int Score
                {
                    get
                    {
                        return intScore;
                    }
                    set
                    {
                        this.intScore = value;
                    }
                }
            }
        }
    }

// Class CSSerial
using System;
using System.Collections;
using System.IO;
using System.Xml;
using System.Xml.Serialization;

namespace CSSerial
{
    class Program
    {
        static void Main(string[] args)
        {
            Program myProgram = new Program();
```

```
    }

    public Program()
    {
        Serialize();
        DeSerialize();
    }

    public void Serialize()
    {
        Person[] myPeople = new Person[3];
        myPeople[0] = new Person("John Q. Public", 32, 95);
        myPeople[1] = new Person("Jacob M. Smith", 35, 67);
        myPeople[2] = new Person("Joe L. Jones", 65, 77);
        XmlSerializer mySerializer = new XmlSerializer(typeof(Person[]));
        TextWriter myWriter = new StreamWriter("person.xml");
        mySerializer.Serialize(myWriter, myPeople);
        myWriter.Close();
    }

    public void DeSerialize()
    {
        Person[] myRestoredPeople;
        XmlSerializer mySerializer = new XmlSerializer(typeof(Person[]));
        TextReader myReader = new StreamReader("person.xml");
        myRestoredPeople = (Person[])mySerializer.Deserialize(myReader);
        Console.WriteLine("My People restored:");
        foreach (Person listPerson in myRestoredPeople)
        {
            Console.WriteLine(listPerson.Name + " is " + listPerson.Age
            + " years old.");
        }
        Console.WriteLine("Press any key to continue...");
        Console.ReadKey();
    }    }
}
```

Objects in Web Services, Mobile Apps, and Hybrids

Perhaps the major reason that objects have become so popular in the software development community today has to do with the Internet. Although object-oriented languages have been around basically as long as structured languages, it was only when the Internet emerged that objects gained wide acceptance. Now, objects are the paradigm of choice for virtually all primary networks today, from the Internet to mobile networks—even the transmission of content such as entertainment and game media to the home via well established infrastructure such as cable and local phone lines.

Although objects were not necessarily in the mainstream until relatively recently (since the late 1990s), the object-oriented language Smalltalk was popular during the 1980s and 1990s, and the object-based language C++ gained widespread acceptance in the 1990s. Smalltalk gained widespread support from object-oriented purists, and C++ became the first object language to become a major force in the marketplace. Java, which was initially targeted specifically for networks, is an object-oriented language that is commercially successful. Now, with the introduction of .NET and Objective-C, object-oriented languages have become part of the mainstream. This chapter covers some of the object technologies that are used on the Internet and other primary networks

Evolution of Distributed Computing

One of the most amazing things about being a professional developer is that change is a constant. Although change is always exciting and keeps the industry forever vibrant, this change comes at a cost—the maintenance of all the great technologies of the past that are now, well, technologies of the past. In short, developers today need to understand how to create all the latest, coolest innovations and integrate these innovations with a lot of legacy technologies. This means that there is always a need to maintain a variety of current and legacy systems. Just think of all the COBOL code written decades ago that is still a vital piece of many companies' IT infrastructure. Relational databases are another good example of decades-old technology that is still amazingly relevant. The history of distributed computing is no different.

In a basic sense, we can trace the beginning of what can be called "distributed computing" to the advent of email. For the purposes of this book, we focus on the process of sending objects between applications that reside on distributed physical platforms. Distributed computing includes many technologies, including the following, which are covered at varied degrees within this chapter:

- HTML
- EDI
- RPC
- CORBA
- DCOM
- XML
- SOAP
- Web services
- ReST

Object-Based Scripting Languages

The primary focus of this book has been on object-oriented programming languages. Languages such as Java, .NET, and Objective-C are used to create complete, potentially standalone, applications. However, these object-oriented languages are not the only domains for programming with objects. We have already mentioned that C++ is not a true object-oriented programming language but is actually an object-based programming language. Remember that C++ is considered to be object-based because object-oriented concepts are not necessarily enforced. You can write a non-object-oriented C program using a C++ compiler. There is also a class of languages called scripting languages—JavaScript, VBScript, ASP, JSP, PHP, Perl, and Python all fall into this category.

Overall Model
Many technologies are used to create web pages. Programming languages, scripting languages, and markup languages all have a place in the model. Although this book focuses primarily on object-oriented programming languages, it is important to understand that programming languages are just part of the puzzle.

At this point, let's pause briefly to cover a few of the Internet-related topics that form the basis for our discussion on the Web and, by extension, web services. First, let's review the concepts of a client/server model. Figure 13.1 shows a typical client/server model.

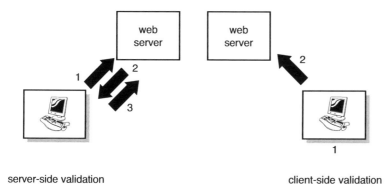

server-side validation   client-side validation

Figure 13.1   The client/server model.

It is important to understand that there are two sides to the client/server story. As the name implies, the two parts of the model are the client side, which in many cases is the browser, and the server side, which is the physical web server. A simple e-commerce example serves as a good study for this discussion.

Suppose you are creating a simple web page that will request the following information from the user:

- Date
- First name
- Last name
- Age

When invoked, the HTML is rendered in the browser, which is considered the client, as shown in Figure 13.2.

This is a very simple HTML document; however, it illustrates the concept of form validation quite well. One of the major issues we must address when developing a client/server system is whether we will do client validation, server validation, or both.

For example, suppose we want to verify that the date entered by the user is valid. We also want the age to be within a valid range—we certainly don't want someone to enter an age of -5. The question is whether to validate on the client side or the server side. Let's explore why this is an important discussion and how it relates to objects.

First, let's address the issue of the Age field. In most business systems, the customer information would be stored in a database that resides with the server. For security reasons, the client is not permitted to access the database directly.

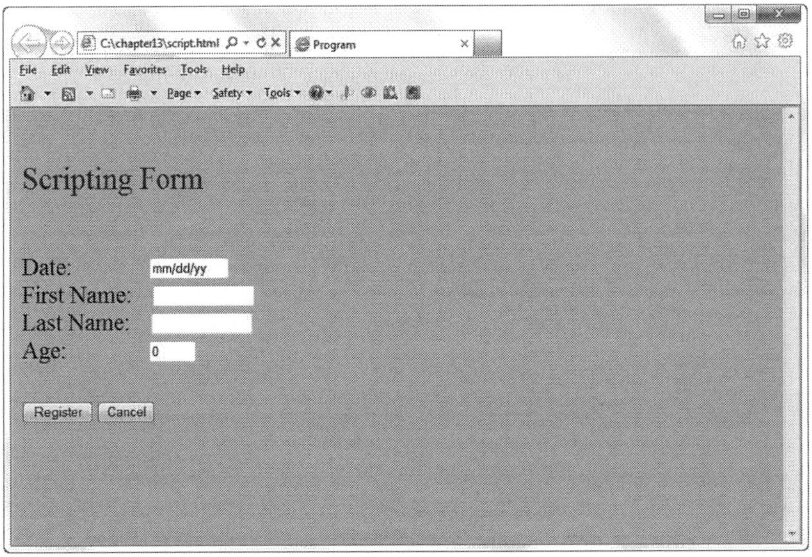

Figure 13.2   Rendering an HTML document.

Client Security

Because anyone can bring up a web browser, it would be very foolish to let the client (browser) access the database directly. Thus, when the client needs to inspect or update the database, it must request the operation from the server. This is a basic security issue.

The reason why this example is so interesting is because it's a perfect example of the interface/implementation paradigm stressed throughout this book. In this case, the client is requesting a service from the server. The software system provides an interface through which the client can literally send messages and request specific services from the server.

In the example relating to the Age field in the HTML document in Figure 13.2, suppose a user named Mary wants to update her age in the database. After bringing up the web page, the user enters the appropriate information on the form (including her age in the Age field) and then clicks the Register button. In the simplest scenario, the information in the form is sent to the server, which then processes the information and updates the database.

How is the information entered in the Date field verified? If no validation is done, the software on the server accesses the Age field in Mary's record and makes the update. If the age that Mary enters is incorrect, the inappropriate age is entered in the database.

If the validation is done on the server, the software on the server checks to make sure that the Age value falls into appropriate ranges. It is also possible that the database itself does some checking to ensure that the age is within proper limits.

However, there is one major limitation to server-side validation—the information must be sent to the server. This might seem counterintuitive, but you can ask this simple question: Why validate something on the server that can be validated on the client?

Redundant Validation

It is important to note that validation should be done on *both* ends for any web applications because there are ways for clients to post results directly to a server without the client validation, or they could shut off the client script and still submit bad values.

Several points address this question:

- Sending things to the server takes more time.
- Sending things to the server increases network traffic.
- Sending things to the server takes up server resources.
- Sending things to the server increases the potential for error.

For these reasons, as well as other possible issues, our goal is to do as much of the validation on the client as possible. This is where the scripting languages come into play.

A JavaScript Validation Example

JavaScript, as are most scripting languages, is considered to be object-based. Just like C++, you can write JavaScript applications that do not comply with object-oriented criteria. However, JavaScript does provide object-oriented capabilities. This is what makes scripting languages, such as JavaScript and ASP .NET, very important in the object-oriented market. You can use objects in a JavaScript application to enhance the capabilities of your web page. In some ways, you can think of these scripting languages as bridges between traditional programming paradigms and object-oriented models. It is important to understand that you can incorporate objects into your web applications, even if you aren't using pure object-oriented technologies.

To understand the power of the scripting languages, we must first understand the limitations of HTML. HTML is a markup language that provides functionality, not inherent programming capabilities. For example, there is no way in HTML to program an IF statement or a loop. Thus, in the early days of HTML, there was little if any way to validate data on the client side. Scripting changed all this.

With the functionality provided by JavaScript and other scripting languages, a web page developer could perform programming logic within the web page. The capability to perform programming logic allows for client-side validation. Let's look at an example of a very simple validation application using HTML and JavaScript. The code for this simple web page is presented as follows:

```
<html>
<head>
```

```
<title>Validation Program</title>
<script type = "text/javascript">
function validateNumber(tForm) {
        if (tForm.result.value != 5 ) {
                this.alert ("not 5!");
        } else {
                this.alert ("Correct. Good Job!");
    }
}
</script>
</head>
<body>
<hr>
<p>
<h1>Validate</h1>
<form name="form">
<input type="text" name="result" value="0" SIZE="2">
<input type="button" value="Validate" name="calcButton"
   onClick="validateNumber(this.form)">
</form>
<hr>
</body>
</html>
```

One of the first things to notice is that the JavaScript is embedded inside the HTML code. This is different from how a programming language is used. Whereas languages like Java and C# exist as independent application entities, on the client side JavaScript is normally considered to "live" within the confines of a browser. However, JavaScript files can exist independently as external code file and libraries (jQuery for example).

Java Versus JavaScript
Although Java and JavaScript are both based on C syntax, they are not directly related.

When presented in the client browser, the web page is very straightforward, as shown in Figure 13.3.

In this application, a user can enter a number in the text box and then click the Validate button. The application then checks to see whether the value is 5. If the entered value is not 5, an alert box will appear to indicate that there was a validation error, as shown in Figure 13.4.

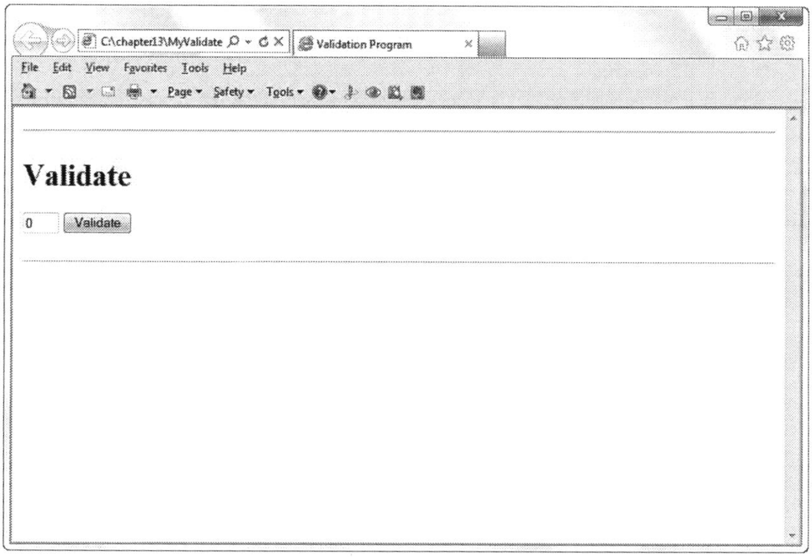

Figure 13.3   JavaScript validation application client.

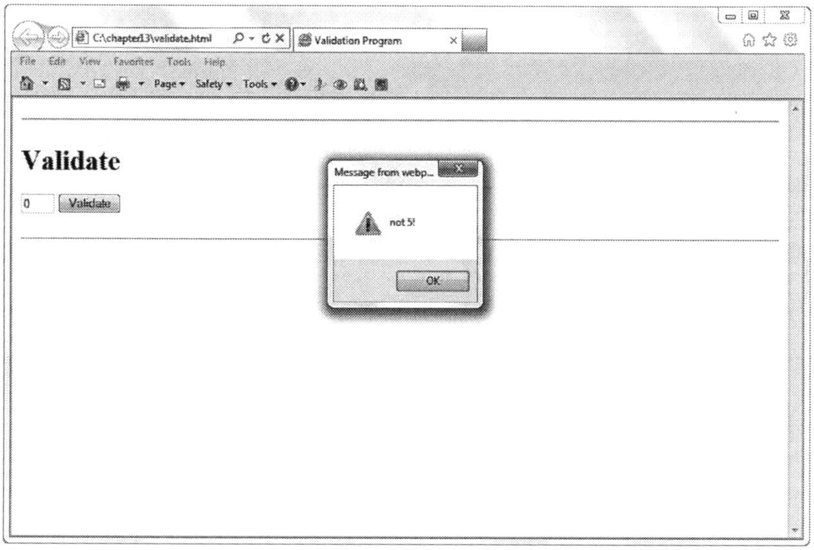

Figure 13.4   JavaScript validation alert box.

If the user enters 5, an alert box indicates that the value was as expected.

The mechanism for performing this validation is based on two separate parts of the JavaScript script:

- The function definitions
- The HTML tags

As with regular programming languages, we can define functions in JavaScript. In this example, we have a single function in the application called validateNumber():

```
<script type = "text/javascript">
function validateNumber(tForm) {
        if (tForm.result.value != 5 ) {
                this.alert ("not 5!");
        } else {
                this.alert ("Correct. Good Job!");
    }
}
</script>
```

> **JavaScript Syntax**
>
> Because we are more concerned with the concepts in this book, you should refer to a JavaScript book for the specifics of the JavaScript syntax.

The function is actually called when the Validate button is clicked. This action is captured in the HTML form definition:

```
<input type="button" value="Validate" name="calcButton"
   onClick="validateNumber(this.form)">
```

When the Validate button is clicked, an object that represents the form is sent via the parameter list to the validateNumber() function.

Objects in a Web Page

There are many ways you can utilize objects within an HTML file for use in a web page. Objects can be implemented via a scripting language, as in the JavaScript validation example in the previous section. External objects can also be included within an HTML file.

There are many examples of these external objects. Some play various media, like music and movies. Others can execute objects created by third-party software such as PowerPoint or Flash.

In this section, we take a look at how objects are embedded within a web page.

JavaScript Objects

Object programming is inherent to the process of the JavaScript example illustrated in the previous section. We can see this by looking at the code within the `validateNumber()` function. Although many names, such as component, widgets, controls, and so on, describe the parts of a user interface, they all relate to the functionality of an object.

You can use several objects to create this web page. Consider the following as objects:

- The text box
- The button
- The form

Each of these has properties and methods. For example, you can change a property of the button, such as the color, as well as change the label on the button. The form can be thought of as an object made up of other objects. As you can see in the following line of code, the notation used mimics the notation used in object-oriented languages (using the period to separate the object from the properties and methods). In the line of code, you can see that the `value` property of the text box object (result) is part of the form object (`tForm`):

```
if (tForm.result.value != 5 )
```

Additionally, the alert box itself is an object. We can check this by using a `this` pointer in the code:

```
this.alert ("Correct. Good Job!");
```

The this Pointer

Remember the `this` pointer refers to the current object, which in this case is the form.

JavaScript supports a specific object hierarchy. Figure 13.5 provides a partial list of this hierarchy.

As with other scripting languages, JavaScript provides a number of built-in objects. For example, we can take a look at the built-in `Date` class. An instance of this class is an object that contains methods such as `getHours()` and `getMinutes()`. You can also create your own customized classes. The following code demonstrates the use of the `Date` object:

```
<html>
<head>
<title>Date Object Example</title>
</head>
<body>
<script language="JavaScript" type = "text/javascript">

    days = new Array ( "Sunday", "Monday", "Tuesday",
                       "Wednesday", "Thursday", "Friday",
```

```
                            "Saturday", "Sunday");

    today=new Date

    document.write("Today is " + days[today.getDay()]);

</script>

</body>
</head>
</html>
```

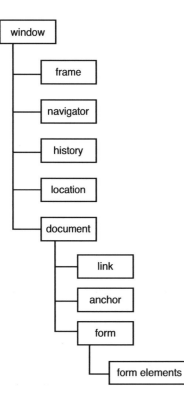

Figure 13.5   JavaScript object tree.

Note that in this example, we create an `Array` object that holds the string values representing the days of the week. We also create an object called `today` that holds the information pertaining to the current date. This web page displays the current day of the week based on the date in your computer's memory.

Web Page Controls

Many types of objects can be embedded directly into an HTML document. Web page controls consist of a wide array of prebuilt objects. To utilize these objects, an `<object>` tag is provided. As an example, we will use a `Slider` control to include in a simple web page. The following HTML code shows how to use this `Slider` control:

```
<html>
<head>
<title>Slider</title>
</head>
<body>

<object classid="clsid:F08DF954-8592-11D1-B16A-00C0F0283628" id="Slider1" width="100"
height="50">
  <param name="BorderStyle" value="1" />
  <param name="MousePointer" value="0" />
  <param name="Enabled" value="1" />
  <param name="Min" value="0" />
  <param name="Max" value="10" />
</object>

</body>
</html>
```

When you open this file in a browser, you'll see the results shown in Figure 13.6.

Note that this is a true object. It has attributes, such as height and width, and behaviors, such as the slider. Some of the attributes are set via the parameters passed from within the `<object>` tag.

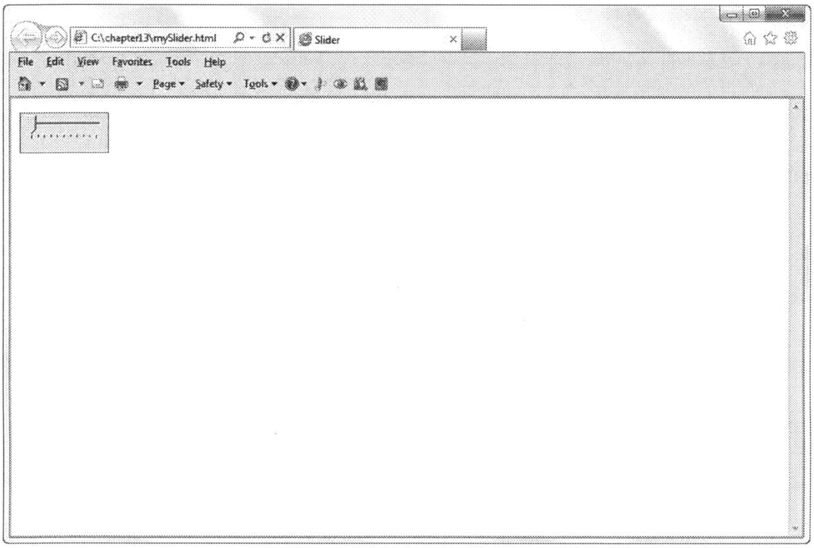

Figure 13.6   Web page control.

Browser Compatibility

As always, be aware that not all objects work with all browsers or on all operating systems. These examples are provided using Internet Explorer 8 on Windows 7.

Sound Players

The `<object>` tag can also be used to embed and launch various sound players from within the browser. In most cases, the player launched depends on the default player loaded by the browser.

For example, the following HTML code loads and plays the sound file specified within the `<object>` tag. In this case, the audio file must be in the appropriate directory—although the file can be accessed over the Internet:

```
<html>
<head>
<title>SoundPlayer</title>
</head>

<body>

<object
classid="clsid:22D6F312-B0F6-11D0-94AB-0080C74C7E95">
<param name="FileName" value="fanfare.wav" />
</object>

</body>
</html>
```

Movie Player

Movie players can be included as well, just as a sound player. The following code plays a movie file (.wmv) from within the `<object>` tag. As with any sound file, the movie file must be in the appropriate directory or Internet location:

```
<html>
<head>
<title>Slider</title>
</head>

<body>
<object
classid="clsid:22D6F312-B0F6-11D0-94AB-0080C74C7E95">
<param name="FileName" value="AspectRatio4x3.wmv" />
</object>

</body>
</html>
```

Flash

As our last example, although there are many more, a Flash object can be embedded in a web document by using the `<object>` tag, as shown in the following HTML code:

```
<html>
<head>
<title>Slider</title>
</head>
<body>

<object width="400" height="40"
classid="clsid:D27CDB6E-AE6D-11cf-96B8-444553540000"
codebase="http://download.macromedia.com
/pub/shockwave/cabs/flash/swflash.cab#4,0,0,0">
<param name="SRC" value="intro.swf">
<embed src="bookmark.swf" width="400" height="40"></embed>
</object>

</body>
</html>
```

Distributed Objects and the Enterprise

A decade or so ago, the term *enterprise computing* became a major part of the information technology lexicon. Today, much of the major development in the area of IT technology is that of enterprise computing. But what does *enterprise computing* mean?

Perhaps the most basic definition of enterprise computing is that it's essentially distributed computing. *Distributed computing* is just what the name implies, a distributed group of computers working together over a network. In this context, a network can be a proprietary network or the Internet.

The power of distributed computing is that computers can share the work. In a truly distributed environment, you do not even need to know what computer is actually servicing your request—in fact, it might be better that you don't know. For example, when you shop online, you connect to a company's web site. All you know is that you are connecting using a URL. However, the company will connect you to whatever physical machine is available.

Why is this desirable? Suppose that a company has a single machine to service all the requests. Then consider what would happen if the machine crashes. Now let's suppose that the company can distribute the online activities over a dozen machines. If one of the machines goes down, the impact will not be as devastating.

Also consider the situation when you download files from a web site. You probably have encountered the situation in which the download site provides you with links to a number of sites, and then asks you to choose the site closest to you. This is a means of distributing the load over the network. Computer networks can balance the load themselves. Figure 13.7 provides a diagram of how a distributed system might look.

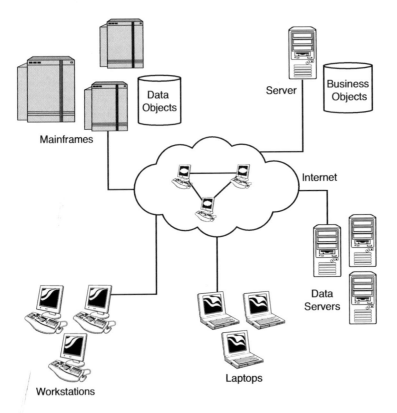

Figure 13.7   Distributed computing.

This book is focused on objects and object-oriented concepts. So in many ways, the entities we are interested in are called distributed objects. That objects are totally self-contained makes them perfect for distributed applications. The thrust of this chapter is this: *If an application (client) requires the service of some object (server), that web service can reside anywhere on the network and doesn't really care what is consuming it.* Let's explore some of the technologies (past and present) that exist for distributed objects.

Remember that many of these technologies are not necessarily considered state-of-the-art but are still in play as legacy systems. For example, CORBA is not nearly as common as it was when the first edition of this book was written in the late 1990s. A shopping cart is now much more likely to be implemented via some sort of web services or maintained directly in the native format of the website rather than use a CORBA interface. SOAP and XML and the

SOA architecture are far more common today; however, a bit of a historical background can be highly instructive to understand how the technologies have evolved.

The Common Object Request Broker Architecture (CORBA)

One of the primary tenets of this book is that objects are totally self-contained units. With this in mind, it doesn't take much imagination to consider sending objects over a network. In fact, we have used objects traveling over a network in many of the examples throughout this book.

The entire premise of the enterprise is built on the concept of distributed objects. Many advantages exist to using distributed objects; perhaps the most interesting is that a system can theoretically invoke objects anywhere on the network. This is a powerful capability and is the backbone for much of today's Internet-based business. Another major advantage is that various pieces of a system can be distributed across multiple machines across a network.

The idea of accessing and invoking objects across a network is a powerful technique. However, there is one obvious fly in the ointment—the recurring problem of portability. Although we can create a proprietary distributed network, the fact that it is proprietary leads to obvious limitations. The other problem is that of programming language. Suppose a system written in Java would like to invoke an object written in C++. In the best of all worlds, we would like to create a nonproprietary, language-independent framework for objects in a distributed environment. This is where CORBA made a major contribution to the development community as the Internet was first becoming a major force in the marketplace in the mid 1990s.

The main premise of CORBA is this: Using a standard protocol, CORBA allows programs from different vendors to communicate with each other. This interoperability covers hardware and software. Thus, vendors can write applications on various hardware platforms and operating systems using a variety of programming languages, operating over different vendor networks.

CORBA, and similar technologies like DCOM, can be considered the middleware for a variety of computer software applications. Whereas CORBA represents only one type of middleware (later we will see some other implementations, like Java's RMI), the concepts behind middleware are consistent, regardless of the approach taken. Basically, *middleware* provides services that allow application processes to interact with each other over a network. These systems are often referred to as *multi-tiered systems*. For example, a three-tiered system is presented in Figure 13.8. In this case, the presentation layer is separated from the data layer by the allocation layer in the middle (middleware is often associated with object-relational mapping systems). These processes can be running on one or more machines. This is where the term *distributed* comes into play. The processes (or as far as this book is concerned, the objects) are distributed across a network. This network can be proprietary, or it might be the Internet.

This is where objects fit into the picture. The OMG states: "CORBA applications are composed of *objects*." So, as you can tell, objects are a major part of the world of distributed computing. The OMG goes on to say that these objects "are individual units of running software that combine functionality and data, and that frequently (but not always) represent something in the real world."

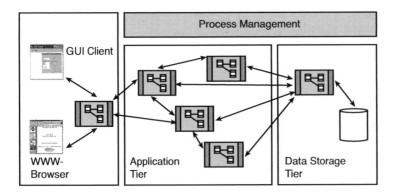

Figure 13.8   A three-tiered system.

One of the most obvious examples of such a system is that of a shopping cart. We can relate this shopping cart example to our earlier discussions on the instantiation of objects. When you visit an e-commerce site to purchase merchandise, you are assigned your own individual shopping cart. Thus, each customer has a unique shopping cart. In this case, each customer will have an object, which includes all the attributes and behaviors of a shopping cart object.

Although each customer object has the same attributes and behaviors, each customer will have different attribute assignments, such as name, address, and so on. This shopping cart object can then be sent anywhere across the network. Other objects in the system represent merchandise, warehouses, and so on.

Wrappers

As we explained earlier in the book, one common use of objects is that of a *wrapper*. Today there are a lot of applications written on legacy systems. In many cases, changing these legacy applications is either impractical or not cost-effective. One elegant way to connect legacy applications to newer distributed systems is to create an object wrapper that interfaces with the legacy system.

One of the benefits of using CORBA to implement a system such as our shopping cart application is that the objects can be accessed by services written in different languages. To accomplish this task, CORBA defines an interface to which all languages must conform. The CORBA concept of an interface fits in well with the discussion we had about creating contracts in Chapter 8, "Frameworks and Reuse: Designing with Interfaces and Abstract Classes." The CORBA interface is called the *Interface Definition Language (IDL)*. For CORBA to work, both sides of the wire, the client and server, must adhere to the contract as stated in the IDL.

Yet another term we covered earlier in the book is used in this discussion—marshaling. Remember that marshaling is the act of taking an object, decomposing it into a format that can be sent over a network, and then reconstituting it at the other end. Thus, by having both the client and the server conform to the IDL, an object can be marshaled across a network regardless of the programming language used.

All the objects that move around in a CORBA system are routed by an application called an Object Request Broker (ORB). You might have already noticed that the acronym ORB is actually part of the acronym CORBA. The ORB is what makes everything go in a CORBA application. The ORB takes care of routing requests from clients to objects, as well as getting the response back to the appropriate destination.

Again, we can see how CORBA and distributed computing works hand-in-hand with the concepts we have studied throughout this book. The OMG states that

> This separation of interface from implementation, enabled by OMG IDL, is the essence of CORBA.

Furthermore,

> Clients access objects only through their advertised interface, invoking only those operations that the object exposes through its IDL interface, with only those parameters (input and output) that are included in the invocation.

To get a flavor of what the IDL looks like, consider the e-business example we used in Chapter 8. In this case, let's revisit the UML diagram of Figure 8.7 and create a subset of the Shop class. If we decide to create an interface of Inventory, we could create something like the following:

```
interface Inventory {
    string[]  getInventory ();
    string[]  buyInventory (in string product);
}
```

In this case, we have an interface that defines how to list and purchase inventory. This interface is then compiled into two entities:

- Stubs that act as the connection between the client and the ORB
- A skeleton that acts as the connection between the ORB and the object

These IDL stubs and skeletons form the contract that all interacting parties must follow. Figure 13.9 shows an illustration of how the various CORBA parts interact.

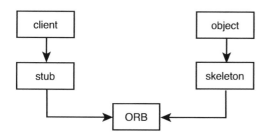

Figure 13.9   CORBA parts.

The really interesting thing about all this is that when a client wants the service of some object, it does not need to know anything about the object it is requesting, including where it resides. The client simply invokes the object (and the service) it wants. To the client, it appears that this invocation is local, as though it's invoking an object that's on the local system. This invocation is passed through the ORB. If the ORB determines that the desired object is a remote object, the ORB routes the request. If everything works properly, the client will not know where the actual object servicing it resides. Figure 13.10 shows how the ORB routing works over a network.

Internet Inter-ORB Protocol

Just as HTTP is the protocol for web page transactions, Internet Inter-ORB Protocol (IIOP) is a protocol for distributed objects that can be written in a variety of programming languages. IIOP is a fundamental piece of standards like CORBA and Java RMI.

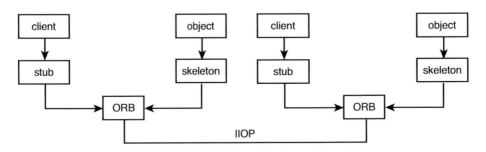

Figure 13.10   ORB routing.

In this section, we have covered some of the original, and fundamental, topics of distributed computing as developed by pioneering technologies such as CORBA, DCOM, and RMI. In the next sections, we continue the discussion with more recent implementations—web services such as SOAP and XML and the SOA architecture are far more common today.

Web Services Definition

Web services have evolved quickly over the past several years. In fact, when the first edition of this book was published, much of the current technology was in its infancy. At this point in time, we will use the W3C general definition of a web service as a "client and a server that communicate using XML messages using the SOAP (Simple Object Access Protocol) standard."

SOAP is a communication protocol used for sending messages over the Internet. SOAP is theoretically platform and language independent and is based on XML. SOAP communicates between applications using the HTTP protocol, because it is common for user client applications to utilize browsers. SOAP extends the functionality of HTTP to provide more functional web services.

Since early on in the evolution of distributed computing, remote procedure calls (RPC) have been a part of the equation. The primary motivation for SOAP is to perform remote procedure calls over HTTP using XML. With all these brief descriptions out of the way, we can describe SOAP in a nutshell: *SOAP is XML-based and is a protocol for distributed applications.*

RPC

Remote procedure calls (RPC) are a communication process that allows the invocation of (*object*) services from another computer on a shared network. When the systems are indeed object-oriented, RPC can also be called remote method invocation (RMI). The method call is seamless in the sense that the developer never knows (or doesn't need to know) whether the service is local or remote. Thus, the actual method call speciation is often a signature that hides the implementation details from the developer. RPC strategies are also often proprietary.

The major drawback with technologies such as CORBA and DCOM is that they are basically proprietary and have their own binary formats. SOAP is text-based, being written in XML, and is considered much simpler to use when compared to CORBA and DCOM. This is similar to the advantages outlined in the section "Using XML in the Serialization Process" of Chapter 12, "Persistent Objects: Serialization, Marshaling, and Relational Databases."

In effect, to work as seamlessly as possible, CORBA and DCOM systems must communicate with similar systems. This is a significant limitation in the current technological environment, because you don't really know what is on the other side of the wire. Therefore, perhaps the biggest advantage that SOAP has going for it is that it has most of the major software companies on board with its standard.

As described over and over in this book, one of the major advantages of object technology is that of wrappers. SOAP can be thought of as a wrapper that, although not an exact replacement for technologies like DCOM, Enterprise JavaBeans, or CORBA, it does "wrap" them for more efficient use over the Internet. This "wrapping" capability allows companies to standardize their own network communications, even though there may be disparate technologies within the company itself.

Whatever the description of SOAP, it is important to note that, as basic HTML, SOAP is a stateless, one-way messaging system. Because of this and other features, SOAP is not a total replacement for technologies like DCOM, Enterprise JavaBeans, CORBA, or RMI—it is a complementary technology.

In keeping with the theme of this book, the following SOAP example focuses on object concepts and not any specific SOAP technology, coding or otherwise.

SOAP

The example presented in this chapter shows the flow of objects through a distributed system. A complete sample application is available electronically on the publisher's web site but is much too large to fit in the pages of this book.

For this example, let's create a Warehouse application. This application utilizes a browser as the client, which then uses a set of web services to transact business with a Warehouse system that resides somewhere on the network.

We use the following model for our SOAP example. Figure 13.11 provides a visual diagram of the system.

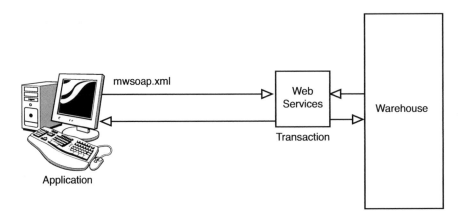

Figure 13.11   SOAP example.

The file mwsoap.xml is the XML description of the structure of the various transactions handled by the web services. This description of Invoice.xsd is shown in the following code:

```
<?xml version="1.0" encoding="utf-8"?>
<xs:schema targetNamespace="http://ootp.org/invoice.xsd"
elementFormDefault="qualified" xmlns="http://ootp.org/invoice.xsd"
xmlns:mstns="http://ootp.org/invoice.xsd" xmlns:xs="http://www.w3.org/2001/XMLSchema">
  <xs:element name="Invoice">
    <xs:complexType>
      <xs:sequence>
        <xs:element name="Address" minOccurs="1">
          <xs:complexType>
            <xs:sequence />
            <xs:attribute name="Street" type="xs:string" />
            <xs:attribute name="City" type="xs:string" />
            <xs:attribute name="State" type="xs:string" />
            <xs:attribute name="Zip" type="xs:int" />
            <xs:attribute name="Country" type="xs:string" />
          </xs:complexType>
        </xs:element>
        <xs:element name="Package">
          <xs:complexType>
            <xs:sequence />
```

```
            <xs:attribute name="Description" type="xs:string" />
            <xs:attribute name="Weight" type="xs:short" />
            <xs:attribute name="Priority" type="xs:boolean" />
            <xs:attribute name="Insured" type="xs:boolean" />
          </xs:complexType>
        </xs:element>
      </xs:sequence>
      <xs:attribute name="name" type="xs:string" />
    </xs:complexType>
  </xs:element>
</xs:schema>
```

The `Invoice.xsd` file describes how an *invoice* is structured and how applications must conform to its definitions. This file is, in effect, a schema in the same way that a schema is used in a database system. Note that, per this `Invoice.xsd` file, an invoice is composed of an `Address` and `Package`. Further, the `Address` and `Package` are built of attributes such as `Description`, `Weight`, and so on. Finally, these attributes are declared as specific data types, such as `string`, `short`, and so on. Figure 13.12 shows graphically what this relationship looks like.

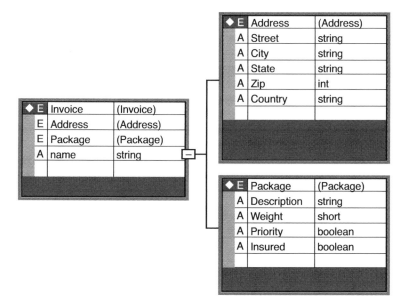

Figure 13.12   Invoice.xsx (visual representation of schema).

In this example, whereas the `Invoice.xsd` file describes *how* the data is structured, the `mwsoap.xml` file represents *what* the data is. An application, written in a language like C# .NET, VB .NET, ASP.NET, or Java, uses the `Invoice.xsd` file to construct valid XML files that are then sent to other applications over the network. These applications would use the same Invoice.xsd file to deconstruct the mwsoap.xml file for its use. In many ways, you can think of the Invoice. xsd file as a sort of *contract*, in a similar way to the concept of a contract covered in Chapter 8.

The following is the mwsoap.xml file that contains specific data embedded in its SOAP/XML format:

```xml
<?xml version="1.0" encoding="utf-8"?>
<soap:envelope xmlns:soap="http://www.w3.org/2001/06/soap-envelope">
  <soap:Header>
    <mySOAPHeader:transaction xmlns:mySOAPHeader="soap-transaction"
soap:mustUnderstand="true">
      <headerId>8675309</headerId>
    </mySOAPHeader:transaction>
  </soap:Header>
  <soap:Body>
    <mySOAPBody xmlns="http://ootp.org/Invoice.xsd">
      <invoice name="Jenny Smith">
        <address street="475 Oak Lane"
                 city="Somewheresville"
                 state="Nebraska"
                 zip="23654"
                 country="USA"/>
        <package description="22 inch Plasma Monitor"
                 weight="22"
                 priority="false"
                 insured="true" />
      </invoice>
    </mySOAPBody>
  </soap:Body>
</soap:envelope>
```

Web Services Code

The only piece of the model left to cover is the code applications themselves. The three classes that correspond to the Invoice, Address, and Package are presented in the following in C# .NET.

It is important to note that the applications can be of any language. This is the beauty of the SOAP/XML approach. Each application must be able to parse the XML file—and that is basically the only requirement, as shown in Figure 13.13. How an application uses the data extracted is totally up to the application.

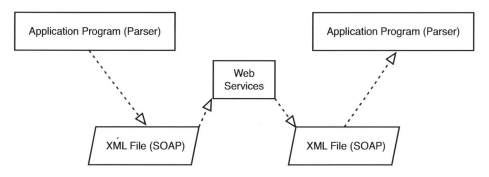

Figure 13.13   Parsing the SOAP/XML file.

As a result of this approach, the specific language, or platform for that matter, is irrelevant. Theoretically, any language can perform a parsing operation, and that is basically what is needed in this SOAP/XML approach.

As developers, it is helpful to take a look at the code directly. In the following sections, the C# .NET code is presented to help illustrate how the system described in Figure 13.12 is implemented. The corresponding VB .NET code is available electronically from the publisher's web site.

Invoice.cs

The following code is the C# .NET implementation of the Invoice class that is represented in Figure 13.12:

```
using System;
using System.Data;
using System.Configuration;
using System.Xml;
using System.Xml.Serialization;
namespace WebServices
{
    [XmlRoot("invoice")]
    public class Invoice
    {
        public Invoice(String name, Address address, ShippingPackage package)
        {
            this.Name = name;
            this.Address = address;
            this.Package = package;
        }

        private String strName;
        [XmlAttribute("name")]
```

```
        public String Name
        {
            get { return strName; }
            set { strName = value; }
        }

        private Address objAddress;
        [XmlElement("address")]
        public Address Address
        {
            get { return objAddress; }
            set { objAddress = value; }
        }

        private ShippingPackage objPackage;
        [XmlElement("package")]
        public ShippingPackage Package
        {
            get { return objPackage; }
            set { objPackage = value; }
        }
    }
}
```

Representational State Transfer (ReST)

Since the days of the first computer program, developers have constantly walked a fine line between complex and simple architectures. It is the nature of developers to want simply, direct approaches, whereas many business managers prefer structured, more established practices. We can see this is the use of programming languages like Java and .NET versus languages such as Perl and PHP, between XML and JSON, and so on. Web services are also a part of this discussion. Many developers consider technologies such as CORBA, RPC, and SOAP to be fairly complex. Thus, a more "simple: approach, called Representational State Transfer, or ReST, is becoming quite popular.

For example, a SOAP implementation may require various tools (and even have trouble communicating with previous SOAP standards), whereas ReST requires only HTTP support and can function with various technologies, including SOAP.

ReST is a stateless protocol that basically relies on HTTP. Because HTTP is the foundation of the Internet itself, in many ways it can be said that the Internet's architecture is based on ReST, often called RESTful architectures.

The fundamental feature of ReST is that it uses HTTP requests to create, update, read, and delete data. As a result, ReST can be utilized in place of other technologies, such as RPC, or web services, like SOAP, because it provides all the necessary underlying functionality. In short, ReST is a lightweight approach to web services; however, it is not in any way a standard in the way that XML is (one description of ReST calls it a "style"). Figure 13.14 illustrates the flow of data that is typical of the HTTP requests/responses in a RESTful implementation.

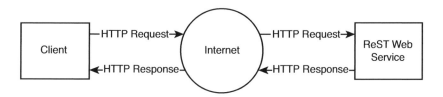

Figure 13.14   RESTful web services.

In fact, although other strategies, such as SOAP, may be considered to be more sophisticated in what they may deliver, a RESTful application will pretty much return either simple text or an XML file. What is delivered is up to the developer. Whereas SOAP is intimately tied to XML, ReST is not. Likewise, ReST requests are primarily simple text parameters and rarely deliver anything more complex. Another point of interest regarding ReST is that it is not inherently object-oriented because it does not really deliver objects, even though objects can be created by parsers by an application.

Conclusion

In this chapter, we have covered some of the technology available for using objects in conjunction with web applications. It is important to differentiate between objects embedded in a web page (such as JavaScript) and objects used in a distributed system and how they relate to each other.

Distributed objects have evolved quickly over the past several years. Now many options exist in the distributed object market; however, the combination of SOAP and XML has made the design of distributed systems much more standard.

References

- Savitch, Walter. 2008. *Absolute Java,* 3rd ed. Boston MA: Addison-Wesley.

- Walther, Stephen. 2008. *ASP.NET 3.5 Unleashed.* Indianapolis, IN: Sams Publishing.

- Skeet, Jon. 2008. *C# in Depth: What You Need to Master C# 2 and 3.* Greenwich, CT: Manning.

- Deitel, et al. 2003. *C# for Experienced Programmers.* Upper Saddle River, NJ: Prentice Hall.

- Deitel, et al. 2003. *Visual Basic .NET for Experienced Programmers.* Upper Saddle River, NJ: Prentice Hall.

- Conallen, Jim. 2000. *Building Web Applications with UML.* Boston, MA: Addison-Wesley.

- Jaworski, Jamie. 1999. *Java 2 Platform Unleashed.* Indianapolis, IN: Sams Publishing.

14

Objects and Client/Server Applications

Chapter 13, "Objects in Web Services, Mobile Apps, and Hybrids," covered the concept of distributed objects as they relate to web services. In that chapter, the Internet was the primary *highway* that the objects navigated. In this chapter, we narrow the scope a bit and explore the topic of sending objects across a client/server network.

Many of the concepts in this chapter tie in well to those of Chapter 13 (because they both involve moving data over a network). I find it very helpful to delve directly into the inner workings of the client/server model, if only for the educational experience of developing a working implementation. In short, in this chapter, we will write a functionally complete client/server application.

Although setting up a small, educational model of a web service is a bit more complicated, we can accomplish the task of creating a small, educational example of a client/server application on a single machine. Although objects in a distributed network do not necessarily follow a specific path, an object on a client/server journey is more of a point-to-point journey—at least in a conceptual sense.

Client/Server Approaches

As we have seen in several of the previous chapters, XML has had a major impact on the development technologies used today. For example, a distributed object model can either be built on a proprietary system or use a nonproprietary approach based on technologies like SOAP/XML.

The same can be said of a client/server model. An application can be built solely on a proprietary system or on a design using an XML. In this chapter, both models are covered. We use Java to describe a proprietary approach that will execute only in a Java environment, even though Java can be used in a nonproprietary solution as well. Then, C# .NET will be used to illustrate the XML-based approach.

Proprietary Approach

In this example, Java is used to illustrate how a direct point-to-point connection is made over a network. To accomplish this, I use an example that I have been using as a teaching technique for many years—sending an object from a client to a server and then printing some of the information contained in the object.

This basic flow of this approach is illustrated in Figure 14.1.

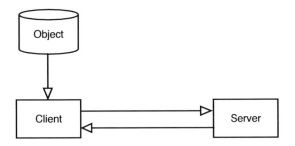

Figure 14.1   Basic client/server flow.

In this design, the client creates an object and then sends it to the server. The server creates a reference to the object to access it. The server then may update the object's attributes and send it back to the client.

Serialized Object Code

We start by creating a simple `TextMessage` class that contains attributes called `name` and `message`. The class also contains a constructor as well as getters and setters. The complete `TextMessage` class is presented in the following code:

```java
import java.io.*;
import java.util.*;

public class TextMessage implements Serializable {

        public String name;
        public String message;

          // TextMessage 's Constructor.
        TextMessage(String n) {
                message = " ";
                name= n;
        }

          // Objects 'getter' function.
```

```
        public String getName() {
                return name;
        }

          // Objects 'getter' function.
        public String getTextMessage() {
                return message;
        }

         // Objects 'setter' function.
        public void setTextMessage(String inTextMessage) {
                message = inTextMessage;
        }
}
```

This is a pretty simple class. The constructor initializes the name attribute via a parameter and sets the message to blanks. The primary item to notice is that the class is serialized in a proprietary Java binary format.

Client Code

The client code uses the TextMessage class to create an object and start it on a journey to the server and back. The client must perform the following tasks:

- Get the user information.
- Create an object.
- Set the attributes.
- Create a socket connection.
- Create the output streams.
- Write the object.
- Close the streams.

The code for this client is presented in the following code. The comments provide most of the code commentary:

```
import java.io.*;
import java.net.*;

/*
 * The Client for TextMessage
 */
public class Client {

    public static void main(String[] arg) {
```

```java
      try {

        String message = " ";
        String name = " ";

        System.out.print("Please enter name: ");
        name = getString();

        // Create a TextMessage object
        TextMessage myTextMessage = new TextMessage(name);

        System.out.print("message: ");

        message = getString();

        // Use the 'setter' to set the TextMessage
        myTextMessage.setTextMessage(message);

        // Create a socket connection
        Socket socketToServer = new Socket("127.0.0.1", 11111);

        // Create the ObjectOutputStream
           ObjectOutputStream myOutputStream = new
              ObjectOutputStream(socketToServer.getOutputStream());

        // Write the myTextMessage object to the OutputStream
        myOutputStream.writeObject(myTextMessage);

        // Close the streams
        myOutputStream.close();

     } catch (Exception e) {System.out.println(e);}
    }

   public static String getString() throws Exception {

        // open keyboard for input (call it 'stdin')
        BufferedReader stdin =
           new BufferedReader(new InputStreamReader(System.in), 1);

        String s1 = stdin.readLine();

        return (s1);


     }
 }
```

The most important points to make about this client code revolve around the network connections. In this example, the following line of code defines where the client will connect to the server:

```
Socket socketToServer = new Socket("127.0.0.1", 11111);
```

When the socket is created, the two parameters passed represent the IP address and the virtual socket the client attempts to connect to.

The IP address 127.0.0.1 is a *loop-back*, meaning that the client attempts to connect to a server that is local. In short, the client and server are running on the same machine. The only obvious condition is that server must be launched first.

Using this *loop-back* IP address is very useful when testing applications. Instead of requiring a connection to a network, the underlying logic of an application can be tested locally—which makes the initial testing much simpler. Later, more general testing can be performed with a *real* IP address.

Besides the IP address, the virtual port must be specified in the parameter list. In this case an arbitrary value of 11111 is chosen. The only condition with this value is that the server that the client attempts to connect to must be listening at this port.

After the client establishes valid communication with the server, and the object is sent and retrieved, the client application terminates.

The only other issue of note in this code is the method at the end of the class that performs the task of retrieving a line from the keyboard. This is the user input, akin to typing in a text message on your cell phone.

Server Code

On the other side of the wire, the server code performs the following tasks:

- Create an object reference.
- Listen to the virtual port 11111.
- Wait for a client to connect.
- Create the Input/Output streams.
- Read the TextMessage object.
- Print the message.

The code for the server is listed here:

```
import java.io.*;
import java.net.*;

/*
 * The Server for TextMessage.
 */
```

```
public class Server {

    public static void main(String[] arg) {

        // create a reference for an object to come from the client.
        TextMessage myTextMessage = null;

        try {

            // Start the Server listening to port 11111
            ServerSocket myServerSocket = new ServerSocket(11111);

            System.out.println("Ready\n");

            // Wait here until a Client attempts to connect
            Socket incoming = myServerSocket.accept();

            // Create an ObjectInputStream
            ObjectInputStream myInputStream = new
                ObjectInputStream(incoming.getInputStream());

            // Read the object from the socket that has the client
            myTextMessage = (TextMessage)myInputStream.readObject();

            System.out.println(myTextMessage.getName() + " : "
                + myTextMessage.getTextMessage()+ "\n");

            // Close the streams
            myInputStream.close();

        } catch(Exception e) {
            System.out.println(e);
        }
    }
}
```

Just as with the client, there is no loop in the code. It is fairly simple to use a loop so that the server can continuously *listen* to the port—but this functionality is not central to the topic here.

It is also possible for the server to update the project and send it back to the client. For example, the client could also create an input stream and read the object back from the server—just as the server can create an output stream and send the object back to the client.

Running the Proprietary Client/Server Example

To simplify matters, the client/server example is run using a basic Command Prompt so we don't have to create a GUI or run it from an Integrated Development Environment (IDE). In the next section, we create modules that will run from within a GUI and an IDE.

The first step in the process is to launch the server. Then, from a second Command Prompt, the client is launched. The server prints out a message indicating that it is ready—and it waits. After launching, the client requests a name and a message that the user must type in.

After the client information is entered and sent, the server displays the message received from the client. Figure 14.2 shows the server session, and Figure 14.3 shows the client session. Again, both the server and the client can contain loops that will allow more than one pass. This example was kept as simple as possible to illustrate the technology.

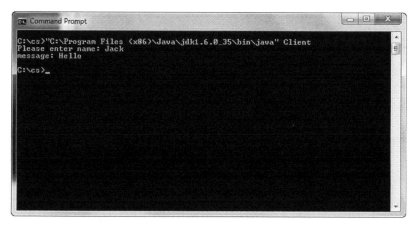

Figure 14.2   Running the server.

The simple user interface of the client requests the name of the user as well as the message that the user wants to send. In a real-world text messaging system, like a cell phone, the server would use the address entered by the user (basically the telephone number) to forward the message to a second user, not simply print it out.

Figure 14.3   Running the client.

> ### Batch Files
>
> To assist in the testing of these types of simple, but functional, educational examples, I like to create an old-fashioned batch file to make the process of using the Java class paths more precise. Not only does it alleviate the need to continuously type in the long and complicated command at the prompt, but it allows you to test for several different versions of Java that may be on the same machine. And this technique works well with many other testing methodologies. For example, you can launch the server by placing the following code in batch file called `server.bat` and then typing `server` at the command prompt:
>
> ```
> "C:\Program Files (x86)\Java\jdk1.6.0_35\bin\java" Server
> ```
>
> This approach works for compiling, as well:
>
> ```
> "C:\Program Files (x86)\Java\jdk1.6.0_35\bin\javac" Client.java
> "C:\Program Files (x86)\Java\jdk1.6.0_35\bin\javac" Server.java
> ```

Nonproprietary Approach

The previous example was handled in a proprietary manner. To create a nonproprietary approach, we can utilize XML technology just like we did with data persistence and distributed object.

Using the XML approach allows us to send the objects back and forth between applications written in various languages and, theoretically, between various platforms. The model can be updated to reflect this, as shown in Figure 14.4.

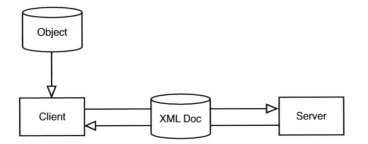

Figure 14.4   XML approach to client/server communication.

Although many of the underlying concepts are the same, the fundamental way that the object is decomposed and reconstituted shifts from a proprietary, binary format to a nonproprietary text-based XML format.

To provide some variety, we use an example based on a `CheckingAccount` class.

Object Definition Code

When creating an XML version of the CheckingAccount class, we can immediately see, by inspecting the code, that the XML definition of the object is embedded directly in the class itself. (See Chapter 11, "Objects and Portable Data: XML and JSON," for a description of this approach.) The C# .NET code for the CheckingAccount class is presented in the following code:

```csharp
using System;
using System.Collections;
using System.IO;
using System.Xml;
using System.Xml.Serialization;

namespace Server
{
    [XmlRoot("account")]
    public class CheckingAccount
    {
        private String _Name;
        private int _AccountNumber;

        [XmlElement("name")]
        public String Name
        {
            get { return _Name; }
            set { _Name = value; }
        }

        [XmlElement("account_num")]
        public int AccountNumber
        {
            get { return _AccountNumber; }
            set { _AccountNumber = value; }
        }

        public CheckingAccount()
        {
            _Name = "John Doe";
            _AccountNumber = 54321;
            Console.WriteLine("Creating Checking Account!");
        }

    }
}
```

Again, the really interesting issue with this class definition is that, although the class contains the requisite attributes and methods, the attributes also contain properties that correspond to the XML definitions of the attributes.

In short, in .NET examples (C# and VB), the class is created around the XML definitions. This approach can be accomplished with Java as well. In fact, by using the XML approach, we can use whatever language or platform we want interchangeably. That is the beauty of the nonproprietary approach.

Also note that for these C# .NET examples, we create a namespace for our projects.

Client Code

For this example, the client performs the following tasks:

- Create the checkingAccount object.
- Create the socket.
- Serialize the object to XML.
- Create the stream.
- Serialize the object to the stream.
- Close the resources.
- Close the streams.

In most case, the comments can provide the explanation of the program flow. The C# .NET client code is presented here:

```
using System;
using System.Collections;
using System.IO;
using System.Xml;
using System.Xml.Serialization;
using System.Net.Sockets;
using System.Net;
using System.Text;

namespace Client
{
    class Client
    {
        public static void Connect()
        {
            CheckingAccount myAccount = new CheckingAccount();
            try
            {
                //Create our TCP Socket
```

```
            TcpClient client = new TcpClient("127.0.0.1", 11111);

            //Prepare to serialize our CheckingAccount object to XML
            XmlSerializer myXmlFactory =
                new XmlSerializer(typeof(CheckingAccount));

            //Create our TCP Stream
            NetworkStream stream = client.GetStream();

            // Serialize our object to the TCP Stream
            myXmlFactory.Serialize(stream, myAccount);

            // Close all of our resources
            stream.Close();
            client.Close();
        }
        catch (Exception ex)
        {
            Console.WriteLine("Exception: {0}", ex);
        }

        Console.WriteLine("Press any key to continue...");
        Console.ReadKey();
    }
  }
}
```

Server Code

In this case we use a loop (in fact, a couple of loops) to implement this version of the server. Again, we can let the code comments provide the flow; however, the server provides the following functions:

- Create the checkingAccount object references.
- Connect to the socket and listen.
- Setup the input stream.
- Create the stream.
- Read the bytes off the stream.
- Serialize the object to the stream.
- Close everything down.

The C# .NET code for the server is listed here:

```csharp
using System;
using System.Collections.Generic;
using System.Text;
using System.Net.Sockets;
using System.Net;
using System.Xml;
using System.Xml.Serialization;
using System.IO;
using System.Runtime.Serialization;

namespace Server
{
    class Server
    {
        public Server()
        {
            TcpListener server = null;
            TcpClient client = null;
            try
            {
                //Create our Socket Listener and start it
                server = new TcpListener(IPAddress.Parse("127.0.0.1"),
                        11111);
                server.Start();

                //Setup our input buffer
                Byte[] bytes = new Byte[256];

                //Loop indefinitely
                while (true)
                {
                    //Begin accepting incoming transmissions in block mode
                    client = server.AcceptTcpClient();
                    Console.WriteLine("Connected!");

                    //Open our stream
                    NetworkStream stream = client.GetStream();

                    //Read all the data from the stream
                    int i;
                    while ((i = stream.Read(bytes, 0, bytes.Length)) != 0)
                    {
                        //Prepare a format that the Serializer can read
                        MemoryStream ms = new MemoryStream(bytes);
                        //Prepare the Serializer
```

```
                    XmlSerializer myXmlFactory =
                        new XmlSerializer(typeof(CheckingAccount));
                    //Create our CheckingAccount from the stream
                    myRestoredAccount =
                        (CheckingAccount)myXmlFactory.Deserialize(ms);
                    //Now demonstrate that the object is indeed created
                    Console.WriteLine("Name: {0}, Account Number: {1}.",
                        myRestoredAccount.Name,
                        myRestoredAccount.AccountNumber);
                    //Throw an exception to exit the loop
                    throw new Exception("ignore");
                }
            }
        }
        catch (Exception ex)
        {
            if (!ex.Message.Equals("ignore"))
                    { Console.WriteLine("Exception: {0}", ex); }
        }
        finally
        {
            //Close our resources
            client.Close();
            server.Stop();
        }
        Console.WriteLine("Press any key to continue...");
        Console.ReadKey();
    }
}
}
```

Running the Nonproprietary Client/Server Example

To execute this example, you can create a project with Visual Studio and launch the C#. NET
code with a simple application, like this:

```
using System;
using System.Collections.Generic;
using System.Text;
using System.Threading;

namespace Server
{
    class Program
    {
        static void Main(string[] args)
        {
```

```
            Server server = new Server();
        }
    }
}
```

Conclusion

In this chapter, we covered the concept of a client/server connection. We took two distinct approaches. First, we used Java to create a proprietary, binary system to move the object along the network connection. The second approach was nonproprietary, using .NET (both C# and VB). Java could also be used in this nonproprietary, XML-based scenario.

The importance of this chapter, as well as Chapter 11 and Chapter 13, is that, along with proprietary solutions, an open standard such as XML can be used to move the objects across various networks, whether a point-to-point network or a distributed network.

References

- Savitch, Walter. 2008. *Absolute Java,* 3rd ed. Boston, MA: Addison-Wesley.

- Walther, Stephen. 2008. *ASP.NET 3.5 Unleashed.* Indianapolis, IN: Sams Publishing.

- Skeet, Jon. 2008. *C# in Depth: What You Need to Master C# 2 and 3.* Greenwich, CT: Manning.

- Deitel, et al. 2003. *C# for Experienced Programmers.* Upper Saddle River, NJ: Prentice Hall.

- Deitel, et al. 2003. *Visual Basic .NET for Experienced Programmers.* Upper Saddle River, NJ: Prentice Hall.

- Jaworski, Jamie. 1999. *Java 2 Platform Unleashed.* Indianapolis, IN: Sams Publishing.

- Flanagan, David, et al. 1999. *Java Enterprise in a Nutshell.* Sebastopol, CA: O'Reilly.

- Farley, Jim. 1998. *Java Distributed Computing.* Sebastopol, CA: O'Reilly.

- Oracle: http://www.oracle.com/technetwork/java/index.html

Example Code Used in This Chapter

The code in this chapter was presented in Java and C# .NET. Code for other languages is available electronically on the publisher's website.

15

Design Patterns

One of the interesting things about software development is that when you create a software system, you are actually modeling a real-world system. For example, in the Information Technology industry, it is safe to say that IT *is* the business—or at least IT *implements* the business. To write the business software systems, the developers must thoroughly understand the business models. As a result, the developers often have the most intimate knowledge of a company's business processes.

We have seen this concept throughout this book as it relates to our educational discussions. For example, when we discussed using inheritance to abstract out the behaviors and attributes of mammals, the model was based on the true real-life model, not a contrived model that we created for our own purposes.

Thus, when we create a mammal class, we can use it to build countless other classes, such as dogs and cats and so on, because all mammals share certain behaviors and attributes. This works when we study dogs, cats, squirrels, and other mammals because we can see patterns. These patterns allow us to inspect an animal and make the determination that it is indeed a mammal, or perhaps a reptile, which would have other patterns of behaviors and attributes.

Throughout history, humans have used patterns in many aspects of life, including engineering. These patterns go hand-in-hand with the holy grail of software development: software reuse. In this chapter, we consider design patterns, a relatively new area of software development (the seminal book on design patterns was published in 1995).

Design patterns are perhaps one of the most influential developments that have come out of the object-oriented movement in the past several years. Patterns lend themselves perfectly to the concept of reusable software development. Because object-oriented development is all about reuse, patterns and object-oriented development go hand-in-hand.

The basic concept of design patterns revolves around the principle of best practices. By *best practices*, we mean that when good and efficient solutions are created, these solutions are documented in a way that others can benefit from previous successes—as well as learn from the failures.

One of the most important books on object-oriented software development is *Design Patterns: Elements of Reusable Object-Oriented Software* by Erich Gamma, Richard Helm, Ralph Johnson, and John Vlissides. This book was an important milestone for the software industry and has become so entrenched in the computer science lexicon that the book's authors have become known as the Gang of Four. In writings on object-oriented topics, you will often see the Gang of Four referred to as the GoF.

The intent of this chapter is to explain what design patterns are. (Explaining each design pattern is far beyond the scope of this book and would take more than one volume.) To accomplish this, we explore each of the three categories (creational, structural, and behavioral) of design patterns as defined by the Gang of Four and provide a concrete example of one pattern in each category.

Why Design Patterns?

The concept of design patterns did not necessarily start with the need for reusable software. In fact, the seminal work on design patterns is about constructing buildings and cities. As Christopher Alexander noted in *A Pattern Language: Towns, Buildings, Construction*, "Each pattern describes a problem which occurs over and over again in our environment, and then describes the core of the solution to that problem, in such a way that you can use the solution a million times over, without ever doing it the same way twice."

The Four Elements of a Pattern

The GoF describe a pattern as having four essential elements:

- The *pattern name* is a handle we can use to describe a design problem, its solutions, and consequences in a word or two. Naming a pattern immediately increases our design vocabulary. It lets us design at a higher level of abstraction. Having a vocabulary for patterns lets us talk about them with our colleagues, in our documentation, and even to ourselves. It makes it easier to think about designs and to communicate them and their trade-off to others. Finding good names has been one of the hardest parts of developing our catalog.

- The *problem* describes when to apply the pattern. It explains the problem and its content. It might describe specific design problems, such as how to represent algorithms as objects. It might describe class or object structures that are symptomatic of an inflexible design. Sometimes the problem will include a list of conditions that must be met before it makes sense to apply the pattern.

- The *solution* describes the elements that make up the design, their relationships, responsibilities, and collaborations. The solution doesn't describe a particular concrete design or implementation, because a pattern is like a template that can be applied in many situations. Instead, the pattern provides an abstract description of a design problem, and how a general arrangement of elements (classes and objects in our case) solves it.

- The *consequences* are the results and trade-offs of applying the pattern. Although consequences are often unvoiced, when we describe design decisions, they are critical for evaluating design alternatives and for understanding the costs and benefits of the applying pattern. The consequences for software often concern space and time trade-offs. They might address language and implementation issues as well. Because reuse is often a factor in object-oriented design, the consequences of a pattern include its impact on a system's flexibility, extensibility, or portability. Listing the consequences explicitly helps you understand and evaluate them.

Smalltalk's Model/View/Controller

For historical perspective, we need to consider the Model/View/Controller (MVC) introduced in Smalltalk (and used in other object-oriented languages). MVC is often used to illustrate the origins of design patterns. The Model/View/Controller paradigm was used to create user interfaces in Smalltalk. Smalltalk was perhaps the first *popular* object-oriented language.

Smalltalk

Smalltalk is the result of several great ideas that emerged from Xerox PARC. These ideas included the mouse and using a windowing environment, among others. Smalltalk is a wonderful language that provided the foundation for all the object-oriented languages that followed. One of the complaints about C++ is that it's not really object-oriented, whereas Smalltalk is. Although C++ had a larger following in the early days of OO, Smalltalk has always had a very dedicated core group of supporters. Java is a mostly OO language that embraced the C++ developer base.

Design Patterns defines the MVC components in the following manner:

> The Model is the application object, the View is the screen presentation, and the Controller defines the way the user interface reacts to user input.

The problem with previous paradigms is that the Model, View, and Controller used to be lumped together in a single entity. For example, a single object would have included all three of the components. With the MVC paradigm, these three components have separate and distinct interfaces. So if you want to change the user interface of an application, you only have to change the View. Figure 15.1 illustrates what the MVC design looks like.

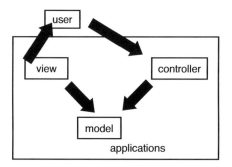

Figure 15.1   Model/View/Controller paradigm.

Remember that much of what we have been learning about object-oriented development has to do with interfaces versus implementation. As much as possible, we want to separate the interface from the implementation. We also want to separate interface from interface as much as possible. For example, we do not want to combine multiple interfaces that do not have anything to do with one another (or the solution to the problem at hand). The MVC was one of the early pioneers in this separation of interfaces. The MVC explicitly defines the interfaces between specific components pertaining to a very common and basic programming problem— the creation of user interfaces and their connection to the business logic and data behind them.

If you follow the MVC concept and separate the user interface, business logic, and data, your system will be much more flexible and robust. For example, assume that the user interface is on a client machine, the business logic is on an application server, and the data is located on a data server. Developing your application in this way would allow you to change the way the GUI looks without having an impact on the business logic or the data. Likewise, if your business logic changes and you calculate a specific field differently, you can change the business logic without having to change the GUI. And finally, if you want to swap databases and store your data differently, you can change the way the data is stored on the data server without affecting either the GUI or the business logic. This assumes, of course, that the interfaces between the three do not change.

MVC Example

As a further example of a listbox, consider a GUI that includes a list of phone numbers. The listbox is the view, the phone list is the model, and the controller is the logic that binds the listbox to the phone list.

MVC Drawbacks

Although the MVC is a great design, it can be somewhat complex in that a lot of attention must be paid to the upfront design. This is a problem with object-oriented design in general—there is a fine line between a good design and a cumbersome design. The question remains: How much complexity should you build into the system with regard to a complete design?

Types of Design Patterns

Design Patterns features 23 patterns grouped into the three categories that follow. Most of the examples are written in C++, with some written in Smalltalk. The time of the book's publication is indicative of the use of C++ and Smalltalk. The publication date of 1995 was right at the cusp of the Internet revolution and the corresponding popularity of the Java programming language. After the benefit of design patterns became apparent, many other books rushed in to fill the newly created market. Many of these later books were written in Java.

In any event, the actual language used is irrelevant. *Design Patterns* is inherently a design book, and the patterns can be implemented in any number of languages. The authors of the book divided the patterns into three categories:

- *Creational patterns* create objects for you, rather than having you instantiate objects directly. This gives your program more flexibility in deciding which objects need to be created for a given case.

- *Structural patterns* help you compose groups of objects into larger structures, such as complex user interfaces or accounting data.

- *Behavioral patterns* help you define the communication between objects in your system and how the flow is controlled in a complex program.

In the following sections, we discuss one example from each of these categories to provide a flavor of design patterns. For a comprehensive list and description of individual design patterns, refer to the books listed at the end of this chapter.

Creational Patterns

The creational patterns consist of the following categories:

- Abstract factory
- Builder
- Factory method
- Prototype
- Singleton

As stated earlier, the scope of this chapter is to describe what a design pattern is—not to describe each and every pattern in the GoF book. Thus, we will cover a single pattern in each category. With this in mind, let's consider an example of a creational pattern and look at the singleton pattern.

The Singleton Design Pattern

The singleton pattern, represented in Figure 15.2, is a creational pattern used to regulate the creation of objects from a class to a single object. For example, if you have a website that has a counter object to keep track of the hits on your site, you certainly do not want a new counter to be instantiated each time your web page is hit. You want a counter object instantiated when the first hit is made, but after that, you want to use the existing object to increment the count.

Figure 15.2   The singleton model.

Although there might be other ways to regulate the creation of objects, it is often best to let the class itself take care of this issue. However, there are many times when using an external factory is very useful or even required—specifically, where patterns like the Factory, Abstract Factory, and Bridge are important.

Taking Care of Business

Remember, one of the most important OO rules is that an object is responsible for itself. This means that issues regarding the life cycle of a class should be handled in the class, not delegated to language constructs like `static`, and so on.

Figure 15.3 shows the UML model for the singleton taken directly from *Design Patterns*. Note the property `uniqueinstance`, which is a static singleton object, and the method `Instance()`. The other properties and methods are there to indicate that other properties and methods will be required to support the business logic of the class.

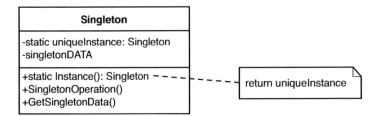

Figure 15.3   Singleton UML diagram.

Any other class that needs to access an instance of a singleton must interface through the `Instance()` method. The creation of an object should be controlled through the constructor, just like any other OO design. We can require the client to interface through the `Instance()` method, and then have the `Instance()` method call the constructor.

The following Java code illustrates what the code looks like for the general singleton:

```java
public class ClassicSingleton {
  private static ClassicSingleton instance = null;

  protected ClassicSingleton() {
   // Exists only to defeat instantiation.
  }
  public static ClassicSingleton getInstance() {
   if(instance == null) {
     instance = new ClassicSingleton();
   }
   return instance;
  }
}
```

We can create a more specific example for the web page counter example that we used previously:

```
public class Counter
{
  private int counter;
  private static Counter instance = null;

  protected Counter()
  {
  }

  public static Counter getInstance() {
      if(instance == null) {
         instance = new Counter ();
        System.out.println("New instance created\n");
      }
      return instance;
  }

  public void incrementCounter()
  {
    counter++;
  }

  public int getCounter()
  {
    return(counter);
  }

}
```

The main point to note about the code is the regulation of the object creation. Only a single counter object can be created. The code for this is as follows:

```
public static Counter getInstance() {
    if(instance == null) {
       instance = new Counter ();
      System.out.println("New instance created\n");
    }
    return instance;
}
```

Note that if the instance is null, it means that an object has yet to be instantiated. In this event, a new Counter object is created. If the instance is not null, it indicates that a Counter object has been instantiated, and no new object is to be created. In this case, the reference to the only object available is returned to the application.

More Than One Reference

There may well be more than one reference to the singleton. If you create references in the application and each reference is referring to the singleton, you will have to manage the multiple references.

Although this code is certainly interesting, it is also valuable to see how the singleton is instantiated and managed by the application. Take a look at the following code:

```
public class Singleton
{
 public static void main(String[] args)
 {
  Counter counter1 = Counter.getInstance();
  System.out.println("Counter : " + counter1.getCounter() );

  Counter counter2 = Counter.getInstance();
  System.out.println("Counter : " + counter2.getCounter() );

 }
}
```

Two References to a Single Counter

Be aware that in this example, two separate references are pointing to the counter. Thus, when the counter changes, both references will reflect the update.

This code uses the `Counter` singleton. Take a look at how the objects are created:

```
Counter counter1 = Counter.getInstance();
```

The constructor is not used here. The instantiation of the object is controlled by the `getInstance()` method. Figure 15.4 shows what happens when this code is executed. Note that the message `New instance created` is output only a single time. When `counter2` is created, it receives a copy of the original object—the same as `counter1`.

Let's prove that the references for `counter1` and `counter2` are the same. We can update the application code as follows:

```
public class Singleton
{
  public static void main(String[] args)
  {
    Counter counter1 = Counter.getInstance();
    counter1.incrementCounter();
    counter1.incrementCounter();
    System.out.println("Counter : " + counter1.getCounter() );

    Counter counter2 = Counter.getInstance();
```

```
    counter2.incrementCounter();
    System.out.println("Counter : " + counter2.getCounter() );

  }
}
```

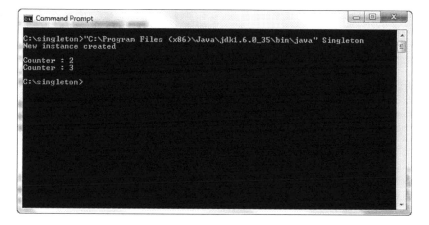

Figure 15.4   Using the Counter singleton.

Figure 15.5 shows the output from the singleton application. Note that in this case, we are incrementing counter1 twice, so the counter will be 2. When we create the counter2 reference, it references the same object as counter1, so when we increment the counter, it's now 3 (2+1).

Figure 15.5   Using the updated Counter singleton.

> **Batch Files Revisited**
>
> As we have demonstrated in earlier chapters, to assist in the testing of these types of simple, but functional, educational examples, I like to create an old-fashioned batch file to make the process of using the Java class paths more precise. You can launch the `Singleton` applications by placing the following code in a batch file called `Singleton.bat` and then typing `Singleton` at the command prompt.
>
> ```
> "C:\Program Files (x86)\Java\jdk1.6.0_35\bin\java" Singleton
> ```

Structural Patterns

Structural patterns are used to create larger structures from groups of objects. The following seven design patterns are members of the structural category:

- Adapter
- Bridge
- Composite
- Decorator
- Façade
- Flyweight
- Proxy

As an example from the structural category, let's take a look at the adapter pattern. The adapter pattern is also one of the most important design patterns. This pattern is a good example of how the implementation and interface are separated.

The Adapter Design Pattern

The adapter pattern is a way for you to create a different interface for a class that already exists. The adapter pattern basically provides a class wrapper. In other words, you create a new class that incorporates (wraps) the functionality of an existing class with a new and—ideally—better interface. A simple example of a wrapper is the Java class `Integer`. The `Integer` class wraps a single `Integer` value inside it. You might wonder why you would bother to do this. Remember that in an object-oriented system, everything is an object. In Java, primitives, such as ints, floats, and so on, are not objects. When you need to perform functions on these primitives, such as conversions, you need to treat them as objects. You create a wrapper object and "wrap" the primitive inside it. Thus, you can take a primitive like the following:

```
int myInt = 10;
```

and wrap it in an `Integer` object:

```
Integer myIntWrapper = new Integer (myInt);
```

Now you can do a conversion, so we can treat it as a string:

```
String myString = myIntWrapper.toString();
```

This wrapper enables us to treat the original integer as an object, thus providing all the advantages of an object.

As for the adapter pattern itself, consider the example of a mail tool interface. Let's assume you have purchased some code that provides all the functionality you need to implement a mail client. This tool provides everything you want in a mail client, except you would like to change the interface slightly. In fact, all you want to do is change the API to retrieve your mail.

The following class provides a very simple example of a mail client for this example:

```
package MailTool;
public class MailTool {
    public MailTool () {
    }
    public int retrieveMail() {

    System.out.println ("You've Got Mail");

        return 0;
    }
}
```

When you invoke the `retrieveMail()` method, your mail is presented with the very original greeting "You've Got Mail." Now let's suppose you want to change the interface in all your company's clients from `retrieveMail()` to `getMail()`. You can create an interface to enforce this:

```
package MailTool;
interface MailInterface {
    int getMail();
}
```

You can now create your own mail tool that wraps the original tool and provide your own interface:

```
package MailTool;
class MyMailTool implements MailInterface {
    private MailTool yourMailTool;
    public MyMailTool () {
     yourMailTool= new MailTool();
        setYourMailTool(yourMailTool);
    }
    public int getMail() {
        return getYourMailTool().retrieveMail();
    }
    public MailTool getYourMailTool() {
```

```
      return yourMailTool ;
   }
   public void setYourMailTool(MailTool newYourMailTool) {
      yourMailTool = newYourMailTool;
   }
}
```

Inside this class, you create an instance of the original mail tool that you want to retrofit. This class implements `MailInterface`, which will force you to implement a `getMail()` method. Inside this method, you literally invoke the `retrieveMail()` method of the original mail tool.

To use your new class, you instantiate your new mail tool and invoke the `getMail()` method:

```
package MailTool;
public class Adapter
{
  public static void main(String[] args)
  {
    MyMailTool myMailTool = new MyMailTool();

    myMailTool.getMail();

  }
}
```

When you invoke the `getMail()` method, you are using this new interface to invoke the `retrieveMail()` method from the original tool. This is a very simple example; however, by creating this wrapper, you can enhance the interface and add your own functionality to the original class.

The concept of an adapter is quite simple, but you can create new and powerful interfaces using this pattern.

Behavioral Patterns

The behavioral patterns consist of the following categories:

- Chain of response
- Command
- Interpreter
- Iterator
- Mediator
- Memento
- Observer
- State

- Strategy

- Template method

- Visitor

As an example from the behavioral category, let's take a look at the iterator pattern. This is one of the most commonly used patterns and is implemented by several programming languages.

The Iterator Design Pattern

Iterators provide a standard mechanism for traversing a collection, such as a vector. Functionality must be provided so that each item of the collection can be accessed one at a time. The iterator pattern provides information hiding, keeping the internal structure of the collection secure. The iterator pattern also stipulates that more than one iterator can be created without interfering with each other. Java provides its own implementation of an iterator. The following code creates a vector and then inserts a number of strings into it:

```java
package Iterator;

import java.util.*;
public class Iterator {
    public static void main(String args[]) {

        // Instantiate an ArrayList.
        ArrayList<String> names = new ArrayList();

        // Add values to the ArrayList
        names.add(new String("Joe"));
        names.add(new String("Mary"));
        names.add(new String("Bob"));
        names.add(new String("Sue"));

            //Now Iterate through the names
        System.out.println("Names:");
        iterate(names );
    }

    private static void iterate(ArrayList<String> arl) {
        for(String listItem : arl) {
                System.out.println(listItem.toString());
            }
    }
}
```

Then we create an enumeration so that we can iterate through it. The method `iterate()` is provided to perform the iteration functionality. In this method, we use the Java enumeration method `hasMoreElements()`, which traverses the vector and lists all the names.

Antipatterns

Although a design pattern evolves from experiences in a positive manner, *antipatterns* can be thought of as collections of experiences that have gone awry. It is well documented that most software projects are ultimately deemed unsuccessful. In fact, as indicated in the article "Creating Chaos" by Johnny Johnson, fully one-third of all projects are cancelled outright. It would seem obvious that many of these failures are caused by poor design decisions.

The term *antipattern* derives from the fact that design patterns are created to proactively solve a specific type of problem. An antipattern, on the other hand, is a reaction to a problem and is gleaned from bad experiences. In short, whereas design patterns are based on solid design practices, antipatterns can be thought of as practices to avoid.

In the November 1995 *C++ Report*, Andrew Koenig described two facets of antipatterns:

- Those that describe a bad solution to a problem, which result in a bad situation

- Those that describe how to get out of a bad situation and how to proceed from there to a good solution

Many people believe that antipatterns are more useful than design patterns. This is because antipatterns are designed to solve problems that have already occurred. This boils down to the concept of root-cause analysis. A study can be conducted with data that might indicate why the original design, perhaps an actual design pattern, did not succeed. It might be said that antipatterns emerge from the failure of previous solutions. Thus, antipatterns have the benefit of hindsight.

For example, in his article "Reuse Patterns and Antipatterns," Scott Ambler identifies a pattern called a *robust artifact*, and defines it as follows:

> An item that is well-documented, built to meet general needs instead of project-specific needs, thoroughly tested, and has several examples to show how to work with it. Items with these qualities are much more likely to be reused than items without them. A Robust Artifact is an item that is easy to understand and work with.

However, there are certainly many situations when a solution is declared reusable and then no one ever reuses it. Thus, to illustrate an antipattern, he writes:

> Someone other than the original developer must review a Reuseless Artifact to determine whether or not anyone might be interested in it. If so, the artifact must be reworked to become a Robust Artifact.

Thus, antipatterns lead to the revision of existing designs, and the continuous refactoring of those designs until a workable solution is found.

Conclusion

In this chapter, we explored the concept of design patterns. Patterns are part of everyday life, and this is just the way you should be thinking about object-oriented designs. As with many things pertaining to information technology, the roots for solutions are founded in real-life situations.

Although this chapter covered design patterns only briefly, you should explore this topic in greater detail by picking up one of the books referenced at the end of this chapter.

References

- Alexander, Christopher, et al. 1977. *A Pattern Language: Towns, Buildings, Construction.* Cambridge, UK: Oxford University Press.

- Gamma, Erich, et al. 1995. *Design Patterns: Elements of Reusable Object-Oriented Software.* Boston, MA: Addison-Wesley.

- Larman, Craig. 2004. *Applying UML and Patterns: An Introduction to Object-Oriented Analysis and Design and Iterative Development,* 3rd ed. Hoboken, NJ: Wiley.

- Grand, Mark. 2002. *Patterns in Java: A Catalog of Reusable Design Patterns Illustrated with UML,* 2nd ed., volume 1. Hoboken, NJ: Wiley.

- Ambler, Scott. "Reuse Patterns and Antipatterns." *2000 Software Development Magazine.*

- Jaworski, Jamie. 1999. *Java 2 Platform Unleashed.* Indianapolis, IN: Sams Publishing.

- Johnson, Johnny. "Creating Chaos." *American Programmer,* July 1995.

Example Code Used in This Chapter

The following code is presented in C# .NET. Code for other languages is available electronically on the publisher's website. These examples correspond to the Java code that is listed inside the chapter itself.

C# .NET

Counter.cs

```
using System;
using System.Collections.Generic;
using System.Text;

namespace Counter
{
    class Counter
    {
        private int counter;
        private static Counter instance = null;

        protected Counter()
```

```
        {

        }

        public static Counter getInstance()
        {
            if (instance == null)
            {
                instance = new Counter();
                Console.WriteLine("New Instance of Counter...");
            }
            return instance;
        }

        public void incrementCounter()
        {
            counter++;
        }

        public int getCounter()
        {
            return counter;
        }
    }
}
```

Singleton.cs

```
using System;
using System.Collections.Generic;
using System.Text;

namespace Counter
{
    class Singleton
    {
        public Singleton()
        {
            Counter counter1 = Counter.getInstance();
            counter1.incrementCounter();
            counter1.incrementCounter();
            Console.WriteLine("Counter = " + counter1.getCounter());

            Counter counter2 = Counter.getInstance();
            counter2.incrementCounter();
            Console.WriteLine("Counter = " + counter2.getCounter());
            Console.WriteLine("Press any key to continue...");
```

```
                Console.ReadKey();
            }
        }
    }
```

MailTool.cs

```csharp
using System;

namespace MailAdapter
{

    class MailTool
    {
        public MailTool()
        {

        }

        public int retrieveMail()
        {
            Console.WriteLine("You've got mail!");
            return 0;
        }
    }
}
```

Mailinterface.cs

```csharp
using System;
using System.Collections.Generic;
using System.Text;

namespace MailAdapter
{
    interface MailInterface
    {
        int getMail();
    }
}
```

MyMail.cs

```csharp
namespace MailAdapter
{
    class MyMailTool : MailInterface
    {
```

```
            private MailTool yourMailTool;
            public MyMailTool()
            {
                yourMailTool = new MailTool();
                setYourMailTool(yourMailTool);
            }

            public int getMail()
            {
                return getYourMailTool().retrieveMail();
            }

            public MailTool getYourMailTool()
            {
                return yourMailTool;
            }

            public void setYourMailTool(MailTool newYourMailTool)
            {
                yourMailTool = newYourMailTool;
            }
        }
}
```

Adapter.cs

```
using System;
using System.Collections.Generic;
using System.Text;

namespace MailAdapter
{
    class Adapter
    {
        public Adapter()
        {
            MyMailTool myMailTool = new MyMailTool();
            myMailTool.getMail();
            Console.WriteLine();
            Console.WriteLine("Press any key to continue...");
            Console.ReadKey();
        }
    }
}
```

Iterator.cs

```csharp
using System;
using System.Collections.Generic;
using System.Text;
using System.Collections;


namespace Iterator
{
    class Iterator
    {
        public Iterator()
        {
            // Instantiate an Arraylist
            ArrayList myList = new ArrayList();

            // Add values to the list
            myList.Add("Joe");
            myList.Add("Mary");
            myList.Add("Bob");
            myList.Add("Sue");

            //Iterate through the elements
            Console.WriteLine("Names:");
            iterate(myList);
        }

        static void iterate(ArrayList arl)
        {
            foreach (String listItem in arl)
            {
                Console.WriteLine(listItem);
            }
        }
    }

}
```

Index